Coordinating Services
to Handicapped Children

C1450

C - Systems, Inc.

Telephone: 703/698-6899

BOOKS N' BOLTS DIVISION

UNIVERSITIES BOOKSTORE IN NORTHERN VIRGINIA

BOOK RETURN POLICY

:books must be returned within <u>THREE</u> weeks from the beginning of fall, winter, and
Ing terms, and during the <u>FIRST</u> week of each of the summer terms, carrying our price
k and CASH REGISTER RECEIPT. The last day to return books is posted in the book-
ce each term. This date is calculated from the date classes begin as scheduled in
University Course offering. A 10% fee will be charged. A fee will not be charged
the course is cancelled.

UNIVERSITY OF VIRGINIA STUDENTS: The above policy applies only to courses
offered during the <u>REGULAR SEMESTER</u> program.

The Bookstore strongly recommends attending class <u>before</u> buying books for any
of the following special course offerings: MINI-COURSES, CONTINUING EDUCATION
COURSES, NON-CREDIT COURSES, CERTIFICATE PROGRAMS, SPECIAL INTEREST PROGRAMS
and REVIEW COURSES. Books for these courses are non-returnable and will have
USED BOOK value.

CASH REFUND will be given for ten working days if purchase was paid by check.

** <u>Caution</u>: Returns will be accepted without a cash register receipt
   only upon presentation of a drop-add slip or written verification
   from the department that the book is not required.

** <u>Caution</u>: New books returned for any reason must be ABSOLUTELY FREE
   of ALL markings. Do not mark your book until you are sure you have
   the correct book and until you are sure you will remain in the course.
   Books must be returned with jacket cover, shrink wrapper, or carton
   intact.

e Bookstore employee handling returns is the sole judge in determining whether books
e in new or used condition.

fective books will be replaced at no charge and should be returned AT ONCE upon
tection.

ED books are non-returnable.

COMMENDED books are non-returnable.

neral books, sale books, special orders, and paperbacks are non-returnable.

oks distributed by a publisher with a NO RETURN POLICY are non-returnable.

LL US YOUR USED BOOKS. DATES ARE POSTED IN THE BOOKSTORE.

SUPPLIES RETURN POLICY

pply items which need to be returned must have a current cash register receipt and be in
e original packaging. They must be returned within one week. If defective, return
ONCE upon detection of defect.

Coordinating Services to Handicapped Children

A Handbook for Interagency Collaboration

Edited by

Jerry O. Elder, M.A.
Assistant Professor, Crippled Children's Division;
Director, Interagency Collaboration Project,
Crippled Children's Division,
Child Development and Rehabilitation Center,
University of Oregon Health Sciences Center, Portland

Phyllis R. Magrab, Ph.D.
Associate Professor of Pediatrics, Georgetown University;
Director, Georgetown University Child Development Center;
Chief Pediatric Psychologist, Georgetown University Hospital,
Washington, D.C.

·P A U L·H·
BROOKES
PUBLISHERS

Baltimore • London

Paul H. Brookes, Publishers
Post Office Box 10624
Baltimore, Maryland 21204

Copyright 1980 by Paul H. Brookes Publishing Company, Inc.
All rights reserved.

Typeset by The Composing Room of Michigan, Inc. (Grand Rapids)
Manufactured in the United States of America by Universal Lithographers,
Inc. (Cockeysville, Maryland)

Library of Congress Cataloging in Publication Data

Main entry under title:

Coordinating services to handicapped children.

Bibliography: p.
Includes index.
1. Handicapped children—Services for—Addresses,
essays, lectures.   I. Elder, Jerry O.   II. Magrab,
Phyllis R.
HV888.C66   362.4′088054   80-16033
ISBN 0-933716-11-7 (pbk.)

Contents

Contributors

Robert H. Audette, Ph.D., Consultant, N. Lake Road, Cazenovia, New York 13035

Jerry O. Elder, M.A., Assistant Professor, CCD, UOHSC; Director, Interagency Collaboration Project, CCD, UOHSC, P.O. Box 574, Portland, Oregon 97207

Howard B. Hall, D.S.W., Community Liaison, The Neuropsychiatric Institute, University of California, Los Angeles, 760 Westwood Plaza, Los Angeles, California 90024

Denise Humm-Delgado, Ph.D., Assistant Director of Title XX Training, Boston College Graduate School of Social Work, McQuinn Hall, Chestnut Hill, Massachusetts 02167

Elynor Kazuk, M.A., Assistant to the Director, John F. Kennedy Child Development Center, University of Colorado Health Sciences Center, 4200 E. Ninth, Box C234, Denver, Colorado 80262

Phyllis R. Magrab, Ph.D., Associate Professor of Pediatrics, Georgetown University; Director, Georgetown University Child Development Center; Chief Pediatric Psychologist, Georgetown University Hospital, 3800 Reservoir Road, N.W., Washington, D.C. 20007

Janelle Mulvenon, M.S., State Liaison Representative, Early Childhood Education for the Handicapped Project, 111 Colorado, Salina, Kansas 67401

Laura Schmidt, Assistant to the Director, Georgetown University Child Development Center, 3800 Reservoir Road, N.W., Washington, D.C. 10007

Richard W. Zeller, M.A., Director, Northwest Direction Service Consortium; Instructor, Center on Human Development, College of Education, University of Oregon, 1590 Willamette Street, Eugene, Oregon 97401

Preface

The very nature of categorical human service programs, each with its own planning and reporting system often unrelated to any other system, leads to fragmented service delivery. The complexity of each of the major service delivery systems was examined in *Planning for Services to Handicapped Persons: Community, Education, Health* (Magrab and Elder, 1979), and the topic of coordinating services across those systems was addressed. The need for such coordination is even more critical in times of shrinking resources, which appears to be the outlook for human services in the 1980s.

Numerous attempts have been undertaken in all of the human service delivery systems to foster interagency collaboration. These efforts have been referred to by such terms as service coordination, services integration, and networking, to mention but a few. The existence of clear operating guidelines for these interagency collaboration efforts, however, is rare. The resources required to develop such guidelines have been limited, and little attempt has been made to collect and integrate the findings of researchers, theorists, and practitioners working in this area.

The subject of interagency collaboration that was introduced in *Planning for Services to Handicapped Persons: Community, Education, Health* is examined in more detail in this volume by focusing on the problems and issues encountered in providing educational and related services to handicapped children. Solutions to these numerous, complex, and controversial problems and issues are sought by coordinating services though interagency collaboration. The subject of interagency collaboration is examined both as a "process" and as an "attitude." The process involves concepts, policies, and procedures required to make the mechanics work. However, of equal, if not more, importance is the creation of positive attitudes and behaviors on the part of the players involved in interagency collaboration. It is critical to recognize and to promote the idea, to be kept in mind at all times, that both the "process" and the "attitude" of working cooperatively together should be directed toward the benefit of the individual client, not the agencies providing services.

This book is designed for educators, professionals, paraprofessionals, and administrators in all of the human service delivery systems for use as a handbook to promote and initiate workable solutions to the problems and issues of delivering services to handicapped children across the various delivery systems. Such efforts will result in comprehensive, coordinated services for handicapped children at the community level.

Jerry O. Elder
Phyllis R. Magrab

Dedication

---

to Carl Lewis Henderson

to Brendan, Ryan and Kylee

Coordinating Services
to Handicapped Children

Introduction and Overview

Jerry O. Elder and Phyllis R. Magrab

The Education for All Handicapped Children Act (Public Law 94-142), enacted in November of 1975, has had an impact upon the delivery of services to handicapped children greater than that of any other piece of legislation. This act, which has been hailed as a "Bill of Rights for the Handicapped," promises an end to the custom of treating children with disabilities as second-class citizens. It, along with Section 504 of the Rehabilitation Act of 1973, provides a legal mandate to guarantee the same rights enjoyed by children who are fortunate enough not to be afflicted with a handicapping condition to *all* children. The application of the principles mandated by these two pieces of legislation, such as the right to receive a free and appropriate education in the least restrictive environment and the right to receive related services in the same least restrictive environment, have created havoc in the various service delivery systems. These delivery systems are unable to cope adequately with the implementation of these principles. At the same time, debates have been generated over which professional service delivery model—for example, the medical model, the vocational rehabilitation model, the social model, or the educational model—is the best mechanism for delivering this care. Such discussion has concerned groups and agency staffs throughout the country.

The problems and issues in providing educational and related services to handicapped children are numerous, complex, and controversial. This book addresses these problems and issues and seeks solutions to them by coordinating services through interagency collaboration.[1] As was brought out in *Planning for Services to Handicapped Persons: Community, Education, Health* (Magrab and Elder, 1979), services to handicapped persons transgress the traditional boundaries of the educational system, the health delivery system, the community and social service system, or the vocational rehabilitation system. All of these service areas must be considered in planning for services

---

[1]Throughout this book, *services coordination* or *coordination of services* is defined as cooperative efforts made by professionals and administrators within a given agency or organization to ensure that the client is provided the appropriate services to which he/she is entitled, while *interagency collaboration* is defined as coordination efforts made by professionals and administrators across different agencies or organizations to ensure that the client is provided appropriate, nonduplicated services.

to handicapped children. In this book, the authors continue the theme developed in the previous volume that most handicapping conditions require the services of two, three, or all four of these human service delivery systems. Handicapped children normally cannot obtain all of the services they need from any one of these delivery systems. Furthermore, because they are handicapped, and especially because they are children, this segment of the population cannot easily pick and choose the most appropriate delivery mechanisms or systems for the services required. The previous book provided some insight on meeting the challenge of the 1980s to provide and plan for coordinated, collaborative human service delivery systems that will enable the handicapped to receive services in an expeditious and coordinated fashion. This book takes a closer look at how services are delivered to one segment of that population, the handicapped child, and presents some practical solutions to coordinating services for this population through *interagency collaboration*.

Because the authors are addressing the needs of children, the definition of handicapped children for this volume will parallel the definition set forth in PL 94-142:

> ... the mentally retarded, hard of hearing, deaf, orthopedically impaired, other health impaired, speech impaired, visually handicapped, seriously emotionally disturbed, or children with particular disabilities who, by reason thereof, require special education and related services.

NECESSITY FOR LOCAL INTERAGENCY COLLABORATION

In communities across the United States and Canada, scores of organizations and agencies[2] provide services to handicapped children. Public, private, or semi-public, they may be local in nature, branches of state offices, or arms of federal agencies. Some agencies provide services only to handicapped children; others are more generic in the clientele they serve. Some are supervisory; others are regulatory. They vary in competence, size, and justification. Some pay little attention to each other; others try to cooperate. Others, created to provide coordination, instead compound that which must be coordinated. The deficiencies in an uncoordinated system of human services provided by such agencies have been highlighted in *Improving Services for Handicapped Children,* a report generated by a Rand Corporation study (Kakalik et al., 1974). The study found that the system that was delivering services to the nation's handicapped children and youth was so complex and disorganized as to defy efficient and effective operation. It was also shown that services that

---

[2]In most cases, an agency is viewed as a governmental or nongovernmental body organized around the needs of a specific population or group with certain functions designed to benefit that population or group. The term *agency* generally connotes a large governmental organization with multiple functions. In this volume, the terms *agency* and *organization* are used synonymously to mean an administrative and functional structure that is organized to provide services to handicapped children.

are provided without coordination directly underlie a poor system performance.

Making some sense out of this complex service delivery system for
handicapped children can best be handled by coordination efforts at the local
level through interagency collaboration. The initiative for such interagency
collaboration has already been established by the federal government. Joint
policy statements have been negotiated between various key federal agencies
that provide services to handicapped children. These joint policy statements
delineate specific roles and responsibilities of the various agencies. Written
joint policy statements are currently in effect between the Bureau of Education
for the Handicapped and the Bureau of Community Health Services and
between Vocational Education, Vocational Rehabilitation and the Bureau of
Education for the Handicapped. The effort made by these major federal programs to contribute organizational resources to the development of these
agreements shows a commitment to invest renewed energy and resources in
interagency collaborative efforts. This federal incentive should become an
important factor in promoting the development of deliberate, planned efforts
to coordinate the service delivery system.

Because of these federal initiatives and corresponding state level efforts,
along with recent developments at both state and national levels in statutory,
judicial, fiscal, and policy areas, there has been a shift from a voluntary to a
more or less mandatory base for interagency program planning. The federal
government's role should primarily be one of initiating the development of
effective interagency collaboration. This initiative then needs to be taken up
by state agency heads, translated into feasible plans for application, and put
into practice.

The authors of this volume, however, believe that the major interagency
collaborative efforts can best be developed and carried out at the local community level. All of the examples described in Section II of this book are
interagency models developed at the community level. The fact that these real
work situations vary so much from community to community, along with the
environment in those communities, means that detailed working relationships
also will vary greatly from locale to locale. There is no set prescription or
model that can be given or followed in a step-by-step fashion and applied to
every community. Each community has its own unique characteristics, needs,
political and geographic boundaries, and problems, and its own members are
best prepared to address these issues and develop efficient, collaborative
service delivery. General guidelines extracted from the experiences of operating models, such as those described in Section II of this volume, can be
followed, but they need to be tailored to the particular requirements of the
individual community.

At the same time, the importance of efforts at the state level are not to be
overlooked. By focusing on the local effort in this book, no implication
should be inferred that state level efforts are of less import. To the contrary,

without the commitment of the state level to the concept of interagency collaboration, the interagency efforts at the community level would fail. As agencies work collaboratively, so too must local and state organizations.

BASIS FOR INTERAGENCY COLLABORATION

The nature of developing interagency collaborative arrangements at the various levels of federal, state, and local intervention is a complicated topic. This is especially true when one thinks about the purposes, values, and worth of such arrangements as well as the substantive problem areas in the educational, health, social, and vocational environments and "process fields," such as intergovernmental relations, centralization and decentralization of power, and public resource allocation, that necessarily involve forms of interagency collaboration. Can the social scientist, together with the professionals known as behavioral and management scientists, supply special insight into these complicated problems (Steingraph, 1977)? It is the premise of this book that social, behavioral, and management scientists alone *cannot* supply all of the answers in this complex effort. Rather, the following areas need to be considered when studying interagency collaboration: theory and practice, nature of communities, interorganizational analysis, organizational exchange, and independence of agencies.

Theory and Practice

Both empirical and theoretical approaches must be used to sort out the complexities of interorganizational collaboration. The current state of knowledge falls short of satisfying all of the requirements for a theory because of the lack of existing literature on interorganizational studies (Negandhi, 1975). Current interorganization theory can be described more realistically as an approach or a perspective rather than as a theory.

One dimension in solving the problems of interagency collaboration deals with how knowledge is developed through research. Some researchers have observed that organizational theory and concepts follow organizational practice per se. That is, concepts and theory are always trying to catch up with the organizational inventions or innovations of administrators and managers (Galbraith, 1973). In effect, the espousers of the concepts and theories, coupled with empirical work, are in the position of trying to codify effectively what is already in existence in the world of organizations (Steingraph, 1977). This fact is applicable to most interorganizational research. The salient questions for building knowledge become: How effective or credible are the real codifications? Are there possibilities for moving beyond what is to what should be?

The models of interagency collaboration described in Section II of this book speak to the issue of what is already in practice in the world of interagency collaboration. Because most of these models have only been in existence for 2 years, there is, at the present, no way to determine how effective or credible these examples will be. It is up to the reader to synthesize the knowledge presented in this volume by combining the theoretical information provided with the empirical models described to determine an appropriate route to follow for interagency collaboration in his/her own situation.

Nature of Communities

Community-organizing principles summarized by Dunham (1970) contain both substantive assumptions about the nature of communities and prescriptive recommendations for action. According to Dunham's idealogy, communities and the organizations and groups within them are characterized by a relatively high degree of autonomy, changes originate from the actions of individuals at the grass roots level, one should steer as clear from political issues as possible to accomplish community coordination, and an organizing effort should be decentralized and rely on persuasion (as opposed to authoritarianism) in decision making since this guards the individualism and freedom so valued within American culture. Zeitz (1975) suggests that these substantive assumptions about the autonomy of organizations and groups are consistent with the assumptions in the interorganizational literature. These assumptions support the position of the authors in this volume that interagency collaboration needs to be worked out at the local community level.

Interorganizational Analysis

There are three basic approaches to interorganizational analysis (Van de Ven, Emmett, and Koenig, 1975). The environment can be conceptualized 1) as an external, straining phenomenon, 2) as a collection of interacting organizations, groups, or persons, or 3) as a social system. Most of the studies that have been formally classified as interorganizational view the environment as a collection of interacting organizations, groups, or persons. This is the focus followed by the contributors to this volume. The issues outlined in Section I, the examples described in Section II, and the steps for effecting interagency collaboration delineated in Section III all relate to an environment where professionals, groups, and organizations are interacting toward a common goal of delivering coordinated services to children. Such an approach holds that, because organizations can seldom marshall the necessary resources to attain their goals independently, they must establish exchange relationships with other organizations. Such reciprocal or working relationships among agencies have an important bearing on the effectiveness with which services can be provided to handicapped children. Ideally, these agencies should be able to coordinate their services so handicapped children will receive all of the services they need regardless of which agency initially identified and began to provide services to the children.

Organizational Exchange

Levine and White (1961) define *organizational exchange* as "any voluntary activity between two organizations which has consequences, actual or anticipated, for the realization of the respective goals or objectives." By and large, most of the working relationships established among agencies to coordinate services to handicapped children are voluntary in nature, although PL 94-142 almost mandates such activity in order to realize the objectives of the law. Experience with PL 94-142 to date and with the Supplemental Security Income Program for Disabled Children indicates, however, that coordination of services among agencies cannot be mandated through legislation (Pratt and Bachman, 1979). The educational system does not have the total resources required to provide all of the related services mandated in PL 94-142; therefore, schools are forced to establish relationships with other agencies and organizations to provide such comprehensive care. Organizations such as schools, in an effort to obtain additional resources, develop greater interdependencies with the network or set of organizations, groups, and parties with which they establish working relationships (Evan, 1966).

Independence of Agencies

Agencies like to maintain their autonomy (Dunham, 1970, Aiken and Hage, 1978). There is a natural tendency for agencies to avoid creating interdependencies except in relatively safe areas that are auxiliary to the main organizational objective. However, this is not seen as a deterrent to developing interagency collaboration. If anything, this tendency fosters interagency working relationships. An educational agency is more likely to enter into a joint program with agencies in other service delivery areas to provide, for example, health or social services than it would be to develop a joint program with another educational agency. In practical terms, this is good common sense. For example, in developing a client evaluation mechanism, it seems more appropriate for the public school system to develop joint working relationships with the public health department and private physicians in a community for the health component; the local welfare or children's services office for the social component; and possibly the community mental health center for clinical psychology services if the school does not have this capability. It seems less practical for the schools to hire staff in order to develop their own programs and expertise in these areas that are ancillary to education. The level of services in each of these service delivery systems in all geographic areas except large urban districts makes this kind of independent action impractical on a cost-benefit basis. In rural areas, this approach would also be impractical because the small size of the population would not justify the school's developing separate health, social, or psychological components. Therefore, the coordination of services through interagency collaboration as described in this book enables schools and other human service delivery agencies to provide comprehensive programs to handicapped children in a coordinated fashion while still maintaining the autonomy that is so important to their separate identity and purpose.

ORGANIZATION OF THE HANDBOOK

This volume is organized into three sections, each addressing a different aspect of interagency collaboration. The first three chapters examine some of the basic issues relating to interagency collaboration. Magrab and Schmidt (Chapter 1) trace the development of interdisciplinary teams as an evaluation and treatment mode for handicapping conditions and show how some of the basic concepts relating to interdisciplinary care contribute to coordination of services. Audette (Chapter 2) provides an overview to interagency collaboration and looks at the role of various levels of government in this arena. Different classes of interagency agreements are also described. Hall (Chapter 3) concludes the section by examining the human factors involved in interagency collaboration and coordination of services. He stresses the importance of establishing key relationships of trust among agency personnel and the need for effective communication. A model for collaboration is also presented that follows the criteria he is advocating.

Section II describes four models of service coordination for handicapped children and the experiences gained through their operation. Zeller (Chapter 4) develops a rationale for Direction Service, a program with a fixed point of referral and coordination unit for handicapped children. He provides a literature base for the evolution of Direction Service and details the working models in Oregon and southern Washington. An insight into some of the cost-benefits of this project is also presented. The experiences of developing a community interagency effort in Colorado are detailed by Kazuk (Chapter 5). After tracing the steps that were used in establishing this project, the problems that were encountered and how they can be prevented or overcome are examined. Mulvenon (Chapter 6) relates the experiences in Kansas of developing interagency teams centered around the needs of preschool children. She also traces the evolution of the Kansas preschool interagency effort and describes problems encountered and how they were resolved. Experiences at a number of the sites in Kansas are reviewed. The last chapter in this section reviews from a planning perspective the experience of an interagency collaboration demonstration project in Massachusetts. Humm-Delgado (Chapter 7) reviews some of the empirical and theoretical studies in the literature relating to interagency collaboration and describes one interagency planning setting. A delineation and discussion of interagency planning issues and recommendations for dealing with them are also presented.

The last two chapters (Section III) provide information required to effect interagency collaboration. The essential components that must be considered when undertaking an interagency collaborative effort are reviewed by Elder in Chapter 8. The areas covered are a compilation of practices followed in the models described in Section II combined with theoretical elements proposed by researchers and the author's own experience. It provides an overview of the necessary concepts for developing coordinated services to handicapped children through interagency collaboration and closes on a cautionary note.

In the last chapter, Elder provides examples of various types of interagency agreements. Accompanying these samples are recommendations of the elements that should be included in such agreements. Different levels and classes of agreements are also reviewed.

REFERENCES

Aiken, M., and Hage, J. 1968. Organizational interdependence and intra-organizational structure. *American Sociological Review* 33:912–929.

Dunham, A. 1970. *The New Community Organization*. Thomas Crowell, New York.

Evan, W. M. 1966. The organization-set: Toward a theory of interorganizational relations. In: J. D. Thompson (ed.), *Approaches to Organizational Design*, pp. 173–91. University of Pittsburgh Press, Pittsburgh.

Final regulations for the implementation of Part B of the Education of the Handicapped Act. 1977 (August). *Federal Register* Vol. 42, No. 163. U.S. Government Printing Office, Washington, D.C.

Galbraith, J. 1973. *Designing Complex Organizations*. Addison-Wesley, Reading, PA.

Kakalik, J., Brewer, G., Dougharty, L., Fleischauer, P., Genensky, S., and Walker, L. 1974. *Improving Services to Handicapped Children*. The Rand Corporation, Santa Monica, CA.

Levine, S., and White, P. 1961. Exchange as a conceptual framework for the study of interorganizational relationships. *Administrative Science Quarterly* 5:583–601.

Magrab, P., and Elder, J. (eds.). 1979. *Planning for Services to Handicapped Persons: Community, Education, Health*. Paul H. Brookes Publishers, Baltimore.

Negandhi, A. 1975. Interorganization theory: Introduction and overview. In: A. Negandhi (ed.), *Interorganization Theory*, pp. 1–13. Kent State University Press, Kent, OH.

Pratt, M., and Bachman, G. 1979. *Evaluation of the Implementation of the Supplemental Security Income Program for Disabled Children (SSI-DCP), Volume I*. Unpublished report, Information Sciences Research Institute, Silver Spring, MD.

Steingraph, H. 1977. *Interorganizational Theory and Practice: Interpretation and Annotation*. The University of Texas, Austin, TX.

U.S. Department of Health, Education, and Welfare. 1975 (May). *A Summary of Selected Legislation Relating to the Handicapped, 1974*. U.S. Department of Health, Education, and Welfare, U.S. Government Printing Office, Washington, D.C.

Van de Ven, A., Emmett, D., and Koenig, R., Jr. 1975. Frameworks for interorganizational analysis. In: A. Negandi (ed.), *Interorganization Theory*, pp. 19–38. Kent State University Press, Kent, OH.

Zeitz, G. 1975. Interorganizational relationships and social structure: A critique of some aspects of the literature. In: A. Negandi (ed.), *Interorganization Theory,* pp. 39–48. Kent State University Press, Kent, OH.

Coordinating Services to Handicapped Children:
A Handbook for Interagency Collaboration
Edited by Jerry O. Elder and Phyllis R. Magrab
Copyright © 1980   Paul H. Brookes Publishers   Baltimore • London

Section I
ISSUES IN INTERAGENCY COLLABORATION

Chapter 1

Interdisciplinary Collaboration
A Prelude to Coordinated Service Delivery

Phyllis R. Magrab and Laura M. Schmidt

> When the voices of children are heard
>   on the green
> And laughing is heard on the hill,
> My heart is at rest within my breast
> And everything else is still.
>
> —Robert Blake
> *The Nurse's Song*

For professionals working in the area of developmental disabilities and for the parents of handicapped children, the heart is never still. Long after normal children's needs and development have led them to self-sufficient maturity, handicapped children and their families are still groping to adapt to the children's special needs and demands. These are multiple and diverse, often requiring more than the support and understanding of the parents, who usually are the sole advocates for the total care of their children. Primary intervention must be provided by those in the health, education, and social service fields who are trained to deal effectively with mentally retarded and developmentally disabled individuals and who may relieve the burden placed upon the parents.

Due in large part to our nation's commitment to our children and to the conscientious interest of the public in mental health, the educational, health, and social services of the community are being made more readily available to help the parents and families, and, more importantly, the children in adapting to and growing with handicapping limitations. But, in doing so, a greater understanding of interdisciplinary cooperation among service providers must be realized.

In talking about the handicapped child and the need for integrated support systems, it is best to remember that services exist to meet the needs of people. The best interests of the child, evidenced at least in part by a con-

13

tinuum of care, must preclude any concept of separatism among the many professions in the various disciplines that serve these children (Valletutti and Christoplos, 1975, p. 5). The disciplines do not exist in their own right; rather, the professionals in their membership are responsible to the child, to the family, and, lastly, to themselves. Disciplines must be joined cohesively for one purpose: to provide a secure, safe, and self-actualizing environment for the handicapped individual.

It has been proved in the past that a loose structure of disciplinary collaboration does not work. The support services that are required by the families of handicapped children necessitate a varied and complex approach to handicapping conditions. Not only are individual support services often insufficient in meeting these needs—due to fragmented delivery—but frequently they also are lacking in a full perspective for the total care of the child. Through collaboration among the various professional disciplines, a general overview of the life events of the child and family, as well as a focus on individual complexities and personalities, can be achieved. This dual objective is best served through a close bonding of the disciples before a particular patient is even taken under consideration. Without this cooperation, the needs of the handicapped child may be handled arbitrarily and incompletely, being addressed within preexisting treatment or service channels within the organizational structure of the agencies or being met only within the limited capabilities of a few service delivery personnel. The result: needless suffering for child and family.

A CASE STUDY: THE URGENCY OF INTERDISCIPLINARY COLLABORATION

> Beth G. is a 4-year-old white female who has severe developmental delays due in large part to rubella contracted during her mother's pregnancy. Born prematurely (at gestational age of 28 weeks), Beth exhibited signs of gross and fine motor delays within the first year. Audiological impairment and language problems also resulted, and a mild seizure disorder was diagnosed. Tested to be within the mild mentally retarded range, Beth began to show learning, behavior, and emotional problems. Her family—mother, father, and brother (age 9)—needed help in coping with Beth, her limitations and problems, and assistance in defining and planning for her future. Since Beth is an integral member of the family, her future is theirs as well.

Beth—and children like her—are the *raison d'être* for interdisciplinary collaboration.

Although the initial responsibility for the care of the child lies with the parents, the overwhelming task of providing sufficient care for developmentally disabled children like Beth is too much for any parent. Most parents understandably lack full comprehension of the problem, the needs of their child, and the requisite intervention. Beth will have numerous functional requirements including:

Attaining motor milestones
Coping with hearing disability
Developing language
Controlling her seizure disorder
Gaining basic educational skills
Adapting to her peer group

Beth's family will have many adaptations to make in integrating Beth into family life. This family, and others like them, must have a coherent approach to management of such problems. But who will meet these needs and how they will be met become the crucial questions.

Professionals who work with handicapped children usually are trained in generic disciplines to meet functional needs. At times, their skills may overlap; other times, a given professional may have the skills to meet the total needs of the child, but typically, each professional will have a fragmented view. The complexity of the individual's needs and of the decision-making process in dealing with them clearly is beyond the scope of any single professional. Using the case of Beth as an instance of the requirement for diverse services, the potential role of various disciplines is examined below to illustrate the magnitude of the necessity for collaboration.

As in Beth's case, the pediatrician may be the first to notice the deficits of the newborn or young child. Within the sphere of health services, the establishment of early diagnosis for an abnormal condition is fundamental to effecting efficient intervention. The pediatrician has the early knowledge and the channel for input to the family unit to initiate the proper care and treatment. By defining the developmentally handicapped child in terms of individual failure to progress at a normal rate in acquiring skills in motor, adaptive, communicative, and social areas, the pediatrician has opened the door for other disciplines to become involved. The concept of commitment to disciplinary collaboration should be exemplary through his/her work. Since disabilities are not mutually exclusive of each other and often are found in combination, as with Beth, the need for specialization in dealing with these disabilities is apparent. The pediatrician usually can serve as integrator to introduce to the family the various other professional services that are needed for the care of the total child.

Because motor delays like Beth's are usually observed early in the child's life, the physical therapist and the occupational therapist may be among the first professionals to initiate contact with the family. The physical or occupational therapist will be essential in determining the impairment of the motor skills and in gaining treatment for the deficit areas. Fine and gross motor skills, muscle tone, strength, and movement are all part of the total evaluative and treatment process between the physical or occupational therapist and the child.

For a child like Beth, failure to respond to sound or communication may be the result of hearing impairment or intellectual dysfunction. Most children like this will require an audiological evaluation as a first step in the diagnostic process to determine the actual disability. It will be important to define the deficits as they actually exist, not as they appear. Since hearing is essential for the development of normal speech, language, socialization, and other forms of behavior, a child like Beth with hearing problems may face a world of isolation and withdrawal if not treated. In terms of a language delay, the speech-language pathologist can define and provide remedial treatment for deficits. An undetected or untreated language problem can mask other problem areas as well as create new ones. Communication skills have a profound effect on all areas of development.

Beth's seizure disorder will require ongoing monitoring by a pediatric neurologist who will have to work closely with the family pediatrician. The management of medication and crisis situations will be shared primarily by these two professionals.

The psychologist must determine the capabilities for learning of children like Beth. By evaluating the current intellectual functioning and testing for cognitive potential of the child, the psychologist can assist in program and intervention planning. In addition, the psychologist will evaluate the emotional status and interpersonal functioning of the child and assist with social and emotional adaptation. The psychologist usually obtains a preliminary assessment of family dynamics in order to achieve a full picture of how the condition of the child is affecting the individual and the family.

The social worker will deal with the family unit as a whole. Each family member must be integrated into the habilitative and rehabilitative process in order for children such as Beth to gain maximum support and for the family to experience minimal stress. Siblings are an important part of the family unit and must be given special attention in terms of their needs and their problems in being part of a family with a handicapped child. The social worker must be available to the family not only in crisis situations but also throughout the time service delivery and intervention are needed to assist in the coping process of the entire family. The list of professionals needed to address the multiple problems that Beth and her family face may not yet be complete. Nursing care, nutritional services, special education planning, and psychiatric intervention at different points in Beth's life will become special needs.

The extent of professional intervention required by this child and her family serves to highlight the urgency of interdisciplinary collaboration. This family is at great risk for fragmented and uncoordinated services in which a lack of common direction and comprehensive planning can flourish. The first step in providing an optimal, well articulated, cohesive approach is to develop a framework of collaboration among all the professionals involved in the care of the family. It is at the case level that all our discussions of interagency collaboration must begin, and it is for this reason that a concept of interdisciplinary care is essential.

THE CONCEPT OF INTERDISCIPLINARY COLLABORATION

That services to and care of handicapped children must be coordinated and comprehensive is self-evident from cases such as the one outlined above. How to achieve a meaningful collaboration among the various disciplines that have an impact on the process is both a difficult and a complex task.

There are those who view interdisciplinary collaboration in terms of specific mechanisms or a concrete set of procedures that includes team membership requirements, assignment of roles, definition of case managership, and operational formats. All of these clearly do serve as descriptors of the process in which a group of professionals may be engaged, but the concept of interdisciplinary collaboration goes beyond a set of descriptors.

In its most meaningful sense, interdisciplinary care is an attitude (Johnston and Magrab, 1976, p. 9). For professionals to interact in a truly collaborative manner, the elements of trust, respect, and mutual dependence must be present. In order to develop a decision-making and planning process that is interdisciplinary in nature, the professionals involved must recognize each other's competencies, trust each other's opinions, and rely upon each other for the total care of the child and his/her family. Clearly, such a set of relationships does not arise immediately, but rather evolves through a process of shared communication. In part, the generated partnership is based on the particular individuals involved, and, in part, it is based on the history of each individual in his/her understanding and knowledge of the potential role of other disciplines. An interdisciplinary attitude does not emerge magically. There is a knowledge and experiential base that assists any given professional in acquiring this attitude.

An understanding of the role of professionals in other disciplines, experience with the outcome of their work, and appreciation for the intricacies of the group decision-making process are important areas for sensitization when attempting to achieve interdisciplinary collaboration. Some specific goals to foster the interdisciplinary process include each participant's ability to:

1. Identify his/her role in the decision-making process
2. Become sensitive to the role and work style of other participants
3. Establish and maintain a balance between disciplinary identity and interdisciplinary group memberships
4. Develop and exercise a leadership competence
5. Develop and exercise competence in problem solving within an interdisciplinary environment

The barriers to interdisciplinary collaboration often stem from initial confusion about the role of participating professionals and their concerns for territorial domain. The leadership function can also be a prominent issue; biases about a preconceived hierarchy of professional status and responsibility often must be overcome. An array of communication barriers, such as nonparticipation, unresolved conflict, and inadequate decision making, that thwart the collaborative efforts can emerge.

To facilitate interdisciplinary care, open communication among participants must develop. The style of interaction of each of the participants is important in the problem-solving process. The more aware each team member is of his/her own behavioral style in a group and the more sensitive each member is to the work style of others, the more effectively tasks will be accomplished. Table 1 summarizes the types of contributions participants can make to the interdisciplinary communication process.

Interdisciplinary collaboration is strengthened and works more effectively when, in the process of interaction, each participant becomes:

1. More aware of the type of contribution, such as information giving, encouraging, or summarizing, that is needed at any given time
2. More able to provide a range of these interactive functions
3. More skilled in giving feedback to other participants

Table 1. Contributions to the interdisciplinary communication process

Type of contribution to interactive process		Group member				
		A	B	C	D	E
Task roles	Proposes action Gives information Gives opinion Asks information Asks opinion Elaborates Summarizes					
Maintenance roles	Encourages Expresses group feeling "Gate keeping"					
Task-maintenance roles	Evaluates Diagnoses Arbitrates Tests for consensus					
Nonfunctional behaviors	Actively aggresses Withdraws Competes					

Team development of professionals working in an interdisciplinary modality should focus on goals, roles, and procedures to develop interdependent relationships among members. Rubin, Plovnick, and Fry (1975) point to the need to manage problems productively and to be alert to the symptoms of inadequately functioning teams, including constant stress, a crisis orientation, and avoidance of conflict.

Team building and interdisciplinary collaboration are complicated phenomena that point to the importance of early training. Knowing that attitudes are difficult to change and that the concept of "interdisciplinary" is basically an attitude, there is a need to foster a receptivity to collaboration as early in the training of professionals as possible. Unfortunately, for most, this aspect of training occurs on the job and the new "attitude" must be developed in team meetings. Most professional training programs attempt to inculcate such strong disciplinary identities that it is difficult to instill an interdisciplinary attitude later. Slowly, professional training programs have come to recognize this problem, and, more and more, changes in basic curricula are occurring that provide a basis for future interdisciplinary collaboration.

HISTORICAL BACKGROUND OF
INTERDISCIPLINARY SERVICES AND TRAINING

Federal health care, social service, and education legislation traces the ability of our society to provide comprehensive, coordinated services to handicapped individuals. The pattern of this legislation reflects the extent to which the various systems developed collaborative strategies. For the United States, prior to the 1960s these systems were specialized, growing independently but not integrally. The schisms among them had bred self-maturing agencies with few or no interrelationships—especially at the point of service delivery.

Yet there had been a growing recognition of the need for comprehensive service programs involving the various disciplines—the precursors to interdisciplinary care (Boggs, 1976, p. 1). As early as 1936, grants were made available for the diagnosis and treatment of "crippled children" and for the creation of maternal and child health programs. During the 1960s, the Children's Bureau gave incentives to states and universities to initiate "comprehensive" diagnostic and evaluative centers for the mentally retarded. The need for changing approaches to treatment came into sharp focus in the late 1950s when statistics at that time showed a marked neglect of the needs of retarded people. In a survey of primary physicians (pediatricians and general practitioners) at the time, 62% indicated that they did not serve the retarded population, as did no less than 88% of the hospitals. Public agencies during this period said that 74% of their professionals did not serve this population (Todd, n.d., p. 1).

By 1960, a number of "comprehensive" diagnostic centers for crippled children and other handicapped persons were in existence in an attempt to service the demanding needs of handicapping conditions. But it was not until 1963 with the signing of PL 88-164, an implementation of recommendations of the President's Panel on Mental Retardation of the previous year, that a concrete outline of interdisciplinary services was developed that would allow for growth in the areas of collaboration and service delivery.

The report of the President's Panel of 1962 was the first major document to deal with the complex, specialized care needed by handicapped individuals, in this case the mentally retarded. The concept of "the continuum of care" was delineated:

> "Continuum of Care" describes the selection, blending and use, in proper sequence and relationship, of medical, educational, and social services required by a retarded person to minimize his disability at every point in his lifespan. Thus "care" is used in its broadest sense and the word "continuum" underscores the many transitions and liaisons, within and among various services and professions, by which the community attempts to secure for the retarded the kind and variety of help and accommodation he requires. A "continuum of care" permits fluidity of movement of the individual from one type of service to another while maintaining a sharp focus on his unique requirements. The ongoing process of assuring that an individual receives the services he needs when he needs them and in the amount and variety he requires is the essence of planning and coordination (U.S. Department of Health, Education, and Welfare, 1976, p. 2).

The panel linked this concept of "continuum of care" with the establishment of new approaches to training, which led to the establishment of University Affiliated Facilities (UAFs) *to provide interdisciplinary training in exemplary service settings*. The panel reported:

> ... such exemplary programs can also serve as a means of demonstrating truly adequate management and new concepts of service—such as the "continuum of care" approach—to leaders and potential leaders in other communities. "Seed personnel" are thus prepared who can extend the concept. In addition, with their emphasis upon quality, both in service and in professional training, they would surely promote the recruitment of desirable personnel who work in mental retardation (President's Panel on Mental Retardation, 1962, p. 197).

In 1963, PL 88-164, which created the UAFs, aimed specifically at correcting those problems that pervaded the generic service delivery systems for mentally retarded individuals. University-based facilities were constructed so that practical clinical training in interdisciplinary diagnosis, care, and treatment of mentally retarded individuals would be available. These facilities were to make possible an interdisciplinary approach to the training of physicians, nurses, therapists of many types, educators, speech-language therapists, nutritionists, and psychologists, with opportunities for clinical exposure at the preservice level.

Over a decade later, a Long-Range Task Force on UAFs (1976) was convened by the Office of the Secretary of the Department of Health, Education, and Welfare to reassess the effectiveness and scope of interdisciplinary training and exemplary services provided by this program. The task force affirmed the continued need for this type of training:

> The UAF program has been most noteable in its development and spreading through the educational establishment of an interdisciplinary team approach to education. At the time of the 1962 Panel report, such an approach to education was rare. Today, the concept is widely accepted as offering the breadth of education necessary to medical and other professionals who work with developmentally disabled persons. Indeed it is fair to say that the federally legislated UAF program has supported the development of an interdisciplinary approach to education in general. The evidence of the magnitude of this achievement is illustrated by the commonplace use today of the term "interdisciplinary" (U.S. Department of Health, Education, and Welfare, 1976, p. 5).

Furthermore, interdisciplinary training was defined by the task force as:

> . . . an integrated educational process involving the interdependent contributions of the several relevant disciplines to enhance professional growth as it relates to training, service and research. The interdisciplinary process promotes the development and use of a basic language, a core body of knowledge, relevant skills, and an understanding of the attitude, values, and method of participating disciplines (U.S. Department of Health, Education, and Welfare, 1976, p. 11).

The task force also enumerated the settings and roles for which interdisciplinary education is especially desirable:

1. Comprehensive diagnosis and evaluation of the developmentally disabled individual for purposes of habilitation program planning.
2. Extended case management and individual program coordination (professional advocacy).
3. Training of parents and caregivers.
4. Administration of facilities and systems which have a significant developmental disabilities component in their service population.
5. Community, state and national program planning and evaluation.
6. Leadership in all areas of service delivery, including policy making at community, regional, and national levels.
7. Quality assurance, including development of performance and other standards, licensing, accreditation, and specific program evaluations.
8. Teaching in programs intended to prepare students for careers in DD services for upgrading the competence of existing workers (U.S. Department of Health, Education, and Welfare, 1976, p. 12).

They stated that persons trained in interdisciplinary settings should:

> . . . be available who have been trained specifically to work in the developmental disabilities service system or in its supportive network. All graduates of UAFs should (1) be competent in a base discipline; (2) be able to apply their disciplinary knowledge and skills in programs for the developmentally

disabled; (3) understand the role and contributions of other disciplines to the services required by the developmentally disabled; (4) work effectively in an interdisciplinary group and (5) possess a conceptual framework which serves to articulate the functional areas represented within the human services network (U.S. Department of Health, Education, and Welfare, 1976, p. 13).

Increasingly, the concept of *interdisciplinary service* and training has become recognized and implemented. Today, service delivery to handicapped individuals more typically is conceived of as an interdisciplinary process, and increasing numbers of professionals are being trained in this regard. Through federal legislation and the expanded commitment of universities for interdisciplinary training, the trend of collaborative services will continue to be enhanced. The success of interagency coordination is dependent on our ability to continue to train and serve in this manner.

SUMMARY

It is at the case level that all discussions of interagency collaboration must begin. The needs of handicapped children and their families almost always extend beyond the scope of any single profession or agency. At the outset, it is the parent who serves as the sole advocate for the total care of the child. This is an awesome task, and it is in relation to this need for comprehension and coordinated services that the concept of interdisciplinary services in born. Through a collaboration approach to care, the various professionals assisting the child and his family can be brought together in a cohesive way to support the parent in caring for the total needs of the child.

"Interdisciplinary" as a concept reflects primarily an attitude—one of respect, trust, and interdependence among professions. To achieve the goal of interdisciplinary services, the attitude and skills required for interdisciplinary services must be introduced early in the training of professionals who will serve handicapped children. Professionals so trained ultimately will serve as change agents in the broader service delivery system. Interdisciplinary collaboration is the prelude to much needed coordinated service delivery.

REFERENCES

Boggs, E. M. 1976. An Abbreviated Legislative History of University Affiliated Facilities for the Mentally Retarded and Developmentally Disabled. April 1. AAUAP Office, Washington, D.C.

Johnston, R., and Magrab, P. (eds.). 1976. *Developmental Disorders: Assessment, Treatment, Education,* University Park Press, Baltimore.

Koch, R., and Dobson, J. C. 1971. *The Mentally Retarded Child and His Family.* Brunner/Mazel, New York.

Mittler, P. (ed.). *Research to Practice in Mental Retardation.* Volume II. University Park Press, Baltimore.

President's Panel on Mental Retardation. 1962 (October). U.S. Government Printing Office, Washington, D.C.

Rubin, I. W., Plovnick, M. S., and Fry, R. E. 1975. *Improving the Coordination of Care: A Program for Health Team Development.* Ballinger Publishing Co., Cambridge, MA.

Todd, S. P., Jr. (n.d.). The Present Role of University Affiliated Facilities. Washington, D.C.

U.S. Department of Health, Education, and Welfare. 1976. *The Role of Higher Education in Mental Retardation and Other Developmental Disabilities.* Washington, D.C.

Valletutti, P., and Christoplos, F. (eds.). 1977. *Interdisciplinary Approaches to Human Services.* University Park Press, Baltimore.

Coordinating Services to Handicapped Children:
A Handbook for Interagency Collaboration
Edited by Jerry O. Elder and Phyllis R. Magrab
Copyright © 1980   Paul H. Brookes Publishers   Baltimore • London

Chapter 2

Interagency Collaboration
The Bottom Line

Robert H. Audette

Increasingly, numbers are playing a determining role in our lives. It has become important to be able to deal effectively with demands for accurate numbers, such as ZIP codes, area codes, and Social Security numbers, to mention only a few, in daily activities.

Numbers can also reflect symbolic as well as utilitarian values. For those who are concerned with the welfare of children with handicaps, numbers have recently taken on a particularly important symbolic value. As PL 94-142 (Education for All Handicapped Children Act of 1975) and Section 504 of the Rehabilitation Act of 1973 raise expectations that, at long last, opportunities for full and meaningful citizenship can be achieved by children and adults who are handicapped, so the specter of Proposition 13 represses that new hope with the increasing possibility of services and programs without funds.

It is in this climate of converging and seemingly conflicting expectations that the old but unfulfilled ideal of interagency collaboration must be considered.

HOW DID WE GET HERE?

The legislative and litigative history of public response to the needs and rights of persons with handicaps is marbled by erratic, knee-jerk responses to the outrage of the moment. Wolfensberger (1969) has vividly detailed the attitudes and changes in public policy toward persons classified as mentally retarded. Gottwald (1970) has further documented the various attitudes of people toward handicapped persons, surveying most of the handicapping conditions prevalent in the United States today. The misunderstanding and the fear of persons with handicaps, which are still far too common, are both a cause and a result of public policy. The history of federal programs directly or indirectly having an impact on persons with handicaps loudly proclaims, "There is no master plan." Of the 35 federal laws relating to handicapped persons passed since 1970, most have responded to problems or crises that in one way or another have created public discomfiture. These outrages (e.g., the Willowbrook exposé) have generated piecemeal program responses without regard to programs already in place or the manner in which services are organized and delivered.

As a result of this chaos, services to children with handicaps are provided on both functional (e.g., mental health, education, social services) and categorical (e.g., services for mentally retarded, emotionally disturbed, physically handicapped) bases. In addition, eligibility for services within the various functions and categories has been based on considerations of age (e.g., 3–21 for special education), family income (e.g., for Medicaid reimbursement), severity of handicap (e.g., services limited to the severely or multiply handicapped), and the organization of state government (e.g., in some states the Early Periodic Screening, Diagnosis, and Treatment (EPSDT) Program is available to all children eligible for Medicaid based on family income, while in other states the program is administered through Aid for Dependent Children which denies health care to children because their unemployed fathers have not abandoned their families), among other factors.

These approaches to serving (or not serving) children with handicaps have resulted in systems with sharply defined areas of agency responsibility and with correspondingly difficult problems in achieving interagency collaboration, and with a population of children with handicaps that receives services in direct proportion to the effectiveness of its advocates in securing funding for those services through the political process, the courts, or both.

There are four particularly debilitating consequences of the current state of affairs:

1. There are still many gaps in the service system where children with handicaps fail to satisfy eligibility criteria.
2. There are still too many instances in which no services are available for certain categories of children with handicaps (particularly adolescents with unmet emotional needs).
3. There are many instances where services are available but limited to a specific program size or an annual appropriation that is insufficient to provide for the eligible population of children. In addition, the services that are available are highly differentiated by an agency, so that interagency services or comprehensive services are the rare exception rather than the rule.
4. The complaints of Proposition 13 proponents that government is wasting the taxpayers' money by duplicating services across various agencies are sadly true.

It is not surprising, therefore, that studies of children's services in many states during the past decade have recommended an expansion of services to fill gaps in the system that serves children with handicaps as well as other children in need of services. These same studies have also stressed the need for an increase in and improvement of interagency collaboration so that the programs providing services are comprehensive and nonduplicative. Phrases like "coordination of services," "interagency cooperation," "comprehensive services," "maximization of funding," and "nondiscrimination in the delivery of services" appear frequently in these studies and have been repeated increasingly over the past several years in federal and state legislation, task force reports, and administration policy statements. The fact that these phrases are so frequently used and that the goals they embody are so infrequently achieved has created an atmosphere of disenchantment among taxpayers concerned about waste in government, of cynicism among political and administrative officials who are all too aware of the "turf" issues that are a major obstacle to the achievement of these goals, and of frustration among policy makers, planners, and program directors who are constantly being pressured to achieve those goals.

It is the leadership of the Proposition 13 movement, however, that has captured the public interest as its proponents accurately point out that we cannot afford the luxury of duplicative and competitive empires, cumbersome and unnecessarily expensive systems, and ultimately a substantially unserved or poorly served handicapped constituency.

Ironically, many of the "definitions" that have been ascribed to persons with handicaps (e.g., nonadaptive, noncommunicative, perseverative) could more aptly be used to describe the array of organizations and agencies that compete to meet the needs of some children and just as actively avoid responding to the various needs of others. The "patchwork quilt" of agencies, their eligibility criteria, intake systems, coordination mechanisms, and paperwork requirements, and the insulation of agency information under the guise of confidentiality—as well as many other factors—have made it necessary for advocates of children with handicaps to be highly skilled in order to successfully piece together a reasonable facsimile of a "program" that can be responsive to the individual needs of eligible persons. Agencies and organizations have evolved into the "indispensable," sole proprietors of needed resources which they dole out in ways that are self-protective of their "turf" or self-aggrandizing to their individual roles in the community.

The Proposition 13 constituency has much data to support their contention that more tax money and more programs have not resulted in the efficient system of services that persons with handicaps require. These angry citizens will no longer tolerate the pacifiers who propose "reorganization," "decentralization," "centralization," and the adoption of other approaches used to forestall the inevitable need to break up the fiefdoms that are well entrenched and effectively resistant to change. If agencies do not work out effective mechanisms to serve cooperatively children and adults with handicaps, they run the serious risk of being eliminated as part of the "cleanup" of government that is growing more likely each day.

PL 94-142 AND § 504: AN OPPORTUNITY

In light of the fractionated policy development described above, PL 94-142 and § 504 of the Rehabilitation Act of 1973 offer the potential to finally set things straight. Together they provide a basis for serving all children with handicaps regardless of family income, severity of disability, type of handicap, or any other limiting criteria. They are comprehensive in the identification of who can be served, and they are broadening their inclusion of related services necessary for the achievement of a free and appropriate public education.

Section 504 transcends all agencies, programs, ages, handicapping conditions, income considerations, and other factors in proclaiming full citizenship and civil rights to all persons who have handicaps. Consequently, an intense conflict is evolving as the expectations of handicapped children and their families are heightened by PL 94-142 and § 504 while the frustration of taxpayers erupts in Proposition 13 movements in response to wasteful government programs. The convergence of PL 94-142, § 504, and Proposition 13 will either create chaos or generate an improved service delivery environment, depending on the response of education and human service administrators and policy makers.

PL 94-142 and § 504 provide a new, motivating force for the achievement of long sought goals of decent access to the benefits of American citizenship for children and adults with handicaps.

PL 94-142 is particularly relevant to the achievement of these goals for four principal reasons. First, its definition of "handicapped children" is virtually unprecedented in its inclusiveness, with regard to both age and category of handicaps. Read together with the various state statutes and regulations, the only group it overlooks are children less than 3 years of age, although even this group is included in the "child find" requirements and may actually receive special education services which are federally reimbursible after all "first priority" children are served. With regard to category of handicap, its list of eligible handicapping conditions is so broad as to be virtually all-inclusive.

Second, its definition of "free appropriate public education" includes the so-called "related services" and thus expands the traditional definition of special education to include a complex of mandated services that traditionally have been the responsibility of non-education agencies. Among the many services to be provided are psychological services, physical therapy, and occupational therapy, to mention but three.

A third reason why PL 94-142 is particularly relevant to these goals is that its full service mandate is not limited to school systems as in the case of other educational legislation. Also included are all public and private agencies that serve children with handicaps. The federal law requires state education agencies to assume a single set of standards for services to children with handicaps without regard to who the provider may be or where the program is located. The role of the state education agency in relation to these other agencies is to monitor the total service delivery system to ensure that the requirements of the law are carried out by all agencies. Furthermore, PL 94-142 makes it clear that funding for special education is to come not only from education sources but also from "whatever state, local, federal and private sources of support are available in the State. . . ." The regulations for the implementation of PL 94-142 are careful to specify that nothing contained in them "relieves an insurer or similar party from an otherwise valid obligation to provide or to pay for services provided to a handicapped child." Thus, PL 94-142 clearly envisions an extensive and coordinated involvement by "non-education" agencies and the use of "non-educational sources of funding" for the implementation of its full-service mandate.

The fourth reason why PL 94-142 is particularly relevant to these goals is that the result of its inclusiveness with regard to eligibility for services is that states and local communities are faced with a complex and costly mandate to expand and improve services. The financial reward for satisfying this mandate is an increasing level of federal financial assistance for the education of children with handicaps. The stated congressional intent of PL 94-142 is to increase federal support for special education to 40% before the close of the 1980s. Yet, because of the current overlap of federal (and state) programs, *there are significant numbers of children for whom all or parts of their program could be supported with 50% to 100% federal funds now.*

Thus, both PL 94-142 and § 504 offer a legal breadth of mandate for a partnership with the Proposition 13 movement. Such a partnership envisions the implementation of a comprehensive, coordinated, and *cost-effective* system for the delivery of services to children with handicaps. The possibility of such a broadened public constituency has great potential for increased funding by way of interagency agreements with heightened federal financial assistance to facilitate public education for all children, including those with handicaps.

BUILDING THE PARTNERSHIP

The taxpayers' revolt has, as a dominant feature, a frustrated quality of "no nonsense." The merging of forces supportive of quality education and other necessary services for children with handicaps with those who wish to eliminate waste in government requires the application of certain principles in developing and carrying out new forms of interagency collaboration. The methods proposed here are based on the important assumption that *the need for expansion of existing resources and the development of new ones can be accurately determined only after a full exploration of the potential for effective cooperation among public schools and other public and private agencies in the utilization and management of existing resources for these children.*

DEVELOPMENT OF AGREEMENTS

The idea of interagency collaboration in serving children and their families is not new. The cooperative approach to serving persons with handicaps has been tried many times and in many ways. Unfortunately, the success stories are too few and the instances of "paper cooperation" too many. Many of the agreements that have been written to document this collaboration are simply promises to cooperate. Cooperation, however, has not necessarily resulted in implementation of more or better services. In many instances, the spirit of cooperation was not supplemented with the concepts and procedures necessary to overcome the many governance, organizational, and functional barriers that characterize all levels of bureaucracy. A properly designed interagency agreement reflects the constraints, requirements, and discretionary authority of each participating agency. Such a design is based on analysis of common purposes across agencies and acceptable options for meeting those responsibilities through cooperative efforts.

There are more options available to public schools and other agencies in meeting their statutory responsibilities than are generally recognized. More importantly, the options that can be exercised by public school administrations can be multiplied by carefully designed interagency efforts. In the final analysis, all agencies including the constituency of weary taxpayers can be singularly viewed as THE COMMUNITY. The following classifications and concepts are provided to assist local leaders in maximizing their options in serving handicapped children and their families.

Classes of Interagency Agreements

There are three major classes of interagency agreements. The first and most important class centers on common or baseline standards for the conduct of similar programs by different agencies. These agreements are commitments by public schools and other agencies to adopt common and specific criteria in the provision of services to handicapped children and their families. Essentially, these standards reflect multiple-agency adoption of explicit program understandings regarding who does what to whom, when, where, how often, under whose supervision, and to whose advantage. Commitments that address such standards are prerequisite to any and all other agreements regarding the provision of services to handicapped children and their families.

The second class of agreements consists of commitments concerning the allocation of public school and other agency resources in the accomplishment of mutually agreed upon objectives. There are at least six methods of cooperatively allocating resources:

1. _First dollar agreements:_ When a handicapped child or family is eligible for certain services from the public school and one or more agencies, a promise is made regarding which organization pays first. For example, when a Medicaid-eligible, handicapped child needs physical therapy, Medicaid agrees to pay. Education only pays for physical therapy when a child is not eligible for Medicaid.

2. _Complementary dollar agreements:_ When a handicapped child or family is eligible for certain services from the public school and one or more other agencies, a commitment is made for each organization to pay for certain services. For example, when a Medicaid-eligible, handicapped child needs speech therapy and reconstructive dental surgery, the public school pays for the speech therapy and Medicaid pays for the surgery.

3. _Complementary personnel/dollar agreements:_ When a handicapped child or family is eligible for certain services from the public school and one or more agencies, one organization commits personnel to directly serve the child while the other reserves sufficient funds to pay for other services. For example, when a Medicaid-eligible, handicapped child needs speech therapy and reconstructive dental surgery, the public school directly provides (through a school employee) the speech therapy and Medicaid pays for the surgery.

4. _Shared personnel agreements:_ When children are screened before entering public school, a commitment is made that allows public health nurses and school nurses to work together in administering parts of the screening program. For example, family health histories are taken by both public health and school nurses during a preschool screening program.

5. _Shared facility agreements:_ When children are screened before entering public school, a commitment is made to use a community hospital facility for carrying out all or part of the program. For example, when preschool screening is conducted for a certain neighborhood, the local hospital is used as the testing site.

6. _Shared equipment and materials agreements:_ When children are screened before entering public school, a commitment is made to use hospital equipment and/or materials for certain elements of the screening program. For example, when preschool screening occurs, the local hospital does all the blood work analysis for lead paint testing.

The third class of agreements includes commitments to uniform procedures, forms, and activities by public schools and other agencies offering comparable services. Agreements regarding standards (class 1) and allocation of resources (class 2) are absolute prerequisites to procedural and activity (class 3) agreements. Commitments can be made regarding many areas to link directly the needs of individual children and families to the capacity of the public school and other cooperating agencies to respond. Child and family service agreements can be addressed in a systematic manner if the commitment clearly articulates how each participating organization administers client entitlements. The following are some examples of such agreements:

1. *Definitions:* When children and families are evaluated to determine their service needs, the public school and other participating agencies use uniform terminology on all forms to ensure a common understanding of the program requirements. Such definitional agreements are easier to achieve when the terminology is straightforward and free of jargon. For example, when preschool screening is conducted, reports will describe behavior rather than inferred diagnostic classifications.

2. *Forms and formats:* When children are evaluated, reports can be made on a uniform packet of forms. For example, when screening is conducted, all basic information used by the public school and other agencies will be included in a single packet of forms, including those for general as well as specialized information.

3. *Referral:* When children are identified as needing services, a commitment is made to use a single intake system to ensure that all necessary services are provided. For example, when a teacher believes that a child is in need of special services, an interagency evaluation process will be used to establish the child's program needs.

4. *Entitlements:* When individual programs are designed, a commitment is made to coordinate all entitlements offered through various agencies. For example, when a program is designed for a preschool child with severe crippling conditions, a Medicaid-funded, physical therapy program will be included within an individual plan.

5. *Complementarity:* When individual programs are designed, a commitment is made to ensure that services by the public school properly mesh with services from other agencies. For example, the public school will hire an occupational therapist and the health agency will hire a physical therapist.

6. *Transitions:* When long term individual programs are planned, public schools and other agencies are committed to respond to automatic triggering mechanisms for cooperative effort. For example, the public school and the state vocational rehabilitation agency agree that when a 16-year-old student is evaluated for special education services a rehabilitation counselor will participate for purposes of planning programs that will be necessary when the student leaves school at age 22.

Interagency agreements can also be made to ensure that promises to work together are kept.

7. _Planning and budgetary calendars:_ Uniform calendars for planning and budgeting can be used by participating agencies. This procedure will significantly support the promises made by participating agencies.

8. _Coordinated, comprehensive community planning:_ Variously required annual and multi-year community and substate regional plans can be developed in concert so that contributions promised from the public schools and other participating agencies are included in each plan. For example, when the plan for a Health Maintenance Organization (HMO) is prepared, promises for services by public schools and other agencies can be included.

9. _Coordinated staff development:_ Staff who offer similar services, but in different agencies, can be trained together. For example, funds from Title XX of the Social Security Act can be used to train staff from public schools and other agencies who offer eligible services to children who participate in Title XX programs.

10. _Fiscal administration:_ Administrative arrangements can be made so that payment for services follows the child and family regardless of which agency provides services. For example, Title XX funds can be used to pay for community residential services that are prescribed in an individualized education program (IEP).

11. _Integrated data base:_ Information that is collected by the public school and other participating agencies can be stored in a commonly controlled data system, and can be used by each agency for its own purposes or to assist another agency. For example, IEPs can be described and stored in the same computer system as are individualized treatment plans developed by the mental health agency. Both agencies can arrange to search their files to show another agency how a particular program was designed for children with similar needs.

12. _Cooperative evaluations and monitoring:_ Public schools and other participating agencies contribute resources to implement qualitative evaluation and compliance monitoring of their individual and coordinated services. For example, 5% of each program grant for the public school and other participating agencies can be pooled and used to pay the lowest bidder to design and conduct a relevant evaluation program of services offered through the cooperative interagency system.

Thus, interagency agreements can be designed in many ways. It is important that the first steps be discrete and achievable within a reasonable period of time.

CONCLUSION

Time is becoming short for public and private agencies who serve children with handicaps. Historical approaches to establishing task forces or reorganizing the agencies will no longer satisfy the rightful demands of persons with handicaps or stem the outcry of overburdened taxpayers. If organizations do not take the initiative toward establishing cooperative efficiency, they run the risk of jeopardizing their survival and being eliminated for being of no relevance to either the consumer or the taxpayer. It is time to join forces NOW. The bottom line is clear—DO IT or it will be done for you.

REFERENCES

Wolfensberger, W. 1969. The Origin and Nature of Our Institutional Models. In: President's Committee on Mental Retardation, *Changing Patterns in Residential Services for the Mentally Retarded.* U.S. Government Printing Office, Washington, D.C.

Gottwald, G. 1970. *Public Attitudes Toward the Handicapped.* Council for Exceptional Children, Reston, VA.

APPENDIX

What Programs to Consider

Services for handicapped children are provided by public schools, by local, state, and federal agencies, and by private organizations and practitioners, or by some combination of the public and private sectors, as, for example, in the case of a pediatrician in private practice contracting with a public school. Services may be free to the client (as in the case of services provided by public schools), provided on a sliding fee scale based upon the income of the client, paid for by the client who may have no insurance or other third-party coverage, or paid for in whole or in part by a third-party insurer such as Blue Cross/Blue Shield or Medicaid. Certain private philanthropic organizations, such as the United Way, and various foundations provide grants to public and private agencies to enable them to develop new services for handicapped children and others. Usually, such services are ultimately provided at no cost or at a reduced cost to the client. All of these various funding arrangements must be reconsidered in light of the fact that PL 94-142 and § 504 require that all such services must be free to handicapped children.

This appendix is concerned with identifying and describing educational and related services mandated or allowed by federal and some state statutes and regulations that can be utilized in meeting the full service goal of PL 94-142. Thus, the services described in this section are those that have a direct relation to the programs offered by most public school systems. Some of the described services, such as foster care placement and school food services programs, are not among the services mandated by special education statutes and regulations, but they are included because they are key support services that are of particular relevance to whether and how well a handicapped child can progress in a particular special education program. It is important to note that 1) a combination of good special education programs in the public school and specialized foster care offers an attractive fiscal and program alternative in a less restrictive environment than most private residential schools, and 2) a nutritious school breakfast and school lunch program can go a long way toward maximizing the learning benefits of special education programs for handicapped children. In the final analysis, such complementary efforts can determine the usefulness of the many resources expended for the benefit of handicapped children and their families.

In addition, certain "nonmandated" support services are included as a reference point because they are critical to the effectiveness of the mandated services. For instance, an example of a nonmandated support service is foster care placement for a child who is able to attend a public school program, except for the lack of a residence. Also included are services related to the prevention of handicapping conditions because, although not mandated themselves, they directly affect the nature and extent of the mandated services.

Although the focus of this discussion is on services for handicapped children, the services described are usually for broader categories of persons, since very few programs are specifically limited to handicapped children. For example, various health services, such as Maternal and Child Health Services, are not limited to handicapped children from birth through age 6. In general, the following four categories of services are described:

1. Programs for handicapped children
2. Programs for children, which include services for handicapped children
3. Programs for handicapped persons, which include services for handicapped children
4. Comprehensive programs, which include services for handicapped children

Within each category, the programs are grouped according to the administering federal agency. Immediately under the program title is the Federal Catalog of Domestic Assistance identifying number. For some programs the number of the public law that authorized the program's creation is also listed.

Programs for Handicapped Children

1. *Crippled Children's Services*
   HEW 13.211 Health Services Administration
   To provide medical and related services to crippled children and to children suffering from conditions that lead to crippling. Available to all crippled children under 21. Diagnostic services provided regardless of eligibility.
2. *Supplemental Security Income—Disabled Children's Program*
   HEW 13.807 Health Services Administration
   To provide for the delivery of medical, social, developmental, and rehabilitation services to blind and disabled children under 16 years of age who are receiving Supplemental Security Income benefits. The program is responsible for locating these children, getting them into the health care system, and assuming the provision of needed care on an individual basis, which is not available from other sources.
3. *Educationally Disadvantaged Children—Handicapped*
   HEW 13.427 Office of Education (PL 89-313, PL 94-142)
   For handicapped children through age 20 who have not com-

pleted grade 12. To provide educational and related services such as instruction, physical education, mobility training, counseling, and prevocational and vocational training.

4. *Handicapped—Research and Demonstration*
HEW 13.443   Office of Education
Money to fund projects and research to improve the education of handicapped children, including physical education and recreation.

5. *Handicapped Early Childhood Assistance*
HEW 13.444   Office of Education
Programs for children from birth through age 8 who are handicapped. Provides comprehensive therapeutic services.

6. *Handicapped Innovative Programs—Deaf-Blind Centers*
HEW 13.445   Office of Education
Establishes regional centers to provide all deaf-blind children with diagnostic and evaluative services, a program for education, adjustment, and orientation, and consultive services to their parents, teachers, and other caregivers.

7. *Handicapped Preschool and School Programs*
HEW 13.449   Office of Education   (PL 94-142)
A free public education to all handicapped children.

8. *Handicapped Regional Resource Centers*
HEW 13.450   Office of Education
Federal assistance to improve education of handicapped children. Diagnostic and education programming services to handicapped children.

9. *Special Programs for Children with Specific Learning Disabilities*
HEW 13.520   Office of Education
Model centers to provide education services to children with specific learning disabilities.

10. *Handicapped Innovative Programs—Programs for Severely Handicapped Children*
HEW 13.568   Office of Education
To improve and expand education/training services for severely handicapped children. Services to include diagnostic, prescriptive, education/training, and evaluative services; training of staff; construction; and dissemination of information and educational materials.

Programs for Children

1. *School Breakfast Program*
FNS-DOA 10.553   (Section 4 of Child Nutrition Act of 1966)
Nutritious breakfasts provided free or at a reduced price to low income, school-age children.

2. *National School Lunch Program*
   FNS-DOA 10.555
   Nutritious lunches provided free or at a reduced price to low income, school-age children.
3. *Special Milk Program for Children*
   FNS-DOA 10.556
   To make milk available to school-age children.
4. *Special Supplemental Food Program for Women, Infants, and Children*
   FNS-DOA 10.557   (WIC)
   To make supplemental foods available to children 5 years old or younger who are judged to be at risk nutritionally.
5. *Child Care Food Program*
   FNS-DOA 10.558
   To provide nutritious meals to children cared for in institutions.
6. *Summer Food Service Program for Children*
   FNS-DOA 10.559
   To provide food service to low income children attending regularly scheduled summer programs.
7. *Maternal and Child Health Services*
   HEW 13.232   Health Services Administration
   To provide comprehensive health care services to school-age and preschool-age children judged to be vulnerable to health risks. Provides for full range of screening, diagnostic, dental, and medical treatment services; counseling and follow-up are included.
8. *Mental Health—Children's Services*
   HEW 13.259   Mental Health Administration
   To provide a full range of mental health programs to children.
9. *Childhood Lead-Based Paint Poisoning Control*
   HEW 13.366   Center for Disease Control
   Detection and follow-up of lead poisoning in children.
10. *Bilingual Education*
    HEW 13.403   Office of Education   (Title VII)
    To develop and implement preschool, elementary, and secondary programs to achieve competency in English, and to meet educational needs for non-English-speaking children ages 3 through 18.
11. *Educationally Disadvantaged Children –LEAs*
    HEW 13.428   Office of Education   (Title I, Elementary and Secondary Education Act (ESEA), Part A, Subpart I)
    Supplementary services for low income areas.
12. *Educationally Disadvantaged Children—Migrants*
    HEW 13.429   Office of Education   (Title I—Migrants)
    Money used to identify and meet needs of migrant children through educational instruction, health, nutrition, and psychologi-

cal services, cultural development, and prevocational and vocational training.

13. *Educationally Disadvantaged Children in State-Administered Institutions Serving Neglected or Delinquent Children*
     HEW 13.431   Office of Education
     Money for educational or educationally related services. For children under 21 who have not completed grade 12.

14. *Follow-Through*
     HEW 13.433   Office of Education
     To sustain and augment in primary grades the gains children made in Head Start and other preschool programs.

15. *School Library Resources, Textbooks, and Other Instructional Materials*
     HEW 13.480   Office of Education
     To provide library resources, texts, and other materials for public schools, private schools, hospital schools, correctional institutions, and schools for the handicapped.

16. *Strengthening Instruction Through Equipment and Minor Remodeling*
     HEW 13.483   Office of Education
     Primary and secondary schools eligible.

17. *Educationally Disadvantaged Children—Special Education Grants*
     HEW 13.512   Office of Education   (Title I, ESEA, Part B)
     Supplementary money for states exceeding national effort index.

18. *Supplementary Educational Centers and Services, Guidance, Counseling, and Testing*
     HEW 13.519   Office of Education   (Title III, ESEA)
     Money for innovative and exemplary projects to demonstrate solutions to critical education needs of the state; 15% of funds must be reserved for programs for handicapped children.

19. *School Health and Nutrition Services for Children from Low Income Families*
     HEW 13.523   Office of Education
     To coordinate existing health and nutrition services, and to provide comprehensive offering to children kindergarten through age 6 in Title I, ESEA schools.

20. *Elementary and Secondary School Education in the Arts*
     HEW 13.566   Office of Education
     To establish and improve arts programs in public elementary and secondary schools.

21. *Libraries and Learning Sources*
     HEW 13.570   Office of Education
     Money to expand library services in public and private elementary

and secondary schools. Includes purchase of materials and equipment, testing services, and development of programs to offer counseling and guidance services in the schools.

22. *Educational Innovation and Support*
HEW 13.571   Office of Education
Money to strengthen innovative programs in supplementary education centers and services; 15% of funds to be spent on special program of projects for children with learning disabilities and handicapped children.

23. *Child Development—Head Start*
HEW 13.600   Office of Human Development
To provide comprehensive health, educational, nutritional, social, and other services to primarily preschool low income children.

24. *Child Development—Child Welfare Research and Demonstration Grants*
HEW 13.608   Office of Human Development   (Title IV, ESEA, Part B)
Grants for research and demonstration programs in child and family development and welfare.

25. *Child Development—Child Abuse and Neglect Prevention and Treatment*
HEW 13.628   Office of Human Development
Prevention, identification, and treatment of child abuse and neglect. Technical assistance, demonstration projects, and multidisciplinary training.

26. *Child Support Enforcement*
HEW 13.679   OCSE   (Title IV, ESEA, Part D)
To enforce support obligations owed children by their absent parents.

27. *Child Welfare Services*
HEW 13.707   Social and Rehabilitation Service
Preventive and protective services to stem neglect, abuse, exploitation, or delinquency of children. Standard setting for child care institutions, foster care, day care, and homemaker services, runaway centers, and adoptive placement.

Programs for Handicapped Persons

1. *Comprehensive Hemophilia Diagnostic and Treatment Centers*
HEW 13.296   Health Services Administration
Comprehensive diagnostic and treatment centers for persons with hemophilia. Includes social counseling, vocational counseling, written comprehensive care plans, and training in house care.

2. *Handicapped Media Services and Captioned Films*
HEW 13.446   Office of Education

Programs to acquire, produce, and distribute films and other materials and equipment to deaf persons.

3. *Regional Education Programs for Deaf and Other Handicapped Persons*
   HEW 13.560   Office of Education
   To develop and operate specially designed or modified programs of vocational, technical, post secondary, or adult education for deaf or other handicapped persons.

4. *Office for Handicapped Individuals*
   HEW 13.603   Office of Human Development
   Umbrella office to coordinate advocacy, review information and planning for HEW-wide policy, and develop program procedures and activities relevant to the physically and mentally handicapped. Provides information.

5. *Mental Retardation—President's Committee on Mental Retardation*
   HEW 13.613   Office of Human Development
   Coordination of national, state, and local efforts to serve the mentally retarded population. Advisory services, and dissemination of technical information.

6. *Rehabilitation Services and Facilities—Basic Support*
   HEW 13.624   Office of Human Development
   Vocational rehabilitation services to handicapped individuals, including diagnosis, comprehensive evaluation, counseling, training, employment placement, reader service, and interpreter service. Assists with payment for medical and related services, prostheses, transportation, etc.

7. *Vocational Rehabilitation Services for Social Security Disability Beneficiaries*
   HEW 13.625   Office of Human Development
   To enable beneficiaries' return to gainful employment.

8. *Rehabilitation Services and Facilities—Special Projects*
   HEW 13.626   Office of Human Development
   Money for projects and demonstration programs that provide services for the physically and mentally handicapped. To expand and improve services above those provided in the Basic Support Program.

9. *Rehabilitation Research and Demonstration*
   HEW 13.627   Office of Human Development
   To discover, test, demonstrate, and promote use of new concepts and devices to provide rehabilitative services to the handicapped.

10. *Developmental Disabilities—Basic Support*
    HEW 13.630   Office of Human Development
    To develop and implement comprehensive and continuing plans

to meet the needs of developmentally disabled individuals. For direct services, facilities construction, and administration.

11. *Developmental Disabilities—Special Projects*
    HEW 13.631   Office of Human Development
    Money for partial support of services to the developmentally disabled, public awareness programs, and information dispersal; 23% of funding for projects. Demonstration of new or improved services, training, coordination of resources, and technical assistance.

12. *Developmental Disabilities—Demonstration Facilities and Training*
    HEW 13.632   Office of Human Development
    To assist with cost of administration and operation of University Affiliated Facilities (UAFs) and interdisciplinary training for program staff, providing services to the developmentally disabled.

13. *Medical Assistance Program—Title XIX*
    HEW 13.471   Social and Rehabilitation Service
    Provides direct medical services for persons who are over 65, blind, disabled, medically needy, or recipients of Aid to Families with Dependent Children (AFDC) funds. Early Periodic Screening, Diagnosis, and Treatment (EPSDT) part of this.

14. *Medicare—Hospital Insurance*
    HEW 13.800   Social and Rehabilitation Service
    Hospital insurance for persons 65 years of age and older and for certain disabled persons.

15. *Medicare—Supplementary Medical Insurance*
    HEW 13.773, 13.774   Social and Rehabilitation Service
    Provides up to 80% coverage in supplementary medical insurance after $60 deductible for persons 65 years of age and older and for certain disabled persons.

16. *Social Security—Disability Insurance*
    HEW 13.802   Social and Rehabilitation Service
    Disabled workers and their dependents eligible.

17. *Supplemental Security Income*
    HEW 13.807   Social and Rehabilitation Service
    For elderly, blind, and disabled persons.

Comprehensive Programs

1. *Comprehensive Public Health Services—Formula Grants*
   HEW 13.210 314(d)   Health Services Administration
   Money to state mental health and state public health agencies to support comprehensive public health services.

2. *Community Health Centers*
   HEW 13.224   Health Services Administration

To support community health centers serving medically under-served populations.

3. *Community Mental Health Centers—Comprehensive Services Support*
   HEW 13.295   ADAMHA
   Inpatient, outpatient, day care, and alternative residential facility screening and diagnosis. Full range of mental health services.

4. *Vocational Education—Basic Grants to States*
   HEW 13.493   Office of Education
   Individuals requiring vocational education are eligible for pro-grams; 10% of programs must be designated for handicapped persons.

5. *Vocational Education—Special Needs*
   HEW 13.499   Office of Education
   For disadvantaged individuals including the handicapped.

6. *Public Assistance—Social Services*
   HEW 13.754   Social and Rehabilitation Services
   Comprehensive social services for any needy person who is or may be a recipient of welfare funds for the blind, the elderly, or the permanently and totally disabled, or a dependent child.

7. *Public Assistance—Maintenance Assistance*
   HEW 13.761   Social and Rehabilitation Service
   Welfare payments to the indigent.

8. *Social Services for Low Income and Public Assistance Reci-pients*
   HEW 13.771   Social and Rehabilitation Service   (Title XX, So-cial Security Act)
   Social services; avoids inappropriate institutional placement. For AFDC, SSI recipients, and indigent persons.

9. *Social Security—Survivors Insurance*
   HEW 13.805   Social and Rehabilitation Service
   For minor dependents of certain persons on Social Security.

10. *Special Benefits for Disabled Coal Miners*
    HEW 13.888   Health Services Administration
    Special benefits for disabled coal miners and their surviving de-pendents.

11. *Home Health Services Grant*
    HEW 13.888   Health Services Administration
    Comprehensive home health services as defined in the Medicare program.

12. *Community Action*
    NERC 49.002   Community Services Administration
    Includes programs in day care, school-age education, and mental health care.

13. *Community Food and Nutrition*
    NERC 49.005   Community Services Administration
    Money for planning or starting up community food and nutrition
    programs.

Coordinating Services to Handicapped Children:
A Handbook for Interagency Collaboration
Edited by Jerry O. Elder and Phyllis R. Magrab
Copyright © 1980   Paul H. Brookes Publishers   Baltimore • London

Chapter 3

The Intangible Human Factor
The Most Critical Coordination Variable

Howard B. Hall

In the fields of social services and the helping professions, considerations of the human factor—in the most positive sense of the words—have been diminishing in recent years. Perhaps this human factor is best envisioned through description rather than definition. No single definition is adequate; in fact, a definition would, by definition, discount the most basic human elements by giving form and boundary to that which has an indefinite variety of forms and boundless access to reality and opportunity. While we recognize the irony of a society that sends a man to the moon but does not clothe or feed impoverished thousands of people, we tend to discard the issue as a technological problem of modern society. We are caught in an incapacity for feeling within the force of seemingly well entrenched, impersonal systems.

In compensation for this state of affairs we coin such terms as "consumer," "individual advocacy," and "patient rights" with an expressed desire to "attend" to the human factor. Then we proceed to institutionalize such laboriously articulated concepts through methods that flow from the professionally manipulated service system whose philosophies and values echo human concern but whose methodologies are the antithesis of the human factor.

The loss of the human factor in the service coordination and delivery process is more a function of commission than omission. Ironically, the evasive human factor is so pervasive that it is an essential part of any process through which people engage other people. Consequently, the rapidly diminishing quality of the human factor in this service process is primarily the result of conscious or unconscious behaviors, policies, and organizational structures that we have developed to impede its influence. The purpose here is not to dwell on negatives but to identify the types of impeding variables with which we are contending.

DECLINE OF THE HUMAN FACTOR

The growth of bureaucracies is, perhaps, the most commonly expressed barrier to open human exchange in service coordination and delivery. Bureaucracies are designed and run by people with values and objectives that, in their origin, were at least honorable. Consequently, it is not constructive merely to identify bureaucracies as primary impediments to the influence of the human factor.

Consumers, direct service professionals, supervisors, and administrators often express frustration over the increasingly rigid rules, procedures, and guidelines that govern service systems and impede coordination. The loss of individual identity for both the consumer and the provider are consequences of mandates that tend to foster conformity and rigidity within the service system.

Why are such trade-offs to human dignity deemed appropriate as a matter of organization policy? The answer to this question lies partially within the shifting values and demands of our culture and partially within the manner in which services are coordinated in response to such expectations. Expanded social, political, governmental, and, ultimately, organizational policies reflect the many shifts in values during recent years:

1. From a highly select group of clientele toward a large service base
2. From judgment based upon individually expressed service needs toward judgment based upon categories of service needs relative to incidence counts
3. From services delivered through private practitioners or small private service agencies toward services delivered through large public agencies or purchased by public monies
4. From an emphasis upon individual dignity and desires toward policies favoring group or mass equality
5. From programs managed by service-oriented professionals trained in human value systems and ethics to programs administered by business and by fiscal luminaries
6. From a culture placing responsibility for morality and values upon individuals toward a culture placing such responsibility in organizational procedures and courts
7. From a culture valuing independence, individuality, and the inherent responsibility of human risk toward a culture valuing dependency and decreased opportunity for individual judgment and related risk
8. From a culture with a highly humanistic value system toward a culture placing increased emphasis on individual isolation from the broader spectrum of human concern
9. From a culture fostering respect for position, knowledge, and authority toward a culture with increased disrespect for individuals of such knowledge and position

10. From a culture that had a high level of national identity, pride, and dignity toward a culture that discounts most aspects of national identity
11. From a culture that places responsibility for the instilling of social values in children within the family toward a culture that places the responsibility for such guidance within the school system and other institutions
12. From a culture that respects the coordination between individual judgment and risk toward a culture that is tending to remove both judgment and risk from the individual by mandates within public agencies

As such shifts in social and culture values ultimately reflect growing popular acceptance, they become increasingly institutionalized by legislation, by governmental guidelines, and by policies and practices in both public and private service systems. Thus, the expanded bureaucracies are merely mirrors of such value shifts and political trade-offs. Too often services are based on surveys and "incidence counts" related to categories of need. This approach fails to distinguish the individual from the perceived need of the service system. Consequently, it also fails to separate the individual from the group because perceptions of need are based more upon perceptions of classification than upon individual response.

While the rapidly expanding base of human rights legislation has corrected many inequities in our culture, including services for handicapped individuals, it has also tended to remove the loci of moral values responsibility from the individual to service delivery systems and, ultimately, to the courts. Increasingly, groups and individuals are turning to agency policy and the judiciary to determine the boundary of interpersonal responsibility. At one time, families and individuals considered themselves responsible for fostering, and modeling, and perpetuating such values. This time-honored tradition is undermined further by parallel acceleration of group liability for activities and procedures. As a result, many individual professionals and private citizens now avoid kinds of human assistance that were at one time considered personal and moral imperatives.

This pattern has also had an impact on our primary service professions. At one time, medicine, law, and the clergy were the primary professions. They carried deeply rooted moral as well as technical and functional responsibilities. The clergy once provided a broad base of counseling relevant to the emotional and social needs of the family and its individual members. In the past, the legal profession encompassed a variety of responsibilities to society similar to those demanded of the physician in relation to his/her patients. On a different professional level, educators earned and received a level of respect from pupils and parents, and parents sought guidance from teachers as respected authorities in the rearing of children.

Gradually, professions like dentistry, social work, and psychology were established with similarly rooted value systems. However, in more recent years, the proliferation of new professions and paraprofessions has not allowed adequate time for the rooting of such values. Consequently, the hallmark of such professional ethics and standards is rapidly shifting from the preview of the individual professional and the professional association toward legislative regulations and licensing procedures. Again, the basis for moral judgment and responsibility is shifting from individual accountability toward legal and regulatory definition. Such systems monitor and eliminate only a conspicuous level of accountability on the basis of sporadic review and negative response.

Thus, rather than respecting and honoring those who provide public service, we tend to punish those who fail to meet specified criteria. Technically, the boards and systems constructed for such monitoring are frequently tempted with their own forms of internal conception. This further undermines the public respect that was once awarded to individuals of knowledge and authority in the course of their daily functions. The human factor is further undermined and the basis for interpersonal communication is desolving rapidly.

THE HUMAN FACTOR: BETWEEN CONSUMER AND COORDINATOR

This perpetuation of public laws, government procedures, and organization policies results in increased rigidity in service coordination procedures. In recognition of this pattern, alert consumer populations, professionals, and service agencies have supported a recent wave of legislation mandating new levels of individual accountability in the service coordination and delivery process. For example, Public Law 94–142 (Education for All Handicapped Children Act) mandates individualized education programs (IEPs) for all handicapped children. Similar federal and state legislation mandates individualized programs plans (IPPs), individualized habilitation plans (IHPs), and other procedures designed to link efforts between the professional and the consumer in the designation and coordination of services and to hold service delivery systems accountable for generating such procedures. The guidelines backing such legal mandates are detailed and extensive. Generally, the laws mandate a maximum time period between the consumer's request for services and the time in which he/she is determined eligible for such services. Time frames are also established for periods of planning, implementation, and review of service effectiveness as well as initiation of replanning cycles. The procedures for each phase of service planning, coordination, or delivery are replete with regulations and mutual safeguards for both the agency and the consumer. Legislation mandating such individualized service procedures has generally been capped with additional legislation mandating paralleled processes of appeal in the event that the consumer, parent, or advocate does not feel that the initial sequence of procedures was handled in a just and honorable manner. The appeals procedures have their own set of time limits and safeguards for both the consumer and the service agency. Consequently, increasing volumes of professional and consumer time are diverted from service delivery to "paper shuffling" in accounting for services that could have been delivered if goodwill and human integrity had been maintained.

These types of procedures have had a greater impact on the human factor than might at first be envisioned. For example, in the past, if conflict arose between a parent and the school over actions related to a child, the parent generally met with the teacher and perhaps a principal to resolve the conflict. Now, parents of handicapped children are faced with publicly mandated procedures and regulation. While their involvement and potential for appeal are ensured by law, the specified procedures related to each process are overwhelming to the consumer, parents, professionals, and school or agency administrators. Now, in this situation, a parent faces the possibility of having to deal with a group of 10 or more professionals at a formal meeting controlled by rigidly defined guidelines within an atmosphere of mutual defensiveness. While legally constituted for the benefit of the client, such meetings are not highly conducive to a trusting exchange and the human factor is conspicuous in its absence.

Case managers, case coordinators, primary coordinators, or other persons designated by agencies to facilitate the service coordination and delivery process have substantially undermined the managerial responsibilities of the parent and the opportunity for the client to make his/her own choice and to live with the consequence. This pattern of increased dependency on the service system further weakens the family support system and the primary reason that the service is offered—the growing independence of the client. Ironically, the funds, time, and energy expended through the case management model as it is currently practiced also limits the agency resources for delivering more effective services to a broader spectrum of the population. This results in a cancellation between increased dependency and increased management through the coordination activity of service systems.

Recognition of the increased dangers in perpetuating such service coordination patterns has resulted in a variety of current slogans and trends as presumed remedies. "Mainstreaming," "normalization," "least restrictive alternative," and "clients' rights" are reflective of shifts in service patterns that often enhance rather than diminish the dependency they are designed to relieve. There is something distinctly abnormal about "normal" activities being defined for an individual by a professional agency or even his/her family. While created with "good intentions," the simple reality is that such slogans and procedures are more reflective of frustration within current service coordination procedures than of an honest attempt to reinstall the human factor within service coordination and delivery systems.

THE REINTRODUCTION OF THE HUMAN FACTOR THROUGH TRUST

While the purpose of this section is to suggest some avenues through which the human factor may be reintroduced to the service coordination process, the author feels that attitudinal change is a more basic ingredient than shifts in coordination procedures in both recognition and re-engagement of the human factor throughout the service system. Consequently, there are no simple solutions to reinstating the complex human factor in the service coordination process.

As noted, a basic variable in diminishing the human factor is the erosion of trust. Ultimately, no procedures designed to reinstall the human factor can be successful without a supportive growth of trust among all parties concerned with the process. In retrospect, we can recognize that many of our laws, public mandates, and service programs have been implemented in response to a growing distrust among and between professionals, consumers, service agencies, and the general public. The mandate for individualized program plans, individualized education programs, and similar procedures developed out of a growing conviction that the service systems were not effectively addressing and monitoring the needs of specific individuals. The decline of trust has been paralleled by a proliferation of service coordination procedures. Consequently, it would appear counterproductive to recommend a series of procedures designed to counteract this pattern without initially addressing the more basic ingredients: a regenerating of trust among participants in the service coordination and delivery process.

The primary danger in the reintroduction of trust is a concomitant reintroduction of risk. The extension of trust requires a loss or a sense of "giving up something," be it real or imaginative. An individual cannot trust in a vacuum without potential consequence. The consumer's traditional trust of professionals was based upon the belief that these individuals had adequate knowledge, experience, and moral convictions to deal effectively with the issues at question. Alternatives were often limited to seeking other professionals whom the family or consumer felt had a better "reputation" or were more qualified by some criteria. Due to the layman's general lack of knowledge about a specific problem or its remedy, the professional's general "reputation" was often the most significant factor in the extension of trust.

Trust is based upon respect, an intangible yet highly valued commodity to most professionals. Among nonmonetary rewards, respect is perhaps the most highly esteemed and earnestly sought by service providers. Lack of trust signals a lack of respect, which, in turn, diminishes one of the most viable motivators among professionals and other service providers. Consequently, the process becomes self-generating in ensuring its own diminished consequence.

The traditional relationship between the consumer and the provider has implied an extension of trust and respect and an assumption of relevant risk on the part of the consumer toward the service provider. Conversely, most service providers, especially those in private practice, have recognized the potential for the consumer to seek services elsewhere. This option underscores the basic independence of the consumer and demands a level of mutual respect, concern, and communication. While the ultimate responsibility for a treatment procedure may lie in the hands of the professional, the more basic responsibility for determining whether or not to continue with that procedure generally rests in the hands of consumers or their families. While some consumers fail either to recognize or to utilize this reality, the option is implicit in the relationship between the client and the service provider.

The shift during the past two decades toward expanded public responsibility for problems and more comprehensive legislative mandates, however, has contributed to the increased imbalance in this relationship. While having access to a wider variety of professionals and services, the consumer often experiences increased frustration in options related to selection and communication with service providers. This is largely a consequence of rapidly expanding systems with increasingly complex procedures for service coordination. Case managers have assumed many responsibilities previously shouldered by parents or consumers. Processes related to determination of eligibility for services and selection of service providers are now generally considered "in-house" functions of service agencies.

Through this pattern, increased decision-making responsibility has shifted from the consumer or family to the agency and the case manager. This assumption of traditional family responsibilities is placing unwarranted fiscal burdens on agencies as well as time binders on staff. In addition, it is highly questionable whether such responsibilities can be assumed by a person outside of the family with level of care, monitoring, and concern extended by a family member or the individual consumer.

Through increased responsibility for decision making, ultimately the consumer takes the greatest risk while having the least control over options. Legal action, advocacy, and appeal procedures are complex and far too cumbersome as a routine vehicle for interpersonal communication and decision making. Although this was not the designed intent of such procedures, a rapidly increasing number of frustrated consumers are seeking such avenues for recourse on matters that should be handled on a far less complex and more natural level of interpersonal exchange and consensus.

In essence, service professionals and agencies have assumed more responsibility and risk in the service process than may be warranted by public mandate or logical intent. Schools have assumed a variety of responsibilities extending far beyond their basic teaching function, including integration and drug control among others. Many social service agencies now provide an "umbrella" type of case management service which extends the decision-making responsibility of staff members far beyond the level that logically would be required by persons professing a conviction to the adoption of a "normalization" process or advocating that the individual be afforded on opportunity to engage in the "generic" services or "mainstream" elements of our culture.

The problem is further aggravated by the fact that it is frequently more difficult to enter a service system in search of a simple, short term service than to enter and be placed on a waiting list in consideration for ultimate receipt of several complex and integrated long term services. Unwittingly, we may have developed a system for generating a higher level of dependency among the select few receiving a wide array of services, some of which may not be appropriate, while generating long term frustration for individuals who cannot gain entry for resolution of their most basic needs.

Part of the solution to such problems may lie in the redistribution of responsibility between the consumer and the service provider. Perhaps the greatest challenge facing the professional of the current decade is to extend trust to the consumer and risk the consequence. This requires giving up some decision-making responsibilities and functioning more as a consultant or advisor than as a case manager. Conversely, families and consumers would have an opportunity to reassume their traditional responsibilities in the decision-making process. After mutual discussion of the relevant service needs and priorities of an individual, the consumer or family may be encouraged to seek and select among a variety of service options rather than generating a decision through coordinating agencies. Within this context, the client and family assume more responsibilities and more risk. They may make a decision that is less than optimal. They also have the option of nondecision, which reflects its own consequence relevant to the situation. Yet such a consequence may be a primary catalyst in change toward a more appropriate option.

Since current services have conditioned consumers and families to give up such responsibilities, it is incumbent upon the systems to recondition and encourage consumers to reassume such responsibilities; consumers and families must have an opportunity to learn more about the nature, options, and intricacies within the continuum of services. They must be given access to information and procedures relevant to obtaining such services. Consequently, in many situations, procedures for obtaining services must be simplified in both language and action. Both consumers and providers must have access to such systems and their related service components.

This pattern requires a substantial risk on the part of both professionals and consumers. The professional will have to admit that he/she does not know a great deal about substantive areas in which the consumer previously credited the professional with great knowledge. Conversely, the family and consumer will have to take responsibility for a variety of decisions and their inherent consequences, a weight which formerly rested on the shoulders of the professionals and the service sytem. The consumer and family will also often have to deal with the feelings, attitudes, and uncertainties that had been masked in large part when the service system assumed responsibility for planning and coordination of individual programs.

Perhaps, of greatest consequence, both professionals and consumers will have to risk a collaborative rather than a competitive dialogue in addressing and seeking resolution to problems. This requires mutual trust, openness, clarity, and compromise. The necessity of reinjecting the human factor in this process is more critical now than in the previous decade. The consumer may not have the option of merely seeking another professional or service system with which to plan and coordinate a continuum of needed services. During an era of single, insulated service options, such alternatives were feasible. During an era of interdisciplinary practice within complex service continuums, such options may not be practical. In trying to regenerate mutual trust and in seeking a rebalancing of responsibility, avenues for mutual communication and engaging the multifaceted human factor must be regenerated.

THE HUMAN FACTOR IN INTERAGENCY COLLABORATION

Some critical human factors related to mutual trust, risk, and communication between consumers and coordinators in the service delivery process have been examined. Another series of human variables is evidenced in the process of coordinating services among agencies or service systems. The vested interests of service systems tend to go through the same rationales, patterns, and ultimate consequences as do services within individual agencies. Each system and its component agencies tend to expand their boundaries, functions, and their number of consumers with the passing of time. Service systems tend to profess, defend, and justify their activities with the primary intention of self-perpetuation and survival. While one can find fault with this process, the motivations are highly compatible with the most basic human instincts. "Territorial" and "turf" concerns are clearly evidenced among agencies. Mutual support is generated from within the ranks, while external probes are regarded with apprehension. This defensive posture often supports a view of consumers and professionals that agencies are primarily serving their own interests rather than those of the clients.

Such processes and inherent criticisms mask a relatively legitimate, remarkably human aspect of service agencies; namely, service agencies have their needs too. For the most part, they are staffed by individuals who would like to provide, and gain recognition for, quality services. The basis for such recognition frequently is defined by legislative mandate or administratively defined priorities. Within these limits a given agency's staff and administration may receive substantial credit for effectively delivering A, B, and C services while they may receive substantially less credit for delivering D, E, and F services. One of the primary ingredients in effectively engaging the human factor in interagency collaboration is to recognize initially those areas for which the agency receives substantial recognition for delivery of services. While this concept may appear obvious, its implementation requires a high level of interpersonal communication with sensitivity.

There are several pitfalls frequently encountered in seeking interagency agreements. Perhaps the most basic is the tendency to communicate too low or too high in the organizational structure. Attempting to generate interagency policy agreements at a "line" or "supervisory" level is often self-defeating because these individuals frequently are not part of the communication system through which policies are generated. On the other hand, seeking interagency agreements solely at the top of the administrative level often results in procedures that are neither comprehended nor applicable for implementation by persons providing the desired services. During recent years, there has been an increased tendency to elevate negotiations for interagency agreements to higher administrative levels. Frequently, within the public system, for example, negotiations between official agencies at the state level have resulted in agreements that have angered unsuspecting consumers and frustrated service providers who are faced with implementing procedures that are not tuned to other areas of agency practice. Thus, a primary objective in generating interagency agreements should be to develop a pattern of communication that is compatible with both the administrative decision-making process and the pattern of service delivery within the agency.

A second pitfall is in generating agreements that appear compatible among agencies but are neither tested nor monitored relevant to implementation. Often agencies reach closure on agreements and trust one another with the responsibility for implementing "their part of the bargain." While intentions may be honorable, technical modifications and procedures necessitated by such an agreement may prove to be less workable than initially envisioned. Second, it is easier for the personnel of either agency to envision the potential opportunity and pitfall for changes and service patterns within their own system than to envision those elements of the service process that constitute the actual links between two or more agencies.

A third major flaw in such negotiations rests in the fact that the consumer is generally the last person to recognize or experience the shift in agency procedures and the impact relevant to other agencies. Consumers often feel, with strong justification, that they are pawns in such negotiations. Frequently, such negotiations have substantial impact on specific consumer groups and the processes through which they will receive services. For this reason it is essential not to lose sight of the fact that the consumer is a vital human factor in generating interagency agreements and, as such, should be included in the process.

A MODEL FOR COLLABORATION

There are many avenues to reincorporating the human factor in interagency negotiations while maximizing opportunities for successful conclusions. The author developed and successfully implemented the "Interagency Collaboration Model" described below. However, before discussing the model, several principles for negotiating interagency agreements should be considered.

The Interagency Collaboration Model is based upon the following service principles:

1. Effective coordination of services among agencies provides a more effective and meaningful continuum of services for the consumer.
2. Effective interagency collaboration reduces duplications in service costs.
3. Effective interagency collaboration expands the resource knowledge and appreciation of the service providers.
4. Effective interagency collaboration reduces the time and energy that consumers must devote to obtaining effective services.

Effective interagency collaboration requires a basic understanding of and appreciation for the purpose and functions of each participating agency. A mere overview of the agency's charge or detailed experience in one aspect of the agency's operation is not adequate. It is relatively easy to believe that one not only knows but also has an appreciation for what a department of rehabilitation, a public school, or a county health department is charged to do through official mandate. However, rapid acceleration through this phase of getting acquainted frequently causes the collapse of interagency negotiations and violates the most basic components of the human factor. Most agency personnel are pressed by requests from other individuals who do not understand their services. They are often faced with inquiries reflecting too broad an expectation of agency function or lack of clarity relevant to a particular aspect of the agency's operation. An undefined "halo effect" often evolves around agency activities. Most agency personnel are reluctant to discount such images through disclosures of their organizational weakness in areas in which services are not truly provided. Such disclosures require a mutual atmosphere of highly personal exchange based upon a generated feeling of trust and common interest.

A second basic principle in interagency collaboration relates to the selection of the participants to conduct the negotiations. It is generally advisable to receive top level administrative authorization, in writing if possible, for assignment of agencies' representatives. Depending on the size and organizational complexities of the agency, it is generally advisable to select a representative from the administrative ranks or a person who has direct communication with administrative personnel who can assume responsibility for making or endorsing agency policy. In this respect, a basic ground rule would require that the same official representative attend each meeting without substitution. Frequently, it is advisable to suggest that the executive director appoint an official representative if it is anticipated that the executive will not be able to attend meetings on a regular basis.

It is also advisable to select a second representative who has a relatively clear understanding of the line level activities within the agency if the person identified above does not. Many interagency negotiations falter on the inability of an administration to implement a plan due to the plan's incompatibility with daily agency operations. This is a sensitive issue as increasing numbers of agency administrators do not have workable knowledge of their own agency's service delivery level of operations. Supervisory level representatives are occasionally appropriate if their communication with policy level administrators is officially safe and comfortable.

An atmosphere of understanding, clarity, and mutual support should characterize interagency meetings. Avenues of inquiry should be constructed around areas of mutual concern rather than attempts made by more cohesive group members to elicit commitment to a particular action from a specific agency representative. These types of support and mutual consideration are supportive of the most basic human factors since one cannot comfortably give while being pressured. Conversely, one cannot perpetually ask for something without evidencing a capacity and willingness for contribution toward the group objectives.

Evolving administrative agreements should consider the realistic capacities and mandates of participating agencies. They should be stated in a manner that is clear and mutually understood, and such understandings should be functionally implementable. The criteria and responsibility for such implementation should be specified.

The interagency group that creates and defines a working agreement should assume ongoing responsibility for monitoring its implementation, refinement, and incorporation in ongoing agency policy. This is another basic juncture at which many interagency agreements falter. The responsibility for designating procedural criteria and monitoring such activities is frequently assigned to individuals within lower levels of the agency. Generally, such persons do not have the same degree of investment, understanding, or commitment to the activity in question as do the negotiators. Consequently, they may offer a course of action that is closely aligned with routine activities and meets minimal requirements of an interagency agreement. Thus, effective monitoring and follow-up become an essential component of such agreements and illustrate the level of commitment to implementation.

Perhaps the human factors relevant to the Interagency Collaboration Model are best reflected through an illustration. The author implemented this model while developing services for developmentally disabled individuals residing in a large, sparsely populated county. Numerous concerns centered around duplication of services among agencies, cumbersome procedures through which services were obtained, eligibility for services, inequity in patterns through which services were obtained, and a notable lack of outreach to many persons who were eligible for services. An interagency committee was organized, composed of representatives from both public and private agencies, including the county health department, the county schools, three city school districts, the county department of health, the state Department of Employment, the state Department of Vocational Rehabilitation, the County Council of Community Services, two private parent associations, a private school serving retarded children and adults, the March of Dimes, and the Easter Seal Society. Representatives were selected on the basis of criteria specified in the discussion of principles of collaboration.

Interagency meetings were held on a weekly basis at a specified time with meeting locations rotating among participating agencies. The "no substitution of agency representatives" rule was discussed, mutually endorsed, and honored by all participants.

All participants were either agency executives or authorized representatives of the executives. It was understood that such representatives reported content and recommendations of the committee directly to their agency's executives for consultation or endorsement of the committee's recommendations.

The basic purpose and scope of the committee's activities were defined and discussed during the intitial meeting. The atmosphere was one of caution with an overriding sense of defensiveness. Participants were reluctant to make comments that might cast a negative image on their agency or imply some unspecified level of commitment. The defensive patterns appeared when committee members expressed their impressions of the nature, quality, and scope of activities within other participating agencies. Initially, this pattern was overlooked in the group's enthusiasm to define goals and to focus on directions of mutual interest and benefit. Since most of the participants functioned at a middle management or supervisory level, they reflected a high level of concern for the quality and direction of their services and a vested interest in presenting their agencies in a favorable light.

During the third meeting the communication process began to falter. The reason was clear; there was a general lack of understanding and appreciation for the scope, nature, and refinements of services offered by participating agencies as viewed by the representatives of other agencies. Several worthwhile meetings were devoted to resolving this impass. During several meetings one or two representatives would define the scope, functions, and specific services of their agencies in relative detail. Other group members raised questions for purposes of clarification and commented about their previous misunderstandings of the agency's functions. The group benefited substantially from the new understanding of what each agency did not do as well as what services each agency did offer. Through such understandings and mutual appreciation, the defensive tone within the group rapidly diminished.

The committee then proceeded to define areas of mutual concern in service delivery. While such concerns did not always have equal impact on all agencies, most participants made a positive contribution to such discussions. Gradually, differences and conflicts between agency expectations and practices were aired openly. As this occurred, the weak areas of functions within an individual agency were addressed with concern relevant to that agency seeking complementary or supportive services from other agencies represented within the group.

The group then began to identify common issues and formulate interagency policies to enhance the flow of services. For example, substantial progress was made in clarifying the types of services that were actually offered by each agency and the most expeditious methods of obtaining such services. Second, the group began to identify service patterns that were complementary to one another and reached consensus on expedient procedures for gaining access to such services on an interagency basis. The group also initiated a concept of "primary coordinator" as a means of designating a person in specified agencies who would assume overall responsibility for case management services for a client, including those services emanating from another agency.

As the group began to reach consensus on interagency policies and related procedures, the members learned that implementation was a more difficult task than originally envisioned. Although limited funds were a problem, the major concerns were related to suiting the interagency policies with the daily activities of each agency. It was evident that some procedures would have to be modified for such adaptation.

At this juncture the group shifted formats and limited discussion to policy and procedural issues on alternate weeks. During the weeks that followed the committee functioned as an interagency team, discussing case presentations from specific agencies that were related to the kinds of issues, policies, and procedures that the group had been addressing. This practice proved to be a key factor in reaching functional definitions of interagency problems. As a secondary benefit, the level of exchange within the group generated considerable insight and benefit for individual agencies in refining their internal operations.

The organizational structure for the Interagency Collaboration Model was based upon maximizing the human element in the interagency exchange. In retrospect, it was evident that this was the major variable in realizing success in the development and implementation of interagency procedures. Trust and mutual support were gradually developed as a result of open, direct communication. The group recognized and placed confidence in the conviction that all participating agencies and their representatives were working in the best interests of their clients. Second, the ripple effect among personnel of the participating agencies generated through their representatives had substantial impact on service flow among agencies. Consumer representatives made positive contributions in helping their constituencies gain more functional access to agencies and their services. Bureaucratic procedures and red tape were cut significantly. The nature and quality of interagency agreements generated during the initial year resulted in policies that were maintained and expanded for several years thereafter.

THE HUMAN FACTOR IN OBTAINING GENERIC LIFE-STYLES

From the mid 1960s through the late 1970s, service systems evolved from relatively isolated services to coordinated services under "umbrella" structures of service continuums, encompassing programs offered through many public and private agencies. This trend is based on the concept of "generic services." Essentially, the intent of generic services is to tap the potential for obtaining services for any individual through "generic agencies," that is, agencies that traditionally or primarily did not serve, in this case, handicapped persons of a specified classification. Under various circumstances, schools, departments of vocational rehabilitation, departments of health, mental health departments, and other agencies came to be included under the term generic services. Emphasis was placed primarily upon public agencies. If one were to draw a series of concentric circles beginning at the center with those agencies providing the most specialized services for handicapped individuals of a particular category and moving outward toward those agencies providing little or no services to handicapped persons of the same category, the functional response to the term generic services could be visualized. The tendency in seeking services is to approach the agencies assisting the handicapped before approaching those agencies represented by the outer circles. In this sense, the term *generic* has proved to be functionally misleading in its application. Ironically, it has been easier to approach, examine, and criticize an agency that traditionally has extended funds and effort in serving the specified handicapped population than to approach, examine, and criticize an agency that has never offered specific services to this specialized population. This pattern is evident regardless of consideration for the possibility that the greater needs for service were reflected in the activities of the latter group of agencies.

The more generic group of public agencies, such as public transportation services, often greets inquiries of persons seeking services for handicapped individuals with mixed emotions. Since neither party knows the perimeter of expectations of the other, successful initial contacts reflect a rare blend of exploration diplomacy with an implicit backup of legal sanctions. This blend combines humanistic approaches to program coordination with systems and legal concepts of advocacy. Such consideration was part of the ideal under which handicapped persons were "mainstreamed" into patterns of "normalization," exemplifying similarities rather than differences with the mainstream of society. However, ultimately a conflict is generated between the projected image of the individual as "normal" and the express expectation for "specialized services."

In fact the terms *generic* and *services* at times become conspicuously incompatible. If we are addressing patterns of entry for handicapped persons into the mainstream of our culture, the term *services* is distinctly inappropriate as it is traditionally used. An individual attending scuba diving school, taking private dancing classes, going to a ballgame, dining in a restaurant, or merely feeding ducks in a public pond does not reconsider himself obtaining a "service." It is at this level of recognition and shift in strategy that the human factor must be appreciated. Many organiztions providing such "generic" activities for persons in our society recognize the potential free enterprise market represented by handicapped persons. Consequently, they approach various organizations and agencies whom they feel have access to such individuals. They frequently are prepared to provide their range of traditional activities, supported by some specialized arrangements for ease of utilization. Too often the organizations or agencies respond in a defensive and overly protective manner, shielding the very individuals for whom they are professing to seek "normal" experiences from recognizing the fact that such activities are available to them.

A fresh opportunity is presented here to engage the full range of "human" variables in opening avenues toward generic activities for handicapped persons within our communities. This will require practicing what we profess and allowing individuals to take risks based upon their own decisions. Second, it will require a level of interpersonal communication that is devoid of veiled legal threats or a sense of being "planned for." This approach should maximize the opportunity for humanistic exchange and enhance competition, a traditional characteristic of our free enterprise system. The issues of trust, risk, and responsibility must be primary ingredients in the realization and use of the "human" factor within natural patterns of communication.

The growing tendency toward inclusion of handicapped individuals within primary life activities is an extraordinary opportunity to discover and experience interpersonal patterns of communication which we can ultimately reinject into the methods through which we work with specialized services for this population. At that point the cycle will be complete. We will have reintroduced a viable range of human factors into our planning and coordination process, be it among individuals, groups, or agencies. With conscious clarity, we will be able to blend such communication patterns with our current methods of advocacy and services delivery, allowing handicapped individuals to move into the primary activities and struggles of human life.

SUMMARY

In an earlier age, the human factor was abundantly apparent at all levels of communication among consumers and providers in the social services and the helping professions. Most contact was on a one-to-one basis, and problems were addressed with a sense of personal responsibility and commitment to pursue joint decisions actively. For the most part, handicapped individuals functioned in the mainstream of life because there were few tributaries through which they could be channeled. "Normalization" and "mainstreaming" were not issues because we had not fully developed our strategies for segregation of handicapped individuals into segregated services systems. Regardless of the existence or nonexistence of professional assistance, responsibility for life decisions primarily rested upon and was assumed by the family and the consumer as a natural pattern of daily life.

The 1960s and 1970s witnessed a proliferation of specialized services, a broadened base of interdisciplinary involvement with related expertise, and a planning philosophy based upon segregated classes for handicapped children. The "human" factor in the services planning and coordination process began decaying in direct correlation with the expansion of bureaucratic systems and the proliferation of regulatory procedures that transferred the moral, technical, and legal responsibilities from the individual to components of the larger services system. While more individuals received a wider range of services, a personal level of exchange with, and on behalf of, individuals rapidly diminished. Essentially, people begin to fall between the cracks of a larger system that was nearly too encompassing for possible exit.

During the mid 1970s, an additional movement, evidenced by terms like *mainstreaming, normalization, advocacy,* and *least restrictive alternative,* signaled a new trend in the service cycle. Individuals were to be exempt from specialized, segregated programs and directed toward primary generic activities with the inherent risk of community life. Ironically, criteria for "normal" were largely defined by professionals and persons other than those for whom the concept was intended. Implementation manuals and procedures proliferated, which inadvertently reinforced the boundaries of distinctly abnormal avenues for attaining "normal" life-styles.

With increased recognition of these further encroachments upon individuals lost in a maze of potential services and the inherent indignities in loss of personal options and basic communication, an additional wave of legislated procedures was generated. This wave primarily encompassed a wide range of advocacy and appeals procedures, principally defined and implemented through legal procedures. This pattern further reinforced the growing sense of distrust, defensiveness, and conflict between and among both providers and consumers.

The primary concern here is to regenerate avenues of mutual trust and bring about a return of responsibilities to the clients and their families as "natural case managers." There is adequate evidence that a sense of morality and responsibility for the individual not only cannot be legislated but furthermore that such an effort frequently legitimizes the erosion of responsibilities from clients and families. Regardless of our philosophical or legal posture, the ultimate risk of life lies squarely on the shoulders of each individual. Consequently, the consumer and the family should have greater opportunity to make choices, make mistakes, and engage the consequence of their own decision-making process. Professional resources should shift from case management and managerial perspectives back toward greater engagement in the service delivery process while providing consultative and therapeutic support to those families and individuals seeking options for their own lives.

Moving on to the current concept of "generic services," we may ultimately find that the term *services* is not applicable to the wide range of activities in which the individual will choose to be engaged in the course of life activities. Similarly, interagency collaboration can be facilitated through reinjection of the human factor. Negotiations for such collaboration should attend to both the administrative and the direct service concerns as well as to the functional capacities of each agency. This requires a sensitive and personal level of communication which maximizes positive and supportive planning, coordination, and interaction. Procedures emanating from such agreements should be carefully monitored, revised, and simplified to ensure maximum compatibility both with the system from which they emerge and with the consumer they are intended to serve.

Coordinating Services to Handicapped Children:
A Handbook for Interagency Collaboration
Edited by Jerry O. Elder and Phyllis R. Magrab
Copyright © 1980   Paul H. Brookes Publishers   Baltimore • London

Section II
MODELS OF INTERAGENCY COLLABORATION

Chapter 4

Direction Service
Collaboration One Case at a Time

Richard W. Zeller

Interagency collaboration can be conceived of as having two broad goals: 1) to improve the delivery of services to individuals, and 2) to improve the efficiency and effectiveness of service delivery systems. Within the service delivery "system," these two goals can be addressed by strategies that target the system (promoting policy change, reorganization, etc.) and by strategies that target the particular mix of services provided to individuals.

Wolfensberger has argued that in order to pursue the first class of strategies (systematic coordination of service agencies and systems), one must have power over them—legal authority to direct changes at the service system delivery level. Elsewhere in this volume it is argued that much can be done to improve collaboration among agencies on the basis of shared authority rather than through legal enablement. In either case, regardless of the approach one takes to the coordination of service agencies, some coordination mechanism that operates at the level of the individual recipient is needed.

Direction Service (Brewer and Kakalik, 1979) represents one such individual-targeted strategy. Direction Service works with families of handicapped children to put the pieces together, examining the comprehensive needs of the family and child and matching them to that mix of available services that can best meet those needs.

THE NEED FOR DIRECTION

The creation of the President's Committee on Mental Retardation in the early 1960s signaled some fundamental changes in services to handicapped people. Prior to the Kennedy legislation, the federal government spent approximately $125 million per year on handicapped children, mostly through Social Security, Public Assistance, and Medical payments (President's Committee on

Mental Retardation, 1977). By 1970, total annual expenditures nationwide had grown to $635 million, of which the federal, state, and local shares were 54.6%, 34.6%, and 10.8%, respectively (Brewer and Kakalik, 1979). By fiscal 1982, federal PL 94-142 education funding alone for handicapped children could exceed $3.16 billion. Rossmiller, Hale, and Frohreich (1970) estimate total national expenditures just for educating handicapped children in 1980 could exceed $10.6 billion. This substantial increase in support has resulted in an incredible expansion of community-based services to the handicapped. These additional services have come about, in large measure, in response to strong pressure brought by limited interest advocacy groups (Association for Children with Learning Disabilities, Association for Retarded Children, United Cerebral Palsy, etc.). Parents once were faced with service agencies and schools that often closed the doors on handicapped children; they now may be faced with a myriad of fragmented services, each aiding a limited segment of the handicapped population. Faced with the overwhelming complexity of the service system, many individuals and families settle for whatever is offered or stop trying altogether to find assistance.

The Rand Corporation, in exploring the issue of services to the sensory impaired, found that many parents are not able to cope on their own with services as they are currently arrayed (Kakalik et al., 1974). In a follow-up to the study's final report, Brewer and Kakalik (1979) note that most specialized professionals are also unable to cope with the bureaucratic array of special services or are unable to even see the related problems of clients that require another specialist's attention.

THE EVOLUTION OF DIRECTION SERVICE

The concept of "Direction Centers" was offered by the Rand study as a potential solution to this problem. Brewer and Kakalik (1979) outline several characteristics of Direction Centers. Among these is that ". . . the Direction Center should be separate from other major direct service programs in the bureaucracy, so that it is not captured by those programs, and so that too much emphasis is not placed on direction to certain services" (p. 222).

The Bureau of Education for the Handicapped (BEH), in response to the Rand study's findings, has funded 25 Direction Service demonstration sites nationwide. The BEH concept of Direction Service draws heavily upon the Rand study recommendations. Most of these demonstrations, however, are closely affiliated with educational agencies at state, intermediate, or local levels. This alliance affects the concept of direction significantly. It is necessitated, however, by the close relationship between direction and the current legal requirements that schools must meet to implement PL 94-142 (specifically, the provisions concerning individualized education programs).

This quick transition from research to reality (at least, a demonstration reality) is a fairly unique chapter in the history of public policy. Rarely has a concept, developed through intensive research, been so rapidly implemented. But interest in finding a way to ensure that more comprehensive coordinated services are provided to people with special needs is not new.

OTHER CLIENT-CENTERED
APPROACHES TO COORDINATED SERVICES

The direction concept is one example of a client-centered approach to service coordination for the handicapped, although certainly not an idiosyncratic one. Efforts in this area can be traced back at least half a century. Levine and Levine (1970) describe the role of the visiting teacher model, popular in larger eastern school systems prior to the 1920s. The visiting teacher was an agent for the child to link the school, home, and community in order to improve school performance. Dokecki (1977) observes that between 1920 and 1960, however, there was very little interest in this kind of linking role in human services.

More recently, substantial effort has been devoted to the development of service coordination, fixed point of referral, and case management systems which share, with the direction concept, a client-centered approach to comprehensive services. Wolfensberger has argued that services coordination, in the sense of coordinating services to individual lives, is the responsibility of the service provider system. This is quite different from systematically coordinating services provided by agencies. The Pilot Parents Program of the Greater Omaha Association for Retarded Citizens was an early attempt to implement this coordinating function (as well as others) through the use of parent volunteers (Dean et al., 1971).

Dokecki and his colleagues at George Peabody College for Teachers proposed the Human Development Liaison Specialist role (Dokecki, 1975, 1977; Newbrough, 1977; Williams, 1977). This liaison worker examines what ecological systems an individual is currently involved with (e.g., community agencies, family, churches, schools), and identifies and establishes links with needed community resources to support the greatest possible level of independent functioning. Dokecki (1977) describes this role as creative, flexible, and communication oriented. It must involve interagency collaboration, coordination of services, and an interdisciplinary approach and be based on a win-win philosophy (p. 16).

ATSEM (Acquaint, Teach, Support, Expand, Maintain) is a family involvement model developed by Karnes, Teska, and Zehrbach (1972) for school-based programs involving multihandicapped children. The Support component of the model involved identifying community resources outside the school that can assist families through times of emotional, social, or economic crisis. This notion was further developed by Karnes and Zehrbach

(1975) in a model for matching families to services. This latter model includes steps to identify a wide range of needs, to develop lists of alternative programs to meet jointly established goals, and, with the family, to select the most appropriate alternative services. This clearly requires an individual with a broad knowledge of available community resources to assist families.

The above review does not begin to do justice to the extensive work done by a number of states and the Bureau of Developmental Disabilities, U.S. Department of Health, Education, and Welfare, in developing case management systems.[1]

It is, perhaps, a reflection on the fragmentation of human services in general, that all of these efforts, together with the work of the Rand Corporation's researchers, do not necessarily represent a single body of evolving knowledge. It is significant, however, that so many different individuals have drawn essentially the same conclusion: *Some entity or function must be established within the service delivery system that works with families and handicapped individuals to help them identify their needs and gain access to the full range of appropriate services regardless of who provides those services.*

IF IT'S SUCH A GREAT IDEA,
WHY DOESN'T DIRECTION ALREADY EXIST?

The need for direction-like functions seems clear and well supported. Why, if they are so critical to making services work for people, do these linking functions not exist? There may be several reasons (adapted from Newbrough, 1977):

1. The general population believes that the client (or family) has the responsibility for independently obtaining effective services.
2. The separation of services into special purpose groupings allows for the development of highly technical professions which economically benefit their practitioners.
3. There is a competition among service providers for resources to continue their special activities. The method of justifying the award of resources to one provider over another tends to reinforce that separateness.

---

[1] A case management system design can be found in Kahn, L. D. 1978 (October). *A Case Management System for the Mentally Retarded Citizens of Rhode Island: A Model, A Needs Assessment, and Recommendations.* Prepared by Social Planning Services, Inc., under contract to the Rhode Island Department of Mental Health, Retardation and Hospitals. Included in a DHEW, Office of Human Development Services, Request for Proposal 105-78-5004, August, 1978, is *A Comprehensive Review and Evaluation of Individual Habilitation Plans and Case Management Systems.* A three volume set was developed by the Regional Institute of Social Welfare Research, Athens, Georgia, on the case management model. The volumes include concept and process definition, implementation requirements, and a trainer's guide, respectively. ERIC catalog numbers ED 158876, ED 158877, and ED 158878 (1977).

The primary implicit value, Newbrough observes, is in the direct service. Indirect services, like direction, that improve access are less valued, the last funded, and the first cut in times of fiscal crisis. None of this is dismissed or changed easily. The first reason can be countered with ample evidence from several writers—the service system is just too complex for anyone to use very effectively without assistance (Hobbs, 1975; Brewer and Kakalik, 1979). Changing public beliefs, however, is not so easily accomplished. The second and third above-mentioned reasons are dealt with even less easily. They represent systemic problems that are unlikely to change even with substantial service system reorganization. It may, in fact, be part of the nature of all living organisms to seek a protected ecological niche (for humans, a stable place in the economy).[2]

WHO SHOULD PROVIDE DIRECTION SERVICE?

As indicated earlier, Brewer and Kakalik (1979) have argued that direction-like capability should not be affiliated with any existing service bureaucracy. Such a nonaffiliated arrangement would simplify the role of Direction Service and make its relationships to other agencies clearer and placed on a more equal basis. Brewer and Kaklik suggest creating a system reporting directly to a state's governor. They calculate the cost of providing direction to be about $100 per year per individual served. Even if only a fraction of the estimated 7 million handicapped children in the United States were actually to receive direction, the cost would still be staggering (e.g., serving 14% would cost about $100 million). Establishing a separate system for direction may be, at best, difficult.

Of course, the actual marginal cost of implementing Direction Service as a separate entity within the service system would depend on the extent to which existing resources within the system might be redeployed. That is, many service agencies expend considerable effort conducting intake, assessing needs, determining eligibility, referring clients, and so on. If consolidated through broad interagency collaborative efforts (or legislative fiat), these resources could well be adequate to establish comprehensive direction-like capacity. Several states have begun addressing this issue in the area of case

---

[2]The concepts of ecological niche theory (see, for example, Whittaker, R., and Levin, S. (eds.), *Niche Theory and Application*) have not been, to this writer's knowledge, specifically expanded to human economies. In natural science studies, the niche is the particular place in the ecology occupied by a given species. It can be described in terms of a set of variables (e.g., food source, habitat, predators), which, taken together, describe a unique "space" occupied by only that species. In human economies, individuals may behave analogously, seeking a unique and stable economic space not occupied by other individuals. Such behavior (i.e., a drive toward "specialization") may be a necessary result of a competitive environment, but may also, of course, produce effects in opposition to the goals of formal (group) organizations.

management services for the developmentally disabled (Kahn, 1978; Oregon Mental Health Division, 1979).

There are attractions and disadvantages to any choice one might take regarding the proper organizational house for direction. People with developmental disabilities served by case management systems are not the only handicapped people needing direction. A legislative debate on a single integrated system providing direction to any handicapped person who needs it within a state would no doubt raise substantial questions about invasion of privacy, rampaging socialism, and the like.

If one is to consider creating direction, one must be prepared to account for those forces that tend to assign it to the "luxury class" of services. To achieve a stable niche for direction one must meet at least three conditions:

1. Its impact must be high enough on a segment of the population to create a sound constituency (families with handicapped children and handicapped consumer groups may represent that constituency).
2. Its placement must be in a setting where there is substantial counterpressure to a narrow specialist approach to serving children.
3. It must be competitively viable—it must be cost beneficial to the organization that pays for it.

The argument is made in the sections that follow that these conditions can be met by the placement of direction in schools. This position, too, is not without its weaknesses.

If direction is administered by a school, then the school becomes a direction client. A direction worker might then be put in an awkward position if, for example, a family requests a service that school administrators feel is unjustified or too costly. Despite these difficulties, there is ample philosophical and legal rationale for placing direction in schools. These are examined in the next section. Later portions of this chapter deal with a suggested role for direction workers in schools and the cost effectiveness of direction from a school perspective.

THE PHILOSOPHICAL RATIONALE
FOR DIRECTION SERVICE IN SCHOOLS[3]

From an anthropological perspective, education is the preparation of the members of a society to assume contributing adult roles. In our society, as in many others, the function of educating the young has traditionally been a shared one—the family and the school, under ideal circumstances, sharing

---

[3]Major portions of the following two sections were previously included in Devers, D., Lorang, K., Marmont, W., and Zeller, R. 1979. Direction: A tool for the school. In: S. Wapnick and C. Scanlon (eds.), *Toward Least Restrictive Environments,* pp. 29–31. Oregon Council for Exceptional Children, Portland. Used with permission.

complementary responsibilities in educating the child. In the broadest sense, any activity that contributes to a child's development could be considered educational. Families may be seen as controlling many of their children's activities and using the expertise of the school to instruct the child in "basic" (e.g., academic) skills.

The real world is somewhat more complex than this for any child. If the child is seriously handicapped, the complexity of the situation increases substantially. The responsibility for educating handicapped children is now assumed by many different groups in our society: the family, the schools, and a myriad of public and private, local, state, and federal programs provide essentially "educational" services to the handicapped population. The development of vocational skills, physical mobility skills, and recreation and leisure time skills are all important to a handicapped person assuming an adult role in society. With the implementation of PL 94-142, much debate has centered around what constitutes an "educational" service. This question, however, is a technical/political one (i.e., what do schools *think* they *should* provide?). From the broader perspective of the society's need to prepare all its members for the most productive adult life possible, any service that contributes to that end is "educational." From this perspective, then, schools are only one of many agents of society involved in education.

Hobbs (1975) has recommended an expanded role for public schools. Schools cannot be considered the sole proprietor of educational services. But they can, at least, become society's agent to ensure that those services, from all sources, are coordinated to support human development (p. 190). That schools can assume such a role is based on their unique status. Schools are distinguished from other social agencies in that they serve everyone. Basic education is *the primary entitlement* in our society. Other agencies may have mandates to serve handicapped children, but schools are the least stigmatizing element in society to coordinate a comprehensive service program because they serve *total* populations by geographic area (p. 200).

Schools, of course, may see their role as primarily instructional, rather than educational in the broader sense of supporting development. Other professionals may see schools as incapable of dealing with such wide-ranging problems. Hobbs's argument in favor of an extended role for schools (pp. 199–201) is adopted here—it may not be the best conceivable solution, but it is the most feasible one in sight. Direction is a way to operationalize that role, at least in part.

THE LEGAL RATIONALE FOR DIRECTION SERVICE IN SCHOOLS

The legal rationale for schools providing direction-like assistance derives from the regulations, and the interpretation of those regulations, for Public Law 94-142 and Section 504 of the Rehabilitation Act of 1973.

With the passage of PL 94-142, schools received a broadened charge to provide "free appropriate public education" (FAPE) to all handicapped children ages 3 to 21 by September 1, 1980. Under Section 504, FAPE was required to be provided to all identified school-age handicapped children as expeditiously as possible and not later than September 1, 1978.

FAPE is defined in the regulations for PL 94-142 as "... special education *and related services* which... are provided in conformity with an individualized education program..." (Section 121a.4).

"Related service," as defined in the same regulations,

> ... means transportation and such developmental, corrective and other supportive services as are required to assist a handicapped child to benefit from special education, and includes:
>
>> speech pathology and audiology,
>> psychological services,
>> physical and occupational therapy,
>> recreation,
>> early identification and assessment of disabilities in children,
>> counseling services,
>> medical services for diagnostic or evaluative purposes.
>
> The term also includes school health services, social work services in schools, and parent counseling and training (Section 121a.13(a)).

Each of those services is further defined in the regulations. What has struck most educators is that these legal *requirements* to provide "educationally related services" go considerably beyond the traditional role and the capability of most school districts. In their own defense, some school districts have indicated that they will plan in individualized education program (IEP) sessions only for those services that they are able to provide.

In a letter to the country's Chief State School Officers, Dr. Edwin Martin (Deputy Commissioner, Bureau of Education for the Handicapped, U.S. Office of Education) clarified the requirements for IEP planning and related services as follows:

> ... some parties have interpreted the final regulations to mean that a public agency must provide to a handicapped child only those services which are available *in the agency*. This interpretation is not correct.
>
> The regulations under Section 504 state that an appropriate education "... is the provision of regular special education and related aids and services that are... designed to meet the individual educational needs of handicapped persons as adequately as the needs of non-handicapped persons are met...."
>
> ... read together, these two statutes (PL 94-142 and Section 504) and their implementing regulations require that... each handicapped child must be provided all services necessary to meet his/her special education and related needs (Martin, 1977).

As has been pointed out repeatedly by school administrators, such requirements, if read as mandating that schools must assume all costs, place impossible financial burdens on school districts to pay for services they have never provided and can ill afford. There is no requirement, however, in any of the legislation that schools can only plan services in the IEP for which the schools can pay. That is, nothing in law or regulations prohibits schools from meeting IEP requirements by utilizing other nonschool community services where they are available. A special U.S. Department of Health, Education, and Welfare report on the responsibilities under Section 504 of administrators of programs for the disabled emphasized this point. Schools must:

> Provide a free appropriate education regardless of the type of severity of a child's disability. (For example, [the school] may select a public or private residential program for a child with profoundly disabling cerebral palsy. Although the public school district itself may not be able to pay the extra cost of non-medical care, room and board, *it is responsible for finding these funds from other sources*) (*Handicapped Americans Reports,* 1977; emphasis added).

Section 121a.301 of the PL 94-142 regulations, entitled "Free Appropriate Public Education—Methods and Payments," reads:

> (a) Each state may use whatever state, local, federal and private sources of support are available in the state to meet the requirements of this part. A state could use joint agreements between the agencies involved for sharing the cost.... (b) Nothing in this part relieves an insurer or similar third party from an otherwise valid obligation to provide or to pay for services to a handicapped child.

Schools are being asked to become the community's responsible agent for facilitating child development. Schools are not necessarily being asked to "provide everything," but rather to serve as the touch point for children to gain *access* to what the community at large has available to support each child's development.

Further support for this view of the school's role is found in the definition of social work services in schools in the regulations for PL 94-142. This part, in essence, authorizes schools to use PL 94-142 funds to pay for direction-like activities:

> Social work services in schools include:
> (i)   Preparing a social or developmental history on a handicapped child . . .
> (ii) Working with those problems in a child's living situation (home, school, and community) that affect the child's adjustment in school; and
> (iii) *Mobilizing school and community resources* to enable the child to receive maximum benefit from his or her educational program (Section 121a.13(b)(11), emphasis added).

Utilizing staff with general skills to identify community resources that might help meet the needs of a handicapped child is a legitimate and probably necessary function of schools. There seems to be no other way to address child needs fully under the law and to provide all needed services economically.

BASIC FUNCTIONS

Various writers have supported a direction-like approach to promoting coordinated services to individuals. Each model described has certain common elements. In February, 1979, representatives of most of the existing BEH-funded direction service demonstrations met to discuss and debate what was emerging as common to all their efforts. The basic functions, described below, emerged from those discussions. They are not intended as a description of any particular organizational structure. They are common to all direction demonstrations, and to the other client-centered service coordination approaches described above, regardless of differences in delivery strategy. There may be as many valid ways to operationalize these basic functions as there are unique communities into which the three functions may fit (Zeller, 1979):[4]

1. *Assist in the location of and access to the most appropriate combination of services and resources to meet the needs of handicapped children.*
   This assistance is characterized as:

   a. Comprehensive (supports the developmental and maintenance needs of handicapped children and families)
   b. Dynamic (can provide assistance over time at a level of involvement appropriate to the needs, abilities, and desires of the family)
   c. Appropriate in matching (operates so as to ensure that the services matched are appropriate and actualized)

2. *Systematically collect and maintain information on services and resources available to meet the needs of handicapped children.*
   This information capability is characterized as:

   a. Comprehensive (includes or has access to all generic and specialized services that may have an impact on any handicapped child or family)
   b. Nonredundant (uses other information systems when appropriate and efficient)

3. *Assist in the development and support of relationships among agencies that promote coordinated services to children.*
   This assistance is characterized as:

   a. Catalytic (develops relationships with agencies that can help promote new services to fill identified gaps in the service delivery continuum)
   b. Facilitative (involves brokerage of information and the convening of appropriate parties to promote understanding and agreements with or

---

[4]The working paper (Zeller, 1979) from which these basic functions are taken is a product of the National Direction Service Task Force, made up of representatives of many of the current BEH-funded demonstrations. The functions are the carefully worded concensus of all the demonstration sites involved in the February, 1979 discussions.

among agencies which result in improved services to a child or to groups of children)

The last function requires some further comment—it is this aspect of Direction Service that justifies the inclusion of this chapter in a book about interagency collaboration. The kinds of relationships supported here can be of two types: 1) individual-centered relationships can be promoted, as when interagency staffings or planning sessions are arranged for an individual case, and 2) agency-agency relationships can be encouraged to support services to groups of individuals, as when areas of possible program overlap between or among agencies are identified by Direction Service on the basis of summary data on many individuals.

The dependency of this third function on the other two points to the need for interaction among all three functions. An information and referral system that is not used by those working closely with individuals and families cannot satisfy the requirements for good information capability—good information depends on users regularly interacting with and when necessary updating the information. Likewise to perform the first function adequately requires both good information on what resources are available and some cordial, productive relationships with service providers. For Direction Service to exist in a service system, all three functions listed must exist and be interactional.

A CONCEPT ANALYSIS OF DIRECTION

Concept analysis can serve the positive function of clarifying and defining an idea by giving examples of what does and what does not represent that idea. Its application here to the definition of direction (see Table 1) should provide

Table 1. Concept analysis of direction

Direction *is* . . .	Direction *is not* . . .
Compiling all relevant existing records, past assessments, and services histories on a child and family	Preparing extensive family histories using a set format
Arranging additional assessments when needed	Conducting individual assessments on children
Identifying as many potentially appropriate needs-to-service matches as possible (providing good information to decision-makers)	Making decisions about which is the best service for a particular child's need
Systematic, comprehensive matching of needs-to-services over time	An information and referral service
Resource linking and referral facilitation	Assignment to services (control); service resource allocation and management
Child-and-family-centered (facilitating needed services to individual families regardless of who provides them)	Program-centered (concerned substantially with the efficient management of service programs to groups of people)

the reader with an understanding sufficient to distinguish direction from other human services and other approaches to interagency coordination and collaboration.

Each instance provided in Table 1 of what direction is and is not requires further discussion of how one might operationalize the concept. This additional discussion is provided throughout the chapter on more salient issues implied in this analysis (e.g., decision making, quality of services).

It should be clear that all of the "is not" instances listed in Table 1 represent valid operations or concerns within the service agencies ("the system"). Of course, someone must conduct assessments and assign children to specific services. These operations, to one degree or another, are already extant in the various service agencies. They may be rearranged, changed, and so on, through collaborative agreements (and probably should be), but they are not Direction Service and the provision of direction does not rely on their specific configuration.

PROVIDING DIRECTION—IMPORTANT CONSIDERATIONS

Direction Goals Guide Style

There are two broad goals that should guide the provision of direction to every family:

Goal 1: To ensure that each child (family) referred is matched with that set of resources that will best meet identified needs.

Goal 2: To assist families to become more competent and skilled at identifying needs and coping with the service system to obtain appropriate services.

To pursue the first goal, Direction Service provides different levels of support to families depending upon what seems appropriate. This support might range from simple information and referral assistance to intensive direction involvement (see Figure 1). The provision of simple information and referral generally presumes that the family can assess their own needs adequately, can articulate them reasonably well to the information and referral (I & R) provider, and requires only information about who provides the necessary services. At the other extreme, intensive direction assistance involvement (including help in identifying problems; developing and selecting solutions; identifying and selecting appropriate services, assisting with appointment scheduling, the completion of application forms, etc.) presumes that the family is not prepared at that time to make the necessary decisions independently and requires extensive support. The kind of direction support provided to a family depends upon their particular circumstance and need.

Figure 1 shows the relationship of this first goal to the various levels of direction involvement and to the second goal. The provision of intensive

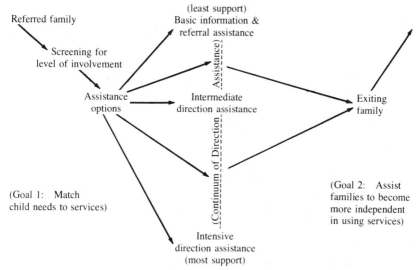

Figure 1. Direction goals and their relation to a continuum of direction assistance.

direction assistance to the family of every handicapped child is neither practical nor necessary. Screening for the level of assistance needed is a critical function but not one for which any inventory can be easily constructed.

The following piece from a document on how to accomplish direction makes the point:

> Families come from different places. They don't all have the same perspective on what constitutes help. In dealing with people, what's true is not nearly as important as what people believe to be true.
>
> Letting the family take the lead in deciding what help they want means that operational procedures can't be easily fixed—they have to remain flexible enough to meet the family where the family is.
>
> Thomas Gilhool, the lawyer in the *PARC* right to education case, said in his arguments: "This is a case where the class must fit the child instead of the child having to fit into any classroom. . . . This is a new language, a new set of facts, and it will mean a new concept of oneself by those with handicaps of any variety."
>
> The same notion seems valid for Direction Service. There may be procedures to assist families, but the procedures should be flexible enough to fit the family, rather than fixed, forcing the family to fit them. It's harder to do well, but nobody consistently makes good bread without attending to the idiosyncracies of each batch (Justice and Zeller, 1977).

Ideally, when families have been successfully matched to services and are "finished" with direction service, they should be able to do all future matching of their child's needs to services utilizing only information and referral assistance. This ideal may not be attainable, but the intent of the second goal, at a minimum, is to make certain that families, through their involvement with Direction Service do not become more "dependent" upon intensive assistance.[5] Achieving this may involve parent training or counseling of a sort, but it can be largely a matter of the style one uses in providing direction to families.

> Anybody who's ever tried to make a living consulting will tell you that one of they keys to staying alive is to make the other guy look good, instead of grabbing the thunder of the success for yourself. Direction Service is in the business of being a good consultant to families. In order to do that well, we have to change our ideas about power and success around a bit. We can achieve a double kind of success if we allow the family to score the winning run. We do the ground work and exercise our skills to explain to a service provider the importance and necessity for reducing the amount of time that a youngster has to wait for service. Then, when we feel there's a better chance they will grant the request or make the exception, we get back on the phone to the parent. Instead of announcing in a subtly triumphant tone:

>> "It's all set. Have Johnny at the Vocational Rehabilitation office at 9:00. They've agreed to waive the waiting period."

> we say something more like:

>> "I think that if you call Jack _____ at Vocational Rehab., you might be able to convince him that it's important to waive the waiting requirement. Here are some things you might mention."

> Now, we might win twice. First, it's likely we can meet the needs of the youngster. And, on top of that, we will make the parents feel more successful, effectual, and powerful. The next time they need something, they may have an increased confidence to deal with the situation and cut down the amount of time we have to spend (Justice and Zeller, 1977).

Family Decisions and the Direction Process

The broad goals of direction set the context for outlining the relationship of family decisions to the direction process. To specify that relationship further we must first outline the flow of decisions in the service process and their relationship to the family. The model depicted in Figure 2 attempts to do this.

The model shows certain influences impinging upon the family and its view of what constitutes a need for services. The family members are constantly weighing their child's "existing condition" against what they see as some "preferred condition." If they view that discrepancy as substantial enough, they will decide to seek some form of assistance. Such a decision, of course, is clearly subject to the knowledge families have about what's possible for the child, what services exist, what cultural values say about seeking

---

[5]There is no simple assumption here that families necessarily can or will become consistently more independent over time. Olshansky (1962) discusses the notion of "chronic sorrow." No parent of a handicapped child is ever likely to get totally beyond the sorrow of their offspring having some severe limits. From time to time the sorrow may emerge and require added support for the family to move forward. The second goal of direction is to help the family cope in spite of that sorrow, while recognizing its presence and burden.

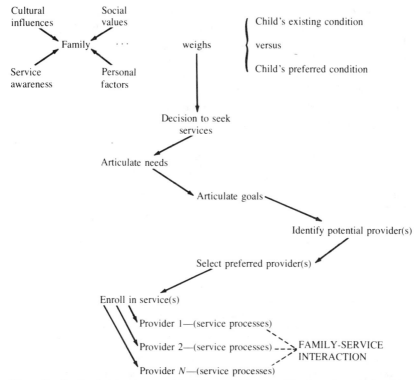

Figure 2. Family decision flow model. (This model is a modification of one designed by Melichar, 1976. Changes have been made for this application, but any clarity this brings the reader is credit to Melichar. Confusion it may promote is this writer's responsibility.)

help from others, and so on. These influences are dynamic and interactive. That is, those influences, being in a continual state of flux, may reverse the decision to seek services at some point, may change perceived need, and so on.

If a family decides to seek services, they must make several other decisions before actually contacting a service agency. These are represented by the points in the model: articulate needs, articulate goals, identify service provider(s), and select service provider(s). Note that this model can describe decisions at any level of sophistication. It is as valid for the less sophisticated family that says

"We heard about your service from our neighbor. (influences)
"We're having trouble managing our son. He's always into everything. (need)
"We want him to do better, (goal) but we don't know what else to try. You are the only place we know to call." (identify and select service provider)

as it is for the more sophisticated family that may have substantial files, developmental profiles, specific learning objectives in mind, good familiarity with existing services, and so on. What is different about the "sophisticated" families is not the decisions per se but the amount of information they apply to those decisions. Sophisticated families may also be better at articulating the decisions they have made and the plans they have for their children.

The major decision steps in Figure 2 can be related to the goals Direction Services has for families, and to the tasks that constitute direction assistance. Table 2 displays these relationships. Family subgoals describe desired levels of independence for each decision model step. Taken together, the achievement of these subgoals constitutes accomplishment of direction goal 2: to assist families to become more competent and skilled at identifying needs and coping with the service system to obtain appropriate services. The "direction

Table 2. Decision steps, subgoals for families, and direction tasks

Decision model steps	Family subgoals	Direction tasks
Decide to seek (change in) service	To be able to identify when current situation (service) is not adequately addressing child needs due to change in needs, inadequate programs, etc.	Receive referrals (complete initial intake, determine initial eligibility, screen for level of involvement, etc.).
Articulate needs	To be able to identify and articulate child's social, educational, health, and other needs on both short term and long term bases.	Compile needs data (consent forms, collect agency records, profile client needs, conduct/participate in staffings).
Articulate goals	To be able to generate appropriate child, service, and family short range and long range goals that address identified needs.	Develop goals with family (identify needed services, develop goal/ expectation statements for each area of service).
Identify service providers	To be familiar with and able to utilize available community resource information banks to identify potential service providers.	Identify appropriate service providers (search information base, select alternative providers, confirm service goals/expectations).
Select preferred providers	To be able to examine and compare available service alternatives in light of their appropriateness to family values, needs, and goals.	Finalize service plan with family (select most appropriate services, plan for enrollment/appointments, establish level of DS support needed to implement services).
Enroll in services	To be able to compile and communicate such information as may be required of provider application/ enrollment processes.	Assist in family enrollment (arrange appointments, transportation for meetings, accompany family to meetings).
Interact with service processes	To be able to communicate with service providers to ensure that family values, needs, and goals are accounted for in all service processes.	Assist in ongoing coordination (serve as fixed point for service providers to coordinate efforts, provide follow-along assistance to families). Follow-up with family and service providers (determine view of service progress, satisfaction with the "match," other needs for DS involvement).

tasks" outline a generic direction assistance process, the outcome of which is the accomplishment of goal 1, ensuring that each family is appropriately matched to services. As a family becomes more independent, the role of direction shifts from the kind of active assistance represented by the tasks to information assistance. That is, the family performs some of the direction tasks relying on direction assistance primarily for service information. Expecting families to become totally independent of information on services (e.g., new programs, changes in what is provided) is probably unrealistic given the way services are currently structured.

The flow of decisions in Figure 2 and the subgoals and direction tasks in Table 2 do not represent simple linear sequences. The decision to seek new services or change existing services is one that will be made by a family many times as their children grow, learn, and mature. Likewise, needs and goals change over time as, of course, do available services. As any of these things changes, the decision process (and direction assistance) can restart where appropriate. If goals and needs for a family remain valid but a new fiscal year brings with it changes in available services, an examination of available service alternatives may be immediately appropriate. If a family and service provider are dissatisfied with service progress, the selection of and matching to another provider may be indicated.

The decisions a family must make to plan for, gain access to, and monitor services to their children represent, like direction, a dynamic, iterative process. The work is never done in any absolute sense—only appropriate to that family's circumstance at any given point in time.

Due Process and Partnership in the IEP—A Direction Orientation

In the above concept analysis of Direction Service a distinction was made between providing to families information needed to make decisions and making decisions about what service is most appropriate. The former constitutes direction; the latter does not. The real issue, however, is much broader than this. Any statement of need is value laden. The determination that a child should receive a particular service is highly value laden—it can say a great deal about the child's place and future in society.

Whose values should guide such decisions? In planning to provide services to any child, there is likely a sharing of expertise applied to each decision, but the family's values should predominate. There may be problems with such an approach if the family's values fall outside some range considered acceptable by society. But our culture subscribes, formally at least, to pluralism—value differences are to be expected and even protected. Congress has enacted several laws to try to ensure that individuals' values will be reflected in the services they receive. The various statutes requiring an individualized planning process are all conspicuously organized to ensure that the service recipients and their families have effective veto power over almost any programmatic decision. Should substantive differences of opinion arise, these laws generally provide some hearing process to mediate the disagreement. Hearing requirements are modeled after judicial due process procedures.

As Kotin (1977) observes, a due process model, in and of itself, may not be well adapted to educational decision making. Kotin also notes that the state has traditionally exercised considerable authority for deciding what is best for children independent of parental wishes (the concept of *parens patriae*).[6] This authority has been defined, however, within the context of the juvenile justice system. Society at large has never had a formalized mechanism for jointly planning for the care of children until an adversarial relationship is declared. The IEP process, however, if it is to be a shared planning responsibility, must reflect a new orientation to "due process." There remains a need, of course, both under law and in practice, for mechanisms to deal with disagreements. These must include a hearings procedure. Mediation through administrative review and other less drastic (and less costly) procedures are also needed, although not required. But mechanisms for managing conflict should not be the starting point for the IEP process.

Sontag (1976) and others have advocated a partnership approach to planning and providing services to handicapped children. Characteristics of a system that promotes partnerships between schools and families might include:

1. Families who are willing and committed to participating actively with professionals in their children's education
2. Professionals who are prepared to meet families:
    a.   As equals in the educational process
    b.   As standard setters in the decision-making process
    c.   As fellow advocates for the child's programs
3. Schools that offer real alternatives in programming based on all available resources, rather than limiting programs strictly to the available educational budget

None of these is easily realized, but all are necessary. The individualized planning process can only be a shared responsibility when some sense of equality exists among the participants. The process can be little more than a sham if real alternatives are not examined and discussed (the "alternatives" cannot be "this program or nothing"). Schools need to offer, and identify in the community, the widest possible range of programs and services. Direction is one way to manage this transition in orientation to a partnership approach to education that still protects due process rights.

---

[6]Kotin (1977) references *Prince* v. *Massachusetts,* 321 U.S. 158 (1944) where the Court defines the doctrine of *parens patriae.* Under that doctrine, the Court said (p. 167), "the state has a wide range of power for limiting parental freedom and authority in things affecting the child's welfare."

Resource Information—An Important Part of Direction

The availability of good, accurate resource information is indispensable to providing quality direction. Even in medium-sized communities, there may be hundreds of service providers offering several times that many services to handicapped children. As Brewer and Kakalik (1979) note, most professionals do not (and, perhaps, cannot) understand the complexity of the service system. Compiling even a fairly small information base, however, can become a full-time job for several people; services change frequently, and staff (and their skills) may change even more often, not to mention locations, telephone numbers, intake procedures, eligibility, and the like.

Many communities have already established I & R services which may be a starting place for compiling resource information. Usually, however, the I & R data bases are of a general nature and may not contain enough information to allow one to identify what kinds of services are actually provided, to whom, and under what conditions.

The northwestern Direction Service sites have used the taxonomy shown in Table 3 to characterize services provided. Each service is fully defined,[7] and an effort has been made to keep the definitions both mutually exclusive and exhuastive. Manual information files are kept along with a service index to facilitate locating providers of needed services.

Figure 3 displays a sample of the kind of data collected on each program. An individual provider may offer several different programs. A private center, for example, may have a school for the mentally retarded, a sheltered workshop, and a vocational training program—each is treated separately. The distinction between primary and secondary services is an important one to appropriate matching. Primary services are those for which a referral can be made to the provider; secondary services are provided only to those receiving a primary service from that provider. Ready access to key contact people, phone numbers, and so on, makes the data more usable.

Several considerations apply to the establishment and maintenance of an accurate information base. In some larger communities, I & R providers may have adequate information to support the provision of direction. Merely collecting available service directories and attempting to use them for an information base is probably a good way to pilot direction. This allows the person interested in developing direction a good idea of what level of information is needed and available.

If a separately maintained information base is needed, think small. Both machine-based and manual needle-sort systems are available that allow one to register and sort service programs based on a large number of variables (service type, age, handicap, income criteria, location, and so on). Usually,

---

[7]To conserve space in this text, definitions for the taxonomy in Table 3 are not provided here. They are available to the interested reader from the author.

Table 3. Direction taxonomy of services

ASSISTANCE/AID/ADVOCACY	**EDUCATION**
AID	ACADEMIC
Equipment	*Alternative
Financial	*Formal/regular
Housing	*Special education
ADVOCACY	*Training (skills)
Legal assistance	Tutoring
Parent/consumer group	OTHER
Parent 1:1	Adult
LIBRARY INFORMATION	Infant stimulation
INFORMATION AND REFERRAL	*Parent
	Preschool
COUNSELING/THERAPY/TREATMENT	**RESIDENTIAL**
COUNSELING	CARE
*Academic	DETENTION
Adult	FOSTER CARE
*Child/adolescent	GROUP HOMES
Crisis	RESPITE CARE
Family	TREATMENT
Genetic	
Vocational	
THERAPY	**SUPPORT SERVICES**
Behavioral/psychological	SOCIAL-RECREATIONAL
*Occupational	Camps
*Physical	Companion
*Speech/language	Social group
*Vision	Sports/recreation
TREATMENT	HOME CARE
Dental	Babysitting
Medical	Day care
	Home attendant
DIAGNOSIS/ASSESSMENT	*TRANSPORTATION
*AUDIOLOGICAL	VOLUNTEER
*EDUCATIONAL	
MEDICAL/DENTAL	**VOCATIONAL/EMPLOYMENT**
Dental	ACTIVITY CENTER
*Medical	JOB PLACEMENT
*Psychiatric	*SHELTER WORKSHOP
*MULTIDISCIPLINARY	*VOCATIONAL TRAINING
*OCCUPATIONAL THERAPY/	
PHYSICAL THERAPY	
*PSYCHOLOGICAL	
*SPEECH/LANGUAGE	
*VISION	
*VOCATIONAL	

*The asterisk indicates "educational and related services," as listed in the PL 94-142 regulations, Section 121a.13. See Figures 5, 6, and 7 and text.

Crippled Children's Services

Phone:	555-3575
Contacts:	Jim Mason Cathy Rennen Pat Kain/Intake
Director:	Dr. Ronald Smythe, Director
Mailing address:	Crippled Children's Services Clinical Services Bldg. 901 East 18th Street Eugene, Oregon 97403

Public

Description: Multidisciplinary screening clinics for the coordination of medical care for cerebral palsy, myelomeningocele, congenital heart, orthopedic, cleft lip and palate, birth defects and genetic counseling. Diane Walkers—Clinic Coordinator. Joanne Marrs—Medical Doctor. Parent education meetings—open to all parents of handicapped, not just clients of CCS.

Master File 7/79

Primary services: AID—Equipment, Financial (Medical); ASSESSMENT—Medical, Total, OT & PT; COUNSELING—Genetic; INFORMATION/REFERRAL; MEDICAL/DENTAL TREATMENT

Secondary services: ASSESSMENT—Educational, Psychological (limited), Speech; COUNSELING—Family; SUPPORT SERVICES—Parent education; THERAPY—Occupational, Physical, Speech/Hearing

Ages: Birth to 21 years

Handicaps: GROSS MOTOR/ORTHOPEDIC, COMMUNICATION DISORDER, HEALTH IMPAIRED (multiple sclerosis, cerebral palsy, myelomeningocele, hydrocephalis, cleft lip, cleft palate, developmental, inherited, congenital, cardiac)

Restrictions: Doesn't serve deaf/blind as primary disability

Fees: none

Figure 3. Sample resource information system format and contents.

however, service type (and possibly handicap) provide enough sort variables to narrow down the choice of available agencies to a manageable number in all but the largest communities. In short, the choice comes down to making the system just complex enough that the manual work is fairly easy. There rarely is one perfect provider, and even an agency's eligibility criteria are sometimes flexible.

The value of interaction between those providing direction and the information base is very high. This interaction allows errors to be spotted and corrected continuously by the primary information users. Without such in-

Table 4. Resource information base—Developmental considerations

What kind of and how much information is needed in order to make adequate direction decisions?

What resources are available for developing and maintaining a service information base (e.g., dollars, staff, reproduction facilities)?

What kind of access to the information is needed? In how many places will the information be kept? Is speed of access important?

What are the available sources of information on agencies, and what has already been collected (e.g., telephone books, service directories, knowledgeable locals, national or local publications)?

Is a budget/funding cycle of providers important to updating service information? What other things may signal updating (e.g., whenever new information comes in, periodically during predictable down-times, as part of family-related agency contact)?

Do post-secondary institutions (community colleges, universities, etc.) have the potential for providing services? Do proprietary organizations or schools have such a potential (e.g., meat-cutting schools may offer dietary help; cosmetology schools may help improve appearance of young adults)?

Will professional groups (e.g., medical society, ministerial society, legal aid) compile information about members who provide services to families with handicapped children?

teraction, the information will quickly become inaccurate and less useful. The bound directory approach to disseminating an information base is particularly weak from this standpoint, unless ways can be found to tap users for needed corrections and to disseminate updates.

Table 4 summarizes the considerations one should examine in undertaking the development of a resource information system to support direction to families.

EXISTING DIRECTION MODELS

BEH-Funded Direction Service Demonstrations

This writer has been involved with three of the Bureau of Education for the Handicapped (BEH)-funded direction service demonstrations. The projects are located in Lane County (Eugene) and Portland, Oregon, and in Educational Service District No. 112 (Vancouver), Washington. At the time of this writing, the projects had been operating approximately 3 years under full BEH funding and were entering the final year of demonstration.

Each site, in a fairly similar fashion, provides direction to some families, information assistance to others, and support to school and agency staff who are seeking resources for handicapped children outside their organizations. Each site began operation somewhat independent of the IEP process in schools. The role was to treat school programs as a resource like any other. It became evident after a short time that the IEP process was critical to providing coordinated services—if the sites helped arrange services independently they would be confounding (or substituting direction for) that process. The second and third project years, then, have concentrated on building the necessary links so that direction can become a part of the school's role in developing IEPs. The receptivity of school districts to this has varied, as is reflected below under the descriptions of "intended futures."

A brief description of each site follows:

Portland Direction Service

Host agency: Portland Public Schools, Portland, Oregon

Service area: Portland schools attendance area; total population is about 380,000, of which approximately 67,000 attend public school. The district is located within a larger population area (approximately 1.2 million population).

Administration: Portland DS is part of the Community Resources Section of the Special Education Division of the district. The project director is also the Community Resources Section Manager. She reports to the Director of Special Education.

Staffing: 0.5 FTE—Director (approximate)

2.0 FTE—Case coordinators

1.0 FTE—Paraprofessional information specialist

1.0 FTE—Secretary/receptionist

Client families served: Approximately 180 intensive cases per year. About 275 active client families at any given time. Less intensive involvement (information only) with about 680 other children per year.

Information base entries: Providers, about 235; Services, about 1,000.

Intended future: Portland Direction Service is very much a school-based model. The main functions of direction are currently being integrated into the district's IEP process. During the final project year and after termination of federal funding, existing school staff will provide basic direction to families when needed. A direction office will continue as a part of the Community Resources Section. Its role will include resource information and consultation support to IEP team members and the provision of direction to families who present particularly difficult and complex problems.

Educational Service District No. 112

Host agency: ESD 112, Vancouver, Washington

Service area: Six southwestern Washington counties (Clark, Cowlitz, Klickitat, Pacific, Skamania, and Wahkiakum). The counties all border the Columbia River from mid-state to the coast (about 220 miles from east to west). The total population is about 240,000. About half live in Clark County (Vancouver), which is a suburb of Portland, Oregon. There are 31 school districts in the target area.

Staffing: 1.0 FTE—Director
2.5 FTE—Professional case coordinators
0.5 FTE—Paraprofessional case coordinator
1.5 FTE—Paraprofessional information specialists
1.0 FTE—Secretary/receptionist

Client families serviced: Approximately 100 intensive cases per year. About 160 active clients at any given time. Less intensive involvement (information only) with about 500 other children per year.

Information base entries: Providers, about 200; Services, about 800. Intended future: ESD 112 has been extensively involved with other agencies in Clark County in the development of interagency agreements. Maintenance after federal funding may involve county funds (for maintenance of the resource information capability), as well as some cooperative funding from local school districts within the target area. Maintenance functions will probably be limited to information support and consultation to agency and school staff who provide direction-like assistance to families.

Lane County Direction Service

Host agency: Center on Human Development, University of Oregon, Eugene, Oregon

Service area: Lane County, Oregon. Total population is about 220,000 with about 140,000 living in the Eugene/Springfield metropolitan area which is located in the center of the county. The county ranges from about 40 to 80 miles north to south and about 120 miles east to west. There are six smaller areas of population concentration around the metropolitan area. Sixteen school districts are within the target area.

Administration: The Center on Human Development (CHD) is a department within the university's College of Education. The project director reports directly to the director of the Center on Human Development.

Staffing: 0.5 FTE—Director
2.5 FTE—Case coordinators
0.5 FTE—Paraprofessional information specialist
1.0 FTE—Secretary/receptionist

Client/families served: Approximately 110 intensive cases per year. About 220 active clients at any given time. Less intensive involvement (information only) with about 275 other children per year.

Information base entries: Providers, about 350; Services, about 1,300.[8]

---

[8]Differences in the numbers of information base entries reflect differences in resource data maintenance procedures rather than real differences in service density. For instance, the Portland and Vancouver sites share their data bases; the Lane County site lists individual day care providers separately.

Intended future: Information base is currently being transferred to machine storage (a word processor with disc storage), and the possibility of maintenance through subscription is being explored. The county's largest school district (Eugene) has implemented a "case management" system that will utilize direction staff support (information and case consultation). The maintenance of a core direction office with these functions is being examined.

Other Direction Models

The above sites are only 3 of the 25 funded by BEH. There is not room in this chapter to attempt even a brief description of each site. There are two other efforts, however, that deserve note because they represent unique approaches to direction.

The Los Angeles Direction Service has developed a parent seminar approach to providing direction called *Directions: Forward by Design* (Justice, 1979). The approach involves a series of eight sessions for parents during which they learn the needs identification, goal-setting, and resource-accessing skills described above in the Family Decision Model. Parents also learn to structure their time and efforts to support both achievement and continuous re-examination of their goals. One critical aspect of this training approach is an emphasis on developing a powerful motivation in parents to pursue goals that benefit their child and family. The seminars involve an eclectic combination of self-awareness experiences, communication skills training, measurable goal-writing exercises, and time management skill development. To what extent these skills can be maintained independently (or with some marginal level of support) remains to be seen. *Directions: Forward by Design,* however, is potentially a powerful cost-efficient approach to parents providing direction independently.

The most rural of the direction demonstrations is located in southeastern Utah. There, two offices serve some of the most sparsely populated land in the country. The target region includes part of the Navajo Indian reservation. Barriers of language, culture, distance, and travel conditions combine to make the delivery of services to handicapped children extremely difficult. The majority of families served in this area live more than 25 miles from the Direction Service office. More than 10% live over 100 miles away. Telephone and mail communication with families is virtually nonexistent. The majority of specialized services in the state are located in Salt Lake City, about 400 miles away. Traveling clinics pass through the area several times a year, but these may get no closer than 100 miles to a family needing service. Cultural and language barriers are somewhat eased by the direction staff members who are both bilingual Navajos. Cultural tradition, however, requires simple acceptance of a handicapped child. Navajo families have no inclination to seek assistance to improve their handicapped child's development.

Two main tasks, then, face this rural direction operation: cultural intervention to modify the willingness of Navajo families to seek assistance, and arranging access to needed services. The latter can be a logistic nightmare, involving travel over huge distances, as well as coordinating service appointments and obtaining culturally acceptable access to services (translators, advocates, etc.). This demonstration is also supporting an interstate agreement between Utah and Colorado so that services closer to the reservation but located in Colorado can be used.

Clearly, this represents a different concept of direction than the one emerging in largely urban, dominant culture areas. It is fraught with questions about the responsibility of the dominant culture to the handicapped people of the Navajo nation. But it is also a demonstration that, even under extreme conditions, direction can facilitate the access of handicapped children to services.

OUTCOMES AND A COST-BENEFIT LOOK AT DIRECTION

The decision of whether or not to implement direction in a school or elsewhere should be made on the basis of its probable cost and anticipated benefit compared with other ways of spending the same amount of money. Any such analysis requires one to specify whose costs are to be considered and from what perspective benefits will be viewed. The cost of establishing direction will vary with the particular cost strategy chosen (e.g., a fully funded center added to a school district budget versus reassigning some existing staff to perform direction functions). Likewise, benefits can be judged from several perspectives. One could look at long term benefits (e.g., preventing higher future costs like institutionalization), at administrative benefits (e.g., avoiding formal hearings and their associated costs), or at accrued service benefits (e.g., the value of services to which access is gained by direction that otherwise would have been paid for by the school or agency). The benefits from a service system viewpoint could also be assessed. Are services somehow better utilized when direction is present? How does one make such a comparison?

Clearly, no simple cost-benefit analysis will satisfy all perspectives. Furthermore, the data required to answer some of the questions well are not available except at high cost. The data available that apply to some of these cost-benefit questions are presented below. The examination here is limited to three questions:

1. How successful has Direction Service been in matching requested services to available resources?
2. To what extent has Direction Service been able to find other than school resources to provide for educational and related services?
3. Who provides those services and at what cost to the resident school district?

Figure 4 shows the number of requests for services and their disposition across the three northwestern Direction Service sites. Three categories of service are displayed, as well as a total. The size of the rectangles and their subdivisions is proportional to the number of services indicated in each case. The divisions of each rectangle, in order from left to right, are: those services received in less than 90 days, those received after more than 90 days, those not received, and those refused by the family. Ninety days was chosen for a division in charting services received because after 90 days the probability of a successful match drops below 0.5. After 180 days, the probability of a successful match is less than 0.24 (the service is effectively unavailable).

The percentages in parentheses represent percent received of the total requested/percent received of the total requested less those refused. The frequency of services refused varies with the type of service requested, counseling being the most common service requested that is subsequently withdrawn. The reason for refusals is not always clear but may stem from a change in the parent's perception of the need, or a change in the nature of the need as it is articulated by the parent. Leaving these out of the calculation of percent received (the second figure in parentheses) provides a better indication of how successful Direction Service can be in matching a service to a stable need.

Using this stable need figure, 92.5% of all requests are successfully matched. This rate is inflated somewhat by the information service match rate (99%)—in those cases information about a service (rather than a service per se) is provided. "Educational and related services," and "all other services" combined are successfully matched 87.1% of the time.

Figure 5 is a similar display breaking down "educational and related services." These services are defined in the PL 94-142 regulations, Section 121a.13, fairly broadly. Table 3 indicates the services that have been included

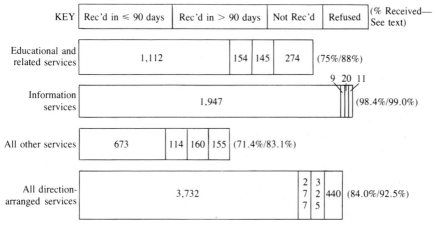

Figure 4. Services requested and received by direction-served families.

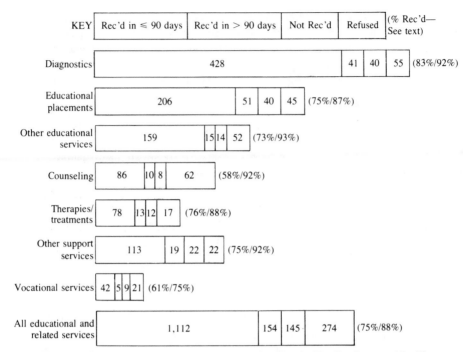

Figure 5. Educational and related services requested and received by direction-served families.

here for purposes of this analysis. Were the regulations interpreted broadly, the data set would be larger but the results with respect to school districts would also be more debatable. Not included in the definition are some services that were provided by school districts although they were not clearly mandated (preschool services, for example). All of the educational and related services listed in Table 3 either have been provided or have been paid for by a school district in at least one case. The definition of related services used here, then, is a fairly conservative one, the validity of which is confirmed by the willingness of schools to pay for or provide those services.

As Figure 5 indicates, the highest success rate in matching is with diagnostic services (92%). The lowest rate of matching is in the vocational area. Adequate vocational preparation for handicapped adolescents, at least among those served by the three projects represented here, is simply not available. The long term cost of not providing such preparation probably far outweighs the expense of adequate programs.

Figure 6 shows the cost of services (free, partial, full) and where they are provided (in-school versus out-of-school). "Cost" in the first five of the categories is the cost to the school district in which the child resides. If the service resulted in any cost to the child's parents, whether or not other sources of funds were involved, the service is indicated as provided "at some cost to

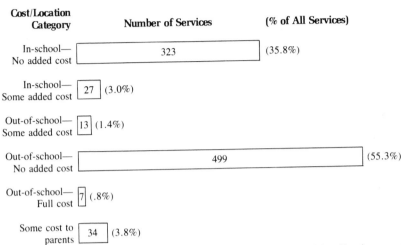

Figure 6. Cost/location of educational and related services received by direction-served families.

the parents." This was the case with only 34 services (3.8% of all related services). The majority of services, however, were arranged without any additional financial burden on either the parents or the district, most of these by agencies outside the school. Only 5.2% of the services required an additional expense on the part of the schools.

Figure 7 tallies services provided by who provided them. Again these are education and related services only. The bulk (49.1%) is provided by the education system. A substantial contribution is also evident from universities and private organizations.[9]

A caution is in order in interpreting these data. Even in the enlightened school districts involved with these Direction Service demonstrations there is a hesitancy to list services provided outside schools on the IEP. Virtually none of the services provided by other agencies results from formalized agreements between agency and school. As IEP processes become more established, and procedures for gaining access to other than school resources become more formalized, the character of these data will likely change. If all IEPs can potentially tap community resources to meet related service needs, more

---

[9]An apparent discrepancy exists between Figures 6 and 7. In Figure 6, 38.8% of the services are listed as provided "in-school." This figure includes both resident district programs and regional or cooperative (intermediate district) programs located in the resident district. Regional and cooperative programs located outside the child's resident district are coded as provided "out-of-school" in Figure 6 (57.5% of all services are provided out-of-school). Of all services, 10.3% are provided by intermediate district programs outside the resident district. Some of these involve added cost to the resident district and some do not. Thus, the 49.1% of all services provided in-school (either a local or intermediate district) shown in Figure 7 are distributed across cost/location categories in Figure 6.

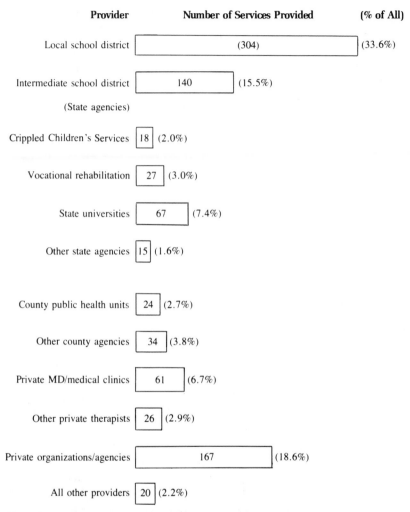

Figure 7. Distribution of providers of related services to direction-served families.

formalized agreements between schools and agencies will become necessary. The role of direction would likewise shift under these circumstances, constrained in its linking functions where formal agreements existed.

An added and very real benefit, but one that is difficult to measure, is cost savings to schools as a result of avoiding due process hearings. Many of the families seen by Direction Service demonstrations have been at odds with school officials. The potential for due process hearings and eventual litigation has been very real. The success of direction in matching those families to services has made proceeding to a hearing moot. The northwestern sites have served over 1,200 families, many referred because they were threatening action against the school. In only three instances have these families requested a due process hearing. In only two of these cases was a hearing actually held. How many of the families served would have requested and proceeded to a hearing without direction assistance is difficult to estimate. If it approaches 10%, however, the savings to schools on the basis of hearing avoidance alone are substantial. Direction diffuses the hostility and arranges services to meet the needs of children and families.

CONCLUSION

It is hard to assign a reliable dollar figure to the value of services matched by direction. It is at least as hard to estimate the public relations value of direction to schools (e.g., hearing avoidance, improved public attitude toward schools). Finally, determining from the experience of the demonstrations the true cost to a school of providing direction is problematic. Of the somewhat less than one million dollars invested in the three northwestern sites to date, a major portion has been spent on development and documentation—trial and error. These costs could be substantially reduced in replication, especially where existing school staff can be assigned a direction role.

Beyond the school, direction has benefits for the community at large. The direction orientation of matching needs to resources extends to the transition from school to independent, or semi-independent, living in the community. The results of failing to attend to this transition have rarely had an impact on schools; the costs of incarceration, other institutionalization, and welfare are more broadly borne. The contribution direction makes avoiding such future cost is again not precisely known, although the northwestern sites have assisted some "institution-bound" families to arrange the support services necessary to keep their child at home.

Whether or not Direction Service can be judged cost beneficial for a given school district or community will depend a great deal on local particulars. The implementation of the concept by schools represents, for some school administrators and school boards, too radical a change in the school's role. But implementing PL 94-142 without something like direction may be virtually impossible, and real costs will depend on how schools approach organizing direction. Clearly, the more service rich a community and the more that direction can be provided by school staff, the more cost beneficial direction appears. Also, as more sanctions are applied to local schools for not fully complying with the law, the easier it will be to justify the relatively small cost of direction. In a sense, it may not be as much a matter of hard figures as it is a matter of time.

REFERENCES

Brewer, G., and Kakalik, J. 1979. *Handicapped Children: Strategies for Improving Services.* McGraw-Hill Book Company, New York.

Bureau of Developmental Disabilities. 1978 (August). *A Comprehensive Review and Evaluation of Individual Habilitation Plans and Case Management Systems.* U.S. Department of Health, Education, and Welfare, Office of Human Development Services, Request for Proposal 105-78-5004, Washington, D.C.

Dean, S., Wolfensberger, W., Porter, F., and Kaiman, R. 1971 (July). *A Proposal for a Pilot Parent Program.* Greater Omaha Association for Retarded Citizens, Inc. Omaha. (Unpublished.)

Devers, D., Lorang, K., Marmont, W., and Zeller, R. 1979. Direction: A tool for the school, or how IEP teams can use non-school community resources to meet the related service requirements of the IEP. In: Wapnick, S., and Scanlon, C. (eds.), *Toward Least Restrictive Environments,* pp. 29-31. Oregon Council for Exceptional Children, Portland.

Dokecki, P. 1975 (April). *A Program for Training Human Development Liaison Specialists: A Prospectus.* George Peabody College for Teachers, Nashville. (Unpublished.)

Dokecki, P. 1977. The liaison perspective on the enhancement of human development: Theoretical, historical and experiential background. *J. Commun. Psychol.* 5:13-17.

Final regulations for the implementation of Part B of the Education of the Handicapped Act. 1977 (August 23). *Federal Register* 42(163).

Handicapped Americans Reports. 1977 (December 16). 1(1):9.

Hobbs, N. 1975. *The Futures of Children.* Jossey-Bass Publishers, San Francisco.

Justice, T. 1979. *Directions: Forward by Design.* Western Los Angeles Direction Service, University of Southern California, Los Angeles. (Unpublished.)

Justice, T., and Zeller, R. 1977. *Making Direction Work.* (Unpublished.)

Kahn, L. D. 1978 (October). *A Case Management System for the Mentally Retarded Citizens of Rhode Island: A Model, A Needs Assessment and Recommendations.* Prepared by Social Planning Services, Inc., under contract to the Rhode Island Department of Mental Health, Retardation and Hospitals.

Kakalik, J., Brewer, G., Dougharty, L., Fleischauer, P., Genensky, S., and Wallen, L. 1974 (May). *Improving Services to Handicapped Children.* The Rand Corporation, Santa Monica, CA.

Karnes, M., Teska, J., and Zehrbach, R. 1972 (June). A family involvement model: Implementation with families of multi-handicapped children. In: *Theory into Practice.* Ohio State University, Columbus.

Karnes, M., and Zehrbach, R. 1975. Matching families to services. *Except. Child.* 42(8):545-549.

Kotin, L. 1977. Due process in special education: Legal perspectives. In: L. Kotin and N. Eager, *Due Process in Special Education: A Legal Analysis.* Research Institute for Educational Problems, Cambridge, MA.

Levine, M., and Levine, A. 1970. *A Social History of Helping Services: Clinic, Court, School and Community.* Appleton-Century-Crofts, New York.

Martin, E. 1977. Informal letter to Chief State School Officers (dated November 17, 1977). Reprinted in: *Education of the Handicapped,* November 23, 1977, pp. 10-12.

Melichar, J. 1977. *Towards a Generalized Model of the Diagnostic Process.* (Presented at a joint meeting of The Institute for Management Sciences and The Operations Research Society). Adaptive Systems Corporation, Inc., San Mateo, CA.

Newbrough, J. 1977. Liaison services in the community context. *J. Commun. Psychol.* 5:24–27.

Olshansky, S. 1962. Chronic sorrow: A response to having a mentally defective child. *Soc. Casework* 43(4).

Oregon Mental Health Division. 1979 (March). *Conceptual Framework for a Specialized Case Management System.* (Initial design draft for a statewide case management system for mentally retarded/developmentally disabled, and mentally/emotionally disturbed persons in Oregon). Portland.

President's Commission on Mental Retardation. 1977. *MR 76—Mental Retardation: Past and Present.* U.S. Government Printing Office, Washington, D.C.

Regional Institute of Social Welfare Research. 1977. *The Case Management Model,* Vols. I, II, and III. Athens, GA.

Rossmiller, R., Hale, J., and Frohreich, L. 1970. *Educational Programs for Exceptional Children: Resource Configurations and Costs.* (National Education Finance Project Study, No. 2.) Department of Educational Administration, University of Wisconsin, Madison.

Sontag, E. 1976. Federal leadership. In: M. Angele Thomas (ed.), *HEY, Don't Forget about Me!* Council for Exceptional Children, Reston, VA.

Whittaker, R., and Levin, S. (eds.). 1977. *Niche Theory and Application.* Dowden, Hutchinson and Ross, Inc., Stroudsburg, PA.

Williams, J. 1977. Liaison functions as reflected in a case study. *J. Commun. Psychol.* 5:18–23.

Wolfensberger, W. n.d. *A Balanced Multi-Component Advocacy/Protection Schema, Law and Mental Retardation: A Monograph Series.* Canadian Association for the Mentally Retarded, Toronto.

Zeller, R. 1979. Perspectives on Direction Service. Working paper of the National Direction Service Task Force. (In press as part of *Direction Service: Concept to Reality,* a publication of the National Association of State Directors of Special Education.)

Coordinating Services to Handicapped Children:
A Handbook for Interagency Collaboration
Edited by Jerry O. Elder and Phyllis R. Magrab
Copyright © 1980   Paul H. Brookes Publishers   Baltimore • London

Chapter 5

Development of a Community-Based Interagency Model

Elynor Kazuk

Countless private and public agencies are involved in the delivery of services to handicapped children. Many of these services overlap and duplicate each other. For example, at least three government programs require that screening be done to identify children who may have chronic handicapping conditions. These programs include: Head Start, Medicaid/EPSDT (Early Periodic Screening, Diagnosis, and Treatment), Child Find (PL 94-142, Education for All Handicapped Children Act). Preschools, community center boards, private physicians, and public health clinics also screen children for disease and handicapping conditions. On the other hand, some services to handicapped children and their families are not provided at all—especially those services that are necessary to handle the diagnostic evaluations and treatment plans that improve or alleviate the problems identified through screening.

If agencies and individuals serving handicapped children can work together to determine what services are available in the community and which ones are needed, then 1) more comprehensive programs might be provided to those in need, 2) resources could be used more efficiently to fill gaps, 3) agencies could serve their clients more informatively, and 4) clients would be assisted through the maze of public programs and services.

This chapter describes how the people in one Colorado county organized an interagency effort. Of course, they emphasized services that filled needs in their community; other communities may want to concentrate on other areas. Nonetheless, the approach is adaptable, and many of the considerations will be the same no matter what specific services are provided or are needed.

INITIAL ORGANIZATION AT THE STATE LEVEL

In 1976, it became apparent to staff at the John F. Kennedy (JFK) Child Development Center in Denver, Colorado, a University Affiliated Facility which provides training to those serving handicapped children, that the increasing number of public programs that were being mandated to serve children were causing numerous problems for the state and community. Basically, these problems fell into four areas:

1. *Lack of screening resources:* Screening implies the application of simple, easy-to-administer tests to a large number of apparently well children in order to identify those at risk. Therefore, screening affects a much larger number of children than the number affected when only unhealthy children are served. In most communities individual agencies and private practitioners do not have the resources to screen adequately all or even part of the preschool children in their jurisdiction.

2. *Lack of diagnostic and treatment services:* With increased emphasis on screening, more diagnostic and treatment facilities than are currently available are needed. This is particularly true with regard to problems of infants and preschoolers. Few professionals in the human service disciplines have received special training in working with this population, and communities are greatly in need of appropriate treatment for the various developmental and physical problems discovered through screening.

3. *Little, if any, interagency collaboration for coordination of services:* Agencies and individual practitioners tend to operate separately in providing comprehensive care to handicapped children and their families. There may be informal communication with some familiar agencies, but no systematic method exists for sharing information among all the professionals and agencies who may be working with the family. Also, agencies are often not aware of other programs and services that could assist the family; it is often up to the parents to make their own way through the maze of possible services.

4. *Finally, there is often duplication and omission of services:* The Child Find effort, for example, may include in its screening package, some of the same areas covered under Medicaid or Head Start. The family may receive duplicate screening from the schools, the health department, and their private physician. On the other hand, families who do not fit under any public assistance program may not receive any type of screening at all. In another sense, if too many providers get involved in the screening process, they may be putting too much effort into *that* step, thus detracting from needed diagnostic and treatment programs.

The first measure taken by the director of the Kennedy Center was to call together state representatives of programs that affected handicapped children. This initial meeting included:

The director of Maternal and Child Health Programs, State Department of Health

High level representatives from the Title XX and Medicaid/EPSDT programs,
State Department of Social Services
The director of the state Division of Developmental Disabilities and the repre-
sentative from the state Division of Mental Health
A state Head Start representative
The director of the Colorado Association for Retarded Citizens
The director of the State Department of Special Education
The director of the Developmental Disabilities Council

At this meeting, three major decisions were made regarding how the problems
presented would be addressed.
The first decision of the group was to meet together on a regular basis as
a State Interagency Committee for the purposes of sharing information and
providing state-level guidance to whatever solutions were implemented. Second, the group agreed that, since the programs involved were all implemented
at a community level, the success of any solution would ultimately depend on
whether it could be operationalized by the community. Finally, it was decided
that the group would identify one or two counties in the state that would be
willing to develop a model for coordinating services at that level. The state
committee would provide whatever support it could to those counties until
such time as they became independent and requested no further assistance
from the state group.
The first county to volunteer to discuss the project was Fremont County,
a small, rural county in south-central Colorado with a total population of
approximately 30,000. The director of the mental health clinic in the county
was interested in coordinating services for the handicapped and volunteered to
take the lead in calling a local meeting and discussing the pros and cons of
organizing an interagency group which would develop a model that might be
used in other counties.
A meeting was arranged in September, 1976, in Canon City, the largest
town in the county. All the counterpart organizations of the state representatives were invited as well as consumers and local providers, such as the local
hospital screening staff and pediatricians. Members of the State Interagency
Committee also attended the meeting to indicate their support and willingness
to cooperate with whatever plans might be developed by the local group.
Although the first meeting in the local area was attended by State Interagency Committee members, it was made very clear to the local group that the
state committee had no intention of controlling the model that might be
developed or interfering in any way unless the local group requested assistance. This was an important point to emphasize, because the local agencies
were very hesitant to become involved if it meant that their activities would be
directed from the "outside."
The initial meeting turned out to be a very successful one and the begin-

ning of a local, organized group (the Interagency Council) of consumers and providers of service to handicapped clients, which now calls its program Project ECHO (Early Childhood/Health Education Outreach). The group has developed a model over the course of 3 years which has survived a number of problems, but which now functions smoothly and satisfactorily to all participants. This chapter describes that model and the major steps that led to where it is today.

INITIAL ORGANIZATION AT THE COUNTY LEVEL

After the joint meeting with the State Interagency Committee, where it was decided that coordination of services was needed in the county and that a model would be developed for bringing this about, the real work began. One of the first orders of business was to create by-laws to formalize the group. These by-laws included the name of the group, its purpose, membership, standing committees, and very general procedures for how the group would function. The by-laws changed as the model evolved, but they have served their purpose well in providing structure and a sense of purpose to a project that has been, at times, elusive and difficult to conceptualize, especially in its beginning stages.

Part of the business of developing by-laws was to become clear on the general services to be coordinated. The public programs affecting handicapped children all emphasized the importance of making sure children progressed through the entire screening, diagnosis, and treatment process if necessary. In addition, many programs emphasized the importance of prevention and getting screening services to children who had no obvious symptoms. Therefore, the Interagency Council agreed that the entire process should be included in the model and the major services to be coordinated should be the following:

OUTREACH—making the public aware of what the project offers and encouraging them to participate by seeing that children are periodically screened

SCREENING—using quick and simple procedures to sort out apparently healthy persons from those who may have a disease or abnormality

DIAGNOSIS—determining whether the person truly does have an abnormality and what the nature or cause of the abnormality might be

TREATMENT—remedying the patient's abnormality

In addition to these services, the council wanted to be able to follow the progress of children through the above process and assist them in obtaining whatever services were needed at any step along the way.

Finally, during the initial organization stage, the group had to establish a role for itself and for the participating members. Was the group to be an advisory council, a planning group, a decision-making body, or all three? Could the participating members make commitments for their respective organizations? How much time would each member need to spend? This group decided that the council would meet once a month for the purpose of planning and coordinating project activities. It would serve as a decision-making body, which would act as a steering committee for the project. The specific tasks of the group would be carried out by standing committees and task forces that would be directed by the council. Initially, there were committees for publicity and community education, identifying community needs, investigating and pursuing funding sources, and planning screening activities. Later, these changed when a coordinator was hired to carry out many of the functions.

In regard to the decision-making powers of each representative, it was agreed that the participating organizations should appoint individuals to the council who either would have the power to make organizational commitments or were very knowledgeable about what exactly the organization could or could not commit and would be able to indicate that during a meeting without having to check back with someone else. In many cases, the local program head served on the council and this was encouraged to every extent possible. Eventually, it became helpful to have organizations make commitments in writing, in regard to the amount of time individuals could spend on the project, the type of materials that could be donated, and other in-kind services that would assist project activities.

CONSIDERATIONS OF THE INTERAGENCY COUNCIL

Throughout the first months of the project, a number of important questions needed to be considered by the Interagency Council—some of them very critical and difficult to answer. Struggling with these questions, however, made the council aware of the differences that had to be overcome and showed where coordination was needed. Questions that were considered included the following:

1. What population would the project serve in terms of age, geographic location, and eligibility?
2. What resources existed in the community for serving children and their families?
3. Who (what agencies or individuals) would provide or assist in provision of services? For example, who would do the screening, where would it be done, and what test would be used?
4. What conditions would be screened for and how severe must these conditions be before the client should be referred for further evaluation?
5. Who would coordinate screening and diagnostic results and make referrals for evaluation?

6. What record-keeping would be done and how would information be shared?
7. What, if any, forms would be needed?
8. How would the project be evaluated?
9. How would the council relate to state level programs and agencies and to the State Interagency Committee?
10. How could a joint effort improve services and lower costs for participating agencies?

To help the group discuss these questions a Guide for Initiating and Maintaining a Comprehensive Screening Program was developed and provided to the council by the JFK Child Development Center.[1] The decisions made in regard to each question provided a place to begin. As the model evolved, more improved methods were identified, and eventually almost all of the original decisions were changed. The important thing was that the council members did not refrain from making decisions just because they were unsure of what would result. They initiated a plan and have stayed receptive to improvements of this plan since the project's inception.

EMPLOYING A COORDINATOR

A major question that arose during the first year of the project was whether a full-time coordinator would be needed to facilitate the project activities. The possible roles and tasks for this person were many, including those in the following list:

Assessing and documenting community's needs
Identifying and developing a better use of available state and federal dollars
Informing and securing cooperation of local agencies, physicians, specialists, parents, and the general community
Arranging in-service training for local agencies
Developing a communication and referral system among professionals and agencies serving the family
Working with parents in locating needed services
Ensuring that diagnostic and treatment services are provided to child and family
Developing innovative plans for delivering services
Developing cooperative arrangements among agencies
Representing the community at state level meetings
Lobbying for relevant legislation

---

[1] This guide and an accompanying slide/tape program is available from the National Audiovisual Center, General Services Administration, Order Section, Washington, D.C. 20409 (Ref. S-3611).

Serving as case manager for each child identified
Keeping records for the purpose of "tracking" and periodic recall
Educating the public in the area of developmental disabilities

Besides the role of the coordinator, the group had to decide whether the coordinator would be an employee from one of the participating agencies, a volunteer, or someone who would be paid through donations from all of the agencies. In Fremont County, it was decided that, for the developmental stages of the project, the group would look for funding for a coordinator from state or federal agencies. The JFK Child Development Center, which had taken the lead in the organization of the state level committee and was hosting State Interagency Committee meetings, agreed to serve as the fiscal agent for the local council and assisted the local group in writing a grant for the state Developmental Disabilities Council. The grant was funded for one year, and an individual from outside the community, but recommended by someone on the local council, was hired. Although the JFK Child Development Center was the official employer, the coordinator reported to the chairman of the local Interagency Council for all activities related to the project.

The Interagency Council chairman appointed a committee to establish specific major objectives for the project for the first year of employment, and it was the job of the coordinator to facilitate activities that would accomplish the objectives. These objectives were ambitious and broadly stated as follows:

1. Identify state and federal funds that have potential to fill gaps identified through the needs assessment.
2. Estimate the baseline number of children screened in the first 6 months and work to increase this number by 50% within a year through a coordinated screening, diagnosis, and treatment model.
3. Conduct a community education program consisting of brochures, lectures, radio spots, and newspaper articles to make the public aware of the importance of screening for developmental delays.
4. Refine, develop, establish, and implement a community referral system.

As it turned out, the objectives as stated above were too broad to be carried out very efficiently. The first coordinator was a very enthusiastic person with much energy to invest in the project. However, her role was not defined clearly as she attempted to fulfill all the roles outlined above. This resulted in a diffused effort that could not be easily defined or seen in its entirety by the participating organizations. Each organization knew that it was contributing personnel and other in-kind services to Project ECHO, that children were being screened, diagnosed, and treated, and that the coordinator was extremely busy, but it was not clear just what all the procedures were and how the model operated as a whole system. The project seemed to depend completely upon the coordinator and only she knew how it all worked.

At the end of the funding period, the coordinator felt overworked and "burned out"; the agencies were not happy with the benefits received for the amount of work invested and the project floundered. Because the question of funding was unsettled for a second year, the coordinator accepted another job and the council carried on again with only a chairperson to hold it all together. This chairperson was a strong leader who thoroughly believed in the potential of interagency coordination. With her lead, a second year of funding was obtained from the state Developmental Disabilities Council for a half-time coordinator and a full-time secretary with the idea that the project work to find local funding for subsequent years. The new coordinator was selected for her abilities to organize and to develop specific procedures to give the model definite structure and direction. These skills were exactly what was needed to revitalize the project and to make the model visible and understandable to the local council members. Described below is the project as it currently functions, with all participating agencies satisfied and committed to making it a permanent part of their community.

DESCRIPTION OF CURRENT MODEL

Outreach

The outreach component of the project is and has always been very strong. Initially, a massive public awareness program took place in the county, where the mayors of the local towns proclaimed June, 1977, as screening month. Banners made by inmates of the Colorado Correctional Institution for Women were spread across main streets and brochures were printed and distributed to every family in the county by inserting them in local newspapers and mailboxes. Since that initial campaign, outreach has continued to be stressed. Radio and television spots advertise screening clinics. Avon and Tupperware representatives distribute brochures and messages about the importance of early and periodic screening. Local ministers and large employers in the area are asked to display posters and spread the word. Local high school students deliver brochures on their motorcycles to rural areas.

An effective outreach approach is a face-to-face message delivered by the coordinator or EPSDT outreach workers, social services caseworkers, or public health nurses. The best approach, especially for hard-to-reach families, is a message delivered by a neighbor who has been through the process and believes in its value. In this regard, the coordinator tries to find an individual from a particular neighborhood who will get a group of volunteers together from the neighborhood to talk to the coordinator about the value of screening. After the talk, the participants are asked to invite their friends to attend the next screening, which is usually scheduled within walking distance of the neighborhood in a nearby church or school.

So that Project ECHO coordinates its activities with Medicaid/EPSDT outreach, families are informed that if they have a Medicaid card they can receive screening services from their Medicaid provider. All families are informed of where screening can be obtained in the county—through ECHO screening clinics, private doctors, or the public health department—and are told it does not matter where they go as long as they go. Through the Interagency Council, all outreach messages are coordinated and an attempt is made to ensure that families do not receive contradictory messages about screening and where it can be done.

Screening

Project ECHO focuses on all children from birth through age 5 in the entire county. This population is estimated to number approximately 2,000, and the council decided that its ultimate goal would be to see that *all* of these children are screened as often as is appropriate for their age. In Fremont County, screening previously had been done primarily by private physicians, the local hospital, and during well-child clinics conducted by the local health department. Head Start did screening every September, as did the schools during the kindergarten "round-up" every summer. It was estimated that each year approximately 500 children were screened through these services.

The Interagency Council felt that many families were not being reached this way, and therefore decided to organize ECHO screening clinics that would be offered regularly in neighborhood churches and schools and at least once a month in the main town of Canon City. The areas screened are vision, hearing, development, medical and social history, and general physical problems. This is based upon the screening resources that are available without charge to the project and that can be done on a mass basis using paraprofessional screeners.

The screening component of this project is generally under the direction of the public health department which provides paraprofessional screeners free of charge to the project for one or two days a month to do screening in vision, hearing, development, and general physical problems. These screeners have been trained and certified by the health department which also sees that there is always a registered nurse available during the screening to provide supervision in all screening activities. A social worker from the Department of Social Services, the school system, or the mental health center is also present at ECHO screening clinics to obtain a medical and social history and information regarding need for assistance, past involvement with other agencies, and pertinent family information.

Screenings are held monthly at the county courthouse in space donated by the county and in private homes, churches, and schools in local neighborhoods.

To coordinate results of the screening and to decide upon referrals, a ''mini-staffing'' is held immediately following the screening. The screeners, nurse, social worker, psychologist, and coordinator attend these staffings and review all results. Parents of children who have positive screening results are invited to attend. Some children are referred for rescreening because a complete test could not be obtained for some reason or because the results were uncertain. Those who fail the vision or hearing test are sent directly to a specialist for a further evaluation. Those who are suspect on developmental testing are sent to the local hospital which provides a more comprehensive developmental screening by professionals, free of charge to the family. All screening results are sent to the family's doctor, who provides physical exams for those who need to go on to a diagnostic step, or to the public health department where a physical exam can also be obtained free of charge. All families are encouraged to obtain regular physical exams whether or not the screening results are suspect.

During the screening step, a release form is completed which gives permission to the coordinator to provide results of the screening to other agencies if necessary. All of these agencies are listed on the release form and families are free to disallow any organization or individual from receiving screening information or to pass along such information. The release form (see Appendix A) is completed each time the family comes in for screening since there is a limit on the length of time the permission holds.

Diagnosis

The diagnostic component of the interagency effort is fulfilled by local programs or agencies available in the county. Those children who are suspect on developmental screening are seen by a professional interdisciplinary team at the local developmental disabilities facility. This team will see all children referred to them and will make appropriate referrals for treatment once the evaluation has been made. To ensure that the interdisciplinary staffing meets the requirements of PL 94-142 (Education for All Handicapped Children Act) and that an individualized education program (IEP) is written to comply with federal regulations, a special educator from the school system is on the team. The family's physician is also included in the staffing when referrals are made for treatment. The coordinator of the interagency project is not a part of the diagnostic team; however, she does track the child through this process and makes certain that the family understands where the appointment is and how to obtain transportation if needed, and is reminded of the appointment date.

Treatment

Treatment is determined by the specialist or team conducting the diagnostic evaluation, and the coordinator of the interagency project offers the family or agency any assistance that might be needed to obtain services. One service might be to locate financial assistance, or transportation to day care facilities.

Since the Interagency Council is comprised of representatives from all public programs serving the handicapped, the council also offers information on available public assistance and eligibility for this assistance. If treatment is not immediately available within the county, the coordinator and the council work together to develop interim plans until more appropriate treatment is located.

Record-Keeping

Throughout the process of screening, diagnosis and treatment, the tracking of the children is done by the project coordinator. This coordinator works closely with the person doing tracking for the Medicaid/EPSDT program so that families are not tracked by both programs. Tracking provides the answer to two basic questions: 1) where, in the process, is an individual child at any given time, and 2) how many children are at each point in the process at any given time?

A card file of all children screened in the county is maintained in the ECHO office and is updated with every screening. This includes children screened through Project ECHO, Head Start, and offices of private physicians who have agreed to participate. The list of children screened and those who have been diagnosed as handicapped is given to the school system for their Child Find efforts and for their own information in future planning for children with special needs *along with the release of information forms from parents.* The card file is a tickler system with one set of cards filed alphabetically by last name and another set filed by the month of the child's next contact. Each month the coordinator calls families filed under that month to remind them that it is time for the child to be rescreened. Children under 2½ are screened twice a year and children over 2½ are screened once a year. The system can also be used in evaluating the accuracy of the screening. It is possible to review the number of referrals that are being made from screening to diagnosis and from diagnosis to treatment. If this number is significantly different from the number of referrals the local or state health department would expect for the community, then the reasons for the difference will be explored. Summary data from the card file are provided regularly to the council so that members are aware of the status of the project. Some general lessons have been learned about record-keeping and tracking which make this part of the project a success. The major ones are the following:

1. Record-keeping and tracking require assigning a specific person to keep track of the child through the entire process. In this case, the secretary is responsible and does all the calling of non-Medicaid families to remind parents of their next appointment. The Medicaid outreach worker contacts all Medicaid families.

2. Responsibility for tracking a child must be assumed by the project rather than expecting outside agencies or providers to make appointments or

initiate feedback for the records. In other words, do not send the screening results to someone and expect that person to carry on from there. Keep the whole tracking process in one agency, under a particular person.

3. It is easier to get information about whether a child will need to be followed after screening or diagnosis from parents than from providers. During the initial parent interview, get a phone number where the parent can be reached during the day, *and an alternate number* so that you can remind parents of appointments.

4. Part of the value of record-keeping is to give data to participating agencies and to other interested parties regarding the status of the program. Project ECHO used the form in Appendix B to provide reports to agencies about screening.

How It All Fits Together

It is difficult to depict visually how the various agencies work together to provide an entire range of services to the families in the county. The flowchart illustrated in Figure 1 attempts to do this. What is not shown, however, is the administrative support provided by the council and the coordinator in planning, scheduling, tracking, and keeping records for all the families participating in the program. This support provides the "glue" that holds it all together, and is the part that has needed funding during the course of the project. It is expected that once the project is functioning to the satisfaction and benefit of the participating local agencies, these agencies will provide all the needed financial support for the coordinator and secretary.

At the present time, agencies are providing the in-kind services discussed below. Some of these services would have been offered without the project; however, they would not have functioned collaboratively, working instead without being coordinated with other programs and progressing in an isolated manner that may or may not have enhanced the entire process and that may have caused duplication of program efforts. With regular coordination and sharing of information, agencies can plan their individual programs to fill existing gaps and utilize other resources in the community more effectively.

Participating agencies have assumed responsibility for the following project activities:

The local Public Health Department provides four paraprofessional screeners for one or two days per month. A Public Health nurse donates her time to serve as co-chairperson of the Interagency Council, as a mini-staffing team member, and on various planning committees. The Public Health Nursing Office provides an audiometer to be used at screenings. The Handicapped Children's Program, which is a component of the Public Health Department, sends their medical social worker to each Interagency Council meeting to act as a resource person.

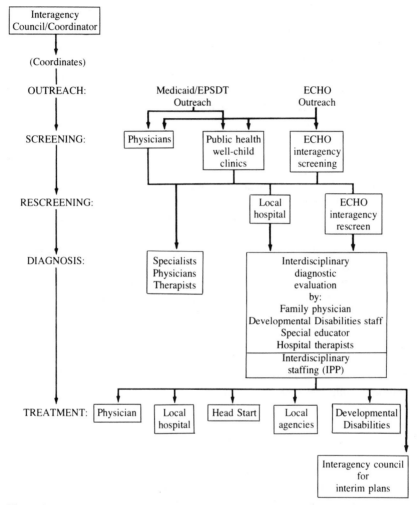

Figure 1. Flowchart of interagency collaboration in Fremont County Project ECHO.

Fremont County makes space available for screenings each month in the courthouse and donates this space for any extra screenings held in Canon City.

The Department of Social Services donates office space, desks, and use of a copying machine. Social Services also makes available a social worker for screenings four times per year. A Social Services' administrator is a member of the Interagency Council. The conference room is also donated for monthly council meetings.

West Central Mental Health Center provides the services of a child psychologist four times per year for screenings. A child psychologist also serves on the Interagency Council. This psychologist, in conjunction with a local pediatrician, writes a series of newspaper articles focusing on preschool development and parenting.

The RE 1 School District's Director of Special Education donates time as co-chairperson of the Interagency Council. The school district also provides a social worker and a psychologist at monthly screenings. The school district contributes time for the Director of Special Education to attend monthly State Interagency Committee meetings in Denver, and to serve on various planning committees. The school district provides some office equipment and supplies.

RE 2 & 3 School Districts supply a social worker and psychologist at screenings involving children from their school districts. Two school nurses are available at screenings and are part of the mini-staffing team. The Director of Special Education gives time to organize and coordinate screenings held in these school districts. These school districts provide space for screenings and some office supplies.

St. Thomas More Hospital provides further assessment of children who have questionable or untestable results from screenings. The hospital provides direct services to some children in the areas of occupational therapy (OT), physical therapy (PT), and speech-language therapy. St. Thomas More Hospital staff representing OT, PT, and speech serve on the Interagency Council. The speech-language pathologist writes a series of newspaper articles addressing various childhood delays and treatments, publicizing the need for early identification through screening.

Developmental Trainers Services (DTS), the local Developmental Disabilities facility, is responsible for an in-depth interdisciplinary evaluation when a child has abnormal or untestable results from a developmental screening. The DTS staff participates in the evaluation as well as the family's physician, an educator, and some therapists from the local hospital. This facility also provides direct services in the infant stimulation program or preschool to a child with two or more delays. The director of DTS serves on the Interagency Council.

The Head Start director serves on the Interagency Council. Children may be referred to Head Start on the recommendation of the mini-staffing team.

Council of Governments handled the cash disbursements for 7 months as part of a CETA grant to fund the position of secretary for the project.

Local ministerial alliances in Florence and Canon City send representatives to the Interagency Council. St. Benedict's Catholic Church in Florence contributes screening space. Local ministers assist in outreach efforts.

Local physicians continue to participate in Project ECHO by screening children and helping with outreach. A pediatrician serves on the Interagency Council and collaborates with the West Central Mental Health Center in writing news articles on childhood delays and parenting.

Evaluation

Evaluation of the project has been done at least annually by the JFK Child Development Center, which serves as the fiscal agent. The intent of the evaluation has been to provide technical assistance where needed rather than to monitor project activities. The criteria used for evaluating success have been 1) the satisfaction of the participating agencies, and 2) the number of children and families served. The steps in the evaluation involve the following:

1. An evaluation form is mailed to each Interagency Council representative and to the directors of the participating agencies. A copy of this form is included at the end of the chapter as Appendix C.
2. JFK Child Development Center staff members visit the site within 2 weeks after the form has been sent and meet individually with the participants to discuss and clarify the responses on the form.
3. Within 2 weeks after the site visit, a formal presentation is made to the council, where the evaluators present the results of the survey and make recommendations for any changes that might improve the project.
4. The council discusses the recommendations and then, as a group, completes the last page of the survey form. This pulls the group together as they strive for a concensus of opinions, and gives a composite picture of where the council stands.

Evaluating the increase in numbers of children and families served has involved gathering much data outside the actual project. Each year the coordinator surveys the agencies offering screening, diagnosis, and treatment services to determine the number of children between birth and 6 years who were screened and followed up during the year and to estimate how many the agencies would have served if the project had not been in existence. Table 1 shows one year's report. It does not include screenings done by private physicians because that information is difficult to collect from each physician's office. Future plans involve making this part of the evaluation as complete and explicit as possible. The council also wants to determine the costs involved per child and any cost savings or cost avoidance to agencies as a result of the project.

FUTURE PLANS OF THE COUNCIL

Funding from the state Developmental Disabilities Council to the JFK Child Development Center for the development of this model ends in August, 1980. In anticipation of that change in the project, the Interagency Council made a number of decisions that are being implemented subsequent to the end of the funding period.

Table 1. Children served by Project ECHO (April, 1978–March, 1979)

Estimated number of preschool children in Fremont County:	1,930
Total number screened since March, 1978:	1,249

Screening facility	Totals
Head Start	71
St. Thomas More Hospital	80
EPSDT	63
Preschools	120
Public Health	140
RE 1 Schools	195
Project ECHO	578
Total	1,247

Estimated number of children who would have been screened for medical problems and developmental delays if project had not been in existence:

Preschools	120
RE 1 Schools	206
Head Start	73
St. Thomas More Hospital	90
EPSDT	63
Public Health	140
	692

Total number of children referred for further evaluation because of abnormal or questionable results, either medical or developmental:	193
Total number of children referred for treatment by all agencies:	179
Total number of children with treatment in process as of March, 1979:	116

1. The council asked the local Developmental Disabilities facility to become the fiscal agent for the group.

2. The council submitted proposals to state and national sources to expand their current effort to nearby counties and to disseminate information and give technical assistance to those who would like to replicate the model. Funding requests in these proposals range from $30,000 to $50,000 for a full-time coordinator and secretary. Requests differ depending upon amount of travel and type of activities.

3. The council obtained tentative commitments from the local school systems to at least partially fund the project during the 1980–81 school year in return for the Child Find efforts which Project ECHO provides the schools. Provisions for this funding were included in 1980–81 budget requests to the state.

4. The council offered to assist the State Department of Special Education in operationalizing state interagency agreements developed during 1979–80. This would give the state an opportunity to see how these general intera-

gency agreements function at a local level. In return, the council asked for partial funding for this project.

5. The council plans to evaluate the project more formally than was done in the past when only the satisfaction of the participating agencies and the number of children served were used as criteria for success. This evaluation will be carried out locally without the involvement of the JFK Center. Included in the evaluation will be an assessment of various outreach methods and their effectiveness.

6. The council plans to document cost savings and specific benefits which have resulted from the project.

7. This is a high energy impact county with an expected growth of up to 40% projected by 1981. Presently, the project screens and tracks over 1,200 children a year. With increases in population, the council is preparing to accommodate almost twice that many children. This means that agencies must be ready to donate more services and manpower and that procedures must be developed to expand the system to make sure it can handle the potential growth.

8. The council will continue to participate in the meetings of the State Interagency Committee to share information and provide whatever assistance is requested for the local group. Other interagency efforts in the state are represented on this committee, and the Fremont County coordinator stays in contact with these projects to share methods and approaches for accomplishing interagency objectives.

This model is still evolving and resolving the many problems of interagency conditions which appear at each stage of the project. Some of these problems and their resolutions are discussed in the following section. Others that are more basic, such as agencies developing trust in each other, sharing of turf, and merging program activities, are in a continuous process of being resolved. At this point the participating agencies are happy with the mechanics of the model that have been developed during the past year, and they believe in the potential benefits that can be achieved through this system.

If nothing else is accomplished, the agencies have gotten to know each other's programs and services better and are becoming familiar with how their activities can interrelate. A resource manual has been compiled for each participating agency and distributed to the members of the council. This manual summarizes basic information about the agency and how its services might be used. Some interagency agreements have already been made as a result of this project. Also, the county and state have become more visible to each other and Interagency Council members are beginning to understand ways to have an impact on state policies and plans for handicapped children.

Perhaps the greatest lesson learned from the effort so far is that interagency coordination takes time if that coordination is going to be more than just sharing information. The forces that are in existence to bring about change are 1) the personalities of the people involved, 2) the commitment to a common problem that is clear to all participants, and 3) the energy and goodwill of the agencies involved. These are subtle ingredients that are difficult to manage when no structure exists to direct them. Only time, careful planning, and a strong sense of purpose and potential benefits can integrate them effectively.

PROBLEMS AND SOLUTIONS

During the initial stages, problems are likely to occur in any interagency effort. It would be impossible to try to anticipate all of them. The following are just a few that had to be resolved in this effort. These might alert others to the types of issues that are raised from an operational standpoint and give them some idea of how they might be approached.

Problem: *Some strategic agencies and individuals believed a funded interagency effort was unnecessary and a waste of taxpayers' money.*

Solution: These individuals were listened to very carefully and assured that the grant to apply for funds would be written only if a definite need could be proved. One of the first items of business, then, was to conduct a thorough needs assessment which would show where duplications and gaps in service exist. The form used was one like the matrix shown in Appendix D. To fill out this matrix, a number was assigned to each agency in the community which provides services to the target population. This number corresponded to a survey that each agency was asked to complete regarding type of services offered, fees, eligibility, ages, and procedures for receiving service. To summarize the data, the matrix was created by placing the numbers of agencies offering services for various handicapping conditions to children ages birth to 6 years in the appropriate boxes on the form. When the summary form was completed, it was easy to see the gaps and duplications that existed and to plan what might be done to alleviate them.

Problem: *Some agencies resented the involvement of "outsiders" such as the JFK Child Development Center and other state representatives.*

Solution: Since Colorado has a system of state government which encourages the autonomy of the counties, it was important for the State Interagency Committee to make it very clear to the local group that it did not intend to plan, direct, or monitor the local project. Throughout the duration of the effort, the JFK Child Development Center maintained this position and did not interfere except when requested to do so. The JFK Child Development Center did ask to observe the process of developing the model and to document this process so that it might be replicated in other counties. It also established itself as a resource and provider of training and technical assistance rather than an agency wishing to control the activities in any way. The State Interagency Committee and other state level representatives worked to maintain this same relationship with their counterpart organizations.

Problem: *The Project lacked a definite goal that was easy for the participants to visualize.*

Solution: This problem was perhaps the most difficult to solve. In fact, another interagency effort that was developing parallel to this one in a more urban county dissolved because of this problem. At the beginning of this type of project, it is easy to lose sight of what should be happening when there is a "successful" model. As mentioned earlier in the chapter, the coordinator or interagency chairperson can end up becoming the only person who knows what the procedures are and how the agencies relate to each other. For this reason it is essential to develop flowcharts, written procedures, and visual models that represent what is happening currently in regard to children going through the screening, diagnosis, and treatment process. Once the present process is depicted visually, it then becomes easier to discuss and to establish what should be done in the future. This project did not work with visual models until after the first site visit. At that time, the evaluator drew a present model, as seen by the evaluation team, and a recommended model. This gave the members a basis for discussion which they had not had previously and allowed them to address themselves to something visible and available for improvement.

Problem: *The coordinator had too many "bosses" as she tried to respond to each participating agency and what each one desired from the project.*

Solution: The coordinator originally tried to organize the project such that each organization could get from it whatever that agency needed. This encouraged fragmentation and hindered the group from developing a common purpose. When it became apparent that the energy of both the group and the coordinator was becoming more and more diffused, the council developed a list of all possible roles for the coordinator (as listed earlier in this chapter) and then asked the participating agencies to select the top three. When that was done, it was possible to determine to what extent there were diverse expectations and how much discussion was needed to bring the group to a consensus in priorities. The important factor in this solution is that the council took the lead in establishing priorities and objectives for the coordinator. The coordinator was then expected to develop methods for implementing the objectives and reporting her progress to the council each month.

Problem: *The issue of confidentiality was a major concern and kept organizations from sharing needed information.*

Solution: Although a release of information form was signed by the parents at the ECHO screenings, agencies were still reluctant to provide information to other agencies even to the extent of releasing names. It was necessary to contact decision makers in various programs at the state level who could, in turn, reassure county staff that they would not be in violation of confidentiality requirements if they had permission from parents at the time of screening. The issue is still a clouded one, however, and a clearer interpretation will be sought from the state during the coming months. In the meantime, the county will use a two-stage release of information form: one form at the screening stage, and another form after a child has been diagnosed and the parent understands the type of information that might be released.

Problem: *County agencies are not ready or able to merge programs or develop interagency agreements to share responsibility for programs without the full cooperation of state level decision makers.*

Solution: Since counties are responsible for implementing the mandates of state and federal law, they are reluctant or unable to make significant changes without state level waivers and agreements. There is a great interest in doing this at state level; however, the way is unpaved and progress is slow. A factor that helped the situation is that the State Department of Special Education received a grant to develop state interagency agreements during the 1979–80 school year. The Fremont Interagency Council offered to serve as a location for implementing these agreements at the county level to test their feasibility and effectiveness. This tightened the relationships between the state and county levels and furthered the cause of significant and cost-saving coordination. Also, the state Developmental Disabilities Council has established state regional councils which will help the county and state work together more effectively. Specifically, the Fremont County model is planning on working closely with the regional Developmental Disabilities Council in their area to expand and refine the project and to influence state policies for the handicapped that have an effect on that part of the state.

Problem: *Agency heads did not attend meetings, but delegated their position to first, second, or third line supervisory staff.*

Solution: Since the delegate was unable, in many instances, to make decisions for the agency, or commit the agency to action, this diminished the effectiveness of the council. Two immediate solutions were initiated. First, it was clearly communicated to agency directors that active representation is necessary for the project to function. Therefore, if a delegate represented the agency, that person should be thoroughly oriented to the project and to his/her own agency as well as vested with the power to make decisions *or* to make immediate contact with the director for a decision. Second, agency directors were asked to keep in close, regular communication with their delegate, and to plan on meeting at least twice a year with the council to review progress and plans of the project at a special meeting planned for that purpose.

Problem: *Attendance at meetings was erratic.*

Solution: Council meetings had been scheduled for different locations and different times each month. Busy council members could not readjust their schedules each month and could not attend regularly. By a majority vote, the council established a definite date and time for regular meetings. Location was more flexible. A tentative agenda for the next meeting was the last order of business at each meeting, thus stirring interest and increasing the involvement of the participants. This agenda was mailed to the members a week in advance of the meeting to remind them of what would be discussed and what to be prepared to accomplish at the meeting.

Problem: *Some providers withdrew from the project because they did not approve of the materials or methods being used.*

Solution: It is good to remember that the reluctance or refusal of one agency will not deter the entire project; however, the reluctance or refusal on the part of many indicates the need for revision. In this case, the withdrawal of two agencies initiated a review of the screening methods. A task force was appointed to establish procedures for Project ECHO screenings. The procedures related to the tests to be used, how the tests would be administered, and by whom. Additionally, they provided guidelines for referral to 1) a rescreening, 2) physical exam, 3) interdisciplinary teams, or 4) further specific diagnostic service. These procedures were placed before the council for approval. Approval indicated support and adherence by project members who would continue to remain a part of the screening program. The procedures are reviewed regularly and the screening process is kept dynamic through agreed upon changes, additions, and deletions. Eventually, when the procedures proved to be successful, both providers rejoined the group and are now very active members.

Problem: *Although use of professionals to staff the screenings would have been expensive, some individuals and some agencies were very hesitant to allow paraprofessionals to perform this service.*

Solution: A statement that paraprofessionals would be properly trained and supervised was not enough. In order to present a valid rebuttal to this concern *and,* in fact, to prepare paraprofessionals to perform the service, a detailed training approach had to be decided upon, carried out, and evaluated. In our project this approach involved the following:

1. The State Department of Health trained and evaluated paraprofessionals to administer screening tests as part of a training program sponsored in various counties throughout the state.
2. University of Colorado Medical Center personnel trained and evaluated Head Start personnel.
3. Trained paraprofessionals performed under the direction of county health nurses who were available to assist the screeners and to counsel parents whenever necessary.

As a review and check, the interpretations and impressions of a team of competent professionals were used. This team reviewed the tests of children failing the screenings and of those who were special concerns of parents, teachers, or any other interested parties. As a result, all of the screenings performed as part of the project fell within the guidelines of the project and met with the approval of the council and the community.

Problem: *Screenings were lacking in adequate administrative personnel or materials. No designated person or agency was responsible for planning or carrying out support details.*

Solution: Written procedures were drawn up for each screening, listing *all* details (time, place, participants, materials needed, person/agency responsible for each task, etc.). This plan was given to each person involved in the screening. A coordinator was assigned for each screening effort. It was agreed that any person or agency unable to carry out his/her portion of service would find a substitute and that the coordinator of that screening effort would be notified of any changes, substitutions, or deletions no later than 2 hours before the screening. Problems at any screening are reviewed by the council in order to prevent recurrence.

Problem: *Very few requests for screening were being received from rural and remote areas.*

Solution: Initially, screenings were held for rural areas of the county at the request of a local group, a school, or parents who had heard about screenings done in other locations. However the number of families who responded to this method was very small. An extensive outreach campaign was initiated, using people-to-people contact. The local school office made appointments for parents who called in, and outreach workers made appointments on the spot when contacting parents. Having the screening locally, and making screening appointments at the time of the initial outreach, increased the response significantly.

Problem: *Publicity, public relations, and an awareness campaign had to be devised at minimal cost.*

Solution: Several approaches were adopted in confronting this problem:

1. A local printing firm, just starting in the business was used to print brochures.

2. Local high schools were asked to incorporate the typing of envelopes as part of typing class.

3. A member service agency used their mailing permit (1½¢ per envelope).

4. A local high school was persuaded to give credit time for young people to go door to door (on foot, bike, motorcycle) to deliver brochures and spread the message of the project. The problems of the handicapped were presented to local high schools via movies from the State Department of Education in order to elicit volunteer help.

5. Donations were obtained from member agencies who gave small amounts of money to purchase paint and material for banners. The women's prison in the major town in Fremont County, Canon City, obtained material and sewed banners. Volunteer high school students painted banners.

6. Free public announcements were arranged on radio; press releases were written, and radio interviews were given on all radio stations in the county.

7. The council worked with the postmaster, who spent a great deal of time advising the project as to the best method of reaching the rural population.

Problem: *A grant to one of the participating agencies, which was anticipated at the beginning of the project for provision of treatment services, did not materialize.*

Solution: Although the lack of this resource left a gap in the project, other agencies in the project made great efforts to supply whatever portion of the service they could. Some restructuring of plans was still necessary, but realistic acknowledgment of the remaining gaps prevented disappointment or dissatisfaction by project members or parents. Everyone worked around the gap in service and avoided failure of the project. Now that the service is available, the entire project has expanded into the originally intended scope of services.

Problem: *The card file used for tracking is gradually become unwieldy as both the project and the county grow substantially.*

Solution: As a pilot project which is still being tested, a computerized tracking system was developed for the Fremont County project by a small company contracted by the JFK Child Development Center to do so. This system, TRAK, used the EPSDT tracking regulation as a basic framework, since these regulations were the most stringent. The system assists the coordinator by reminding her daily, weekly, or monthly which children should be contacted and what their past experience has been with the program. The system also provides the summary data listed on the form in Appendix B. Project staff members have found that the computer saves them much time in filing, scheduling appointments, and summarizing results, even though a relatively small number of children (1,200) are involved at this point. Future plans for the system include testing it with other programs so that it can become an interagency tool that computes data from all programs in the county that serve handicapped children and their families.

SUMMARY

Because so many different private and public agencies are involved in the delivery of services to handicapped children, a number of problems have evolved that need to be addressed at all levels of the delivery system. These problems include: 1) a lack of screening resources to fulfill government mandates for mass screening, 2) a lack of diagnostic and treatment services, particularly for infants and preschoolers, 3) duplication and omission of services, and 4) little, if any, coordination of services to maximize resources, especially in rural areas. This chapter has described an approach to these problems that involves the organization of an interagency collaborative effort at the community level for screening, diagnosing, and treating preschool handicapped children. The description included an explanation of how the approach was initially conceived and initiated, a list of questions and issues that were considered by the local Interagency Council, a description of the components of the project as they currently operate in the community, and a discussion of problems and solutions that arose during the course of the initiation and maintenance of the program. This interagency model currently screens and tracks more than 1,200 children a year between the ages of birth and 6 years. Since the local area expects a growth of 40% over the next 2 years, the project is also expected to grow and to become an integral part of the community. Financial and administrative support for the project has been provided through state and regional Developmental Disabilities grants and contributions from the participating local agencies. In the future, the Interagency Council members expect the project to be locally supported through contracts and contributions from county agencies.

Coordinating Services to Handicapped Children:
A Handbook for Interagency Collaboration
Edited by Jerry O. Elder and Phyllis R. Magrab
Copyright © 1980   Paul H. Brookes Publishers   Baltimore • London

APPENDIX A

Release Form

I/We give my/our permission for _____ to release any information obtained as a result of this screening to the Development Delays Committee. I understand that this information may be made available to an interdisciplinary team (composed of members from the interagency committee: a psychologist, physician, social worker, and educator) and to any agency that is a member of the Developmental Delays Committee.

Child's name _____

Parent's/Guardian's signature _____

Date _____ Witness: _____

Agencies of the Developmental Delays Committee:

Fremont County Nursing Office
West Central Mental Health Clinic
School District RE 1
School District RE 2 J
School District RE 3
Developmental Training Services
Department of Social Services
St. Thomas More Hospital
Canon City Cooperative Preschool
Fremont County Head Start
Developmental Delays Interdisciplinary Team (including physician, social worker, psychologist, educator)

If necessary any of the above described information may be released to the physician of your choice _____.

APPENDIX B

Project Data
Summary Report

Today's Date: _____   Total children enrolled in program since
                                              January 1st: _____
Report period: _____   Total enrolled during this period: _____

Type of screening: _____

I. OF THE CHILDREN ENROLLED IN THE PROGRAM
    THIS PERIOD
        Number screened for this
        condition: _____
            Normal: _____
            Non-normal: _____
            (Abnormal or questionable)
            Untestable: _____
            (Test was started but
            could not be finished
            because of child's mood
            or behavior)

II. OF THE CHILDREN WHO DID NOT PASS
     (Non-normal or untestable)
        Number rescreened because
        of test results: _____
Number waiting for rescreening for
        above reason: _____
Number referred to IDT or to more
        comprehensive evaluation: _____
        Number referred directly to
        treatment: _____
        Others:
        (Explain _____)   _____

III. OF THE CHILDREN RESCREENED
        Number of children referred
        to IDT or to more compre-
        hensive evaluation: _____
        Number referred directly to
        treatment: _____
        Others:
        (Explain _____)   _____

IV. OF THE CHILDREN REFERRED TO IDT OR DIAGNOSTIC
EVALUATION
Number of children receiving
treatment: _____
Number waiting for treat-
ment: _____
Others:
(Explain _____)   _____

APPENDIX C

Evaluation Form
Fremont County   Project ECHO

Organization: _____   Date: _____
Name: _____

	Low	High

I. On a scale of 1 to 5, how would you rate the impact of Project ECHO *on your organization*?

                                               1 2 3 4 5

    Explain your rating:

II. Do you feel Project ECHO could have a stronger impact than it has had during the past 6 months?   1 2 3 4 5

    If yes, explain:

III. To what extent do you feel the concept of an interagency effort is valuable to this community?   1 2 3 4 5

IV. To what extent has the actual operation of the interagency effort met your expectations? 1 2 3 4 5

V. In order of importance to your organization, indicate below, *three* program goals you feel should be emphasized by Project ECHO:

    _____ Increased number of families receiving screening services.
    _____ Improved methods of tracking children through the screening, diagnosis, treatment process.

126

_____ Increased awareness on the part of families regarding child development and the importance of early identification

_____ Addition of new service resources to the county.

_____ Improved communication among agencies and professionals.

_____ Providing outreach for agencies serving handicapped children.

_____ Coordination of special programs and training to allow all agencies to participate in activities that normally would be provided to/for one or two (e.g., special hearing screening).

_____ Locating needed resources for diagnosis and treatment.

_____ Other: _____

_____

	Low	High
VI. To what extent do you feel Project ECHO is now addressing the above program goals?	1 2 3	4 5

Explain your rating:

VII. In order of importance, indicate below *three* primary roles you feel should be assumed by the coordinator.

_____ Assess and document community's need for services.

_____ Identify and develop the best use of available state and federal dollars.

_____ Inform and secure cooperation of local agencies, physicians, specialists, parents, general community.

_____ Develop methods of communication and referral among professionals and agencies serving the family.

_____ Ensure that diagnostic and treatment services are provided to child and family.

_____ Assist agencies in developing cooperative arrangements.

_____ Serve as case manager for each child identified.

_____ Keep records for purpose of "tracking" and periodic recall.

_____ Coordinate screenings.

Name: _____ Date: _____

_____ Plan and implement outreach activities.
_____ Other: _____
      _____

	Low				High
To what extent do you feel the functions you					
have specified are now being addressed:	1	2	3	4	5

Comments:

What suggestions do you have for improving the project to better serve your organization and the target families?

Interagency Council Evaluation

To be completed by Interagency Council

Date: _____

I. What should be the top three goals of Project ECHO in order to improve services to handicapped children in the county?

II. What will be happening in the county when Project ECHO is a success? (In other words, how will you know when the project is "working"?)

III. On a scale of 1 to 5, if 5 represents "success," where do you feel Project ECHO is presently functioning? 1   2   3   4   5

IV. What specifically must be done to make the project successful?

Summary Matrix of Community Resources

Services	Handicapping Conditions								
	Visual Impairment — Blindness	Deafness — Hearing Impairment	Physical Handicap (Orthopedic)	Speech Impairment	Health Impairment	Mental Retardation	Serious Emotional Disturbance	Specific Learning Disability	
1. Counseling									
2. Screening									
3. Diagnosis									
4. Evaluation									
5. Education (classroom or home based)									
6. Follow-up									
7. Referral									
8. Personal Care									
9. Legal (protective/advocate)									
10. Recreation									
11. Staff Training									
12. Transporation									
13. Treatment (specify: PT/ OT/speech)									

14. Equipment									
15. Instructional Materials									
16. Day Care									
17. Foster Care									
18. Parent Training									
19. Case Management									
20. IEP as in PL 94-142									
21. Comprehensive Individualized Planning									
22. Financial Assistance									
23. Health Services									
24. Public Education									
25. Homemaker Service									
26. Home Nursing									
27. Preventive Services									
28. Other									

Chapter 6

Development of Preschool Interagency Teams

Janelle Mulvenon

The Kansas Early Childhood Education for the Handicapped Project and how its organizational structure came into existence are discussed in this chapter. How interest in a preschool team was created is reported, and procedural safeguards, funding schemes, problems encountered, analysis of the effectiveness of the program, and models of service delivery are covered. Nowhere in this chapter can a step-by-step sequence for the development of a preschool interagency team be found. The unique nature of each community would make such a "cookbook" approach, if ever possible to devise, misleading for other communities undertaking an interagency collaborative effort. Rather, the experience in Kansas reported here should be examined and the program's policies and procedures adopted as appropriate and tailored to the individual community's needs.

In August, 1978, the Kansas State Department of Education was awarded a State Implementation Grant for Early Childhood Education for the Handicapped from the Bureau of Education for the Handicapped of the U.S. Department of Health, Education, and Welfare. The grant reflected a felt need to plan and implement preschool services and the recognized problems in so doing. The major thrust of this State Implementation Grant was to coordinate the various agencies serving preschool handicapped children at both the state and local levels.

The state of Kansas has permissive legislation for the provision of services to handicapped children under 5 years of age. Local education agencies in Kansas may organize services for preschool handicapped children in the following ways:

The author would like to acknowledge Phyllis Ellis, project director, and Dr. Lucille Paden, state liaison representative of the Kansas State Department of Education, who have both worked extensively on the project reported in this chapter.

1. They may establish individual programs within their own school district.
2. They may establish a cooperative program with one or more school districts.
3. They may contract with an approved special purpose school or program that has appropriate special education services for preschool level handicapped children.

The current funding system for these programs includes contributions from local funds, state special education categorical funds, and the state entitlement provided through PL 94-142. However, preschool programs do not receive the basic state aid provided to programs for school-age children. One of the ways to overcome the shortfall of funds and to expand services to the preschool handicapped is through the cooperation of various agencies serving young handicapped children. In order to facilitate cooperation and increase the quality and quantity of services available to preschool handicapped children, Kansas is concentrating its efforts in the area of interagency collaboration.

STATEWIDE COORDINATION

State level coordination and planning are addressed through a state Preschool Coordination Committee. This committee participates in short and long range planning, coordinates the state Child Find project, the development of education program standards, and the use of preschool incentive monies, and provides technical assistance to local level interagency planning teams. Local teams are requesting technical assistance on such issues as how to react when agencies and programs increase rates after the school contracts the services, training people to conduct hearing and vision screenings, and early childhood special education teacher certification requirements. Agencies represented include the State Department of Health and Environment, the State Department of Social and Rehabilitation Services, Head Start, local education agencies and special education cooperatives, the State Department of Education, state universities, parents, Developmental Disabilities Centers, and the Cerebral Palsy Research Foundation.

COMMUNITY LEVEL COORDINATION

The most successful component of the present State Implementation Grant is the active involvement of local interagency teams in coordinated planning for preschool services to young handicapped children. In attempting to form a preschool interagency team, it is essential to include:

Representatives of parent advocacy organizations
Directors and teachers from preschools

Developmental Disabilities Centers
Head Start and other private or public centers for preschool children
Representatives from Social Rehabilitation Services offices
Representatives from the public health offices
Regular and special education administrators and teachers
Physicians
Representatives from mental health centers
Physical and occupational therapists

However, it is not necessary that every preschool interagency team be as large as this list indicates. It may be impossible to include one agency or another, but even the smallest communities have the basic components to form a preschool interagency team. There is one basic rule to follow: no agency or program should be excluded on the basis of past prejudices. In some instances, a person or agency thought to be a major hindrance has become the facilitator or chairman of a local team. Even though each program or agency has distinct purposes, goals, policies, and constraints (both fiscal and legal), all can agree with the common goal of increasing the quality and quantity of services to preschool handicapped children.

ROLE OF STATE LIAISON REPRESENTATIVES

In developing the preschool interagency teams, two state liaison representatives were hired through the State Implementation Grant to organize interagency activities in cooperation with the state Preschool Coordination Committee. Initially, the state liaison representatives made personal contacts with local special education directors, superintendents, mental health centers, local offices of the Department of Social and Rehabilitation Services, Head Start, local offices of the Department of Health, community day care centers, preschool programs, parents, the League of Women Voters, PTAs, school board members, and any other agencies serving preschool handicapped children and their families. Thousands of miles were logged making personal contacts in local communities. Regional and local orientation meetings were held to acquaint community members and agency representatives with early childhood education for the handicapped and related state and federal legislation. These meetings introduced the concept of preschool interagency teams and provided general background information. As a result of these meetings, a few special education cooperatives immediately organized preschool interagency teams. However, there were just as many cases in which other agencies or interested people facilitated the formation of the team. The underlying strategy was to have the school district agree to plan and implement services for preschool handicapped children but not to do it in isolation from the other resources.

Early in the development of the Early Childhood Education for the Handicapped Project, a decision was made to capitalize on an existing effort of interagency cooperation, namely the child identification (Child Find) component of PL 94-142. Local Child Find clinics were used extensively to further interagency cooperation. Both the Child Find project and this grant are founded on the concept of cooperation. In fact, both have the same project director, and joint planning meetings are held monthly.

The state liaison representatives were directed to attend the local Child Find clinics where comradeship and *espirit de corps* were witnessed. It was a convenient way to introduce the project to the local people, to observe which agencies and programs have the greatest influence in the community, to assess local needs, and to continue to foster such cooperative relationships. Finally, it was easier to continue interagency cooperation if and when the Child Find clinics were working well.

There is one criticism invariably raised about Child Find. It is the question of the value of identifying young handicapped children without providing educational services. Child Find and the Early Childhood Education project can overcome this criticism since they are complementary programs. The former is the identification arm for the latter. It is impossible to persuade any agency to offer services if it cannot be statistically demonstrated that children are in need of services. Child Find can provide this information.

COMMUNITY NEEDS AND CONCERNS

When the concept of selling a preschool interagency team to a special education cooperative or school district first began, there were usually some recognized needs or problems within a community. They included:

1. Anticipation in the state that the school-age mandate would be extended below the age of 5
2. Financial problems among some developmental centers to the extent that they might have to close
3. If there was a preschool mandate, anticipation by the schools that other agencies would terminate services
4. Recognition that a preschool handicapped child should receive services when diagnosed
5. Recognition that services to preschool handicapped children need to be expanded and improved
6. The opportunity to develop and implement a truly local plan rather than a state-imposed plan

There were some communities where there appeared to be no interest and even resistance to a preschool interagency team. The most viable approach, therefore, was to plant a few seeds of public awareness through community meetings or special interest groups and then waiting to see if an awareness—and interest—developed. In many community meetings, local preschool interagency team members from other communities provided on-site consultation to the emerging preschool interagency teams. They were able to add the local credibility that was needed.

Prior to the State Implementation Grant, *preschool interagency teams* was a foreign phrase. To date, such teams have been formed in 13 Kansas communities and are addressing a variety of concerns. The following list illustrates the scope of the initial concerns that interagency teams often encountered:

1. What community preschool programs already exist?
2. What are their funding sources? Are other sources available?
3. How are these programs staffed?
4. How are children with special needs identified and recruited?
5. What are individual agencies mandated to do for these children?
6. Can a referral network be developed?
7. How does current legislation affect programming?
8. How can a child be evaluated/assessed?
9. Are services duplicated? Are there service gaps?
10. Is joint in-service training feasible?
11. Who is being served?
12. How satisfied are they?
13. Are all children receiving appropriate services?
14. Can interagency program funding agreements be developed?

DEVELOPMENT OF INTERAGENCY TEAMS

Guidelines

Assuming that interest in a preschool interagency team is developing, or already exists, there are many general guidelines to keep in mind when undertaking that process:

1. The team should be an independent committee but with no independent powers.
2. The team must not create another level of bureaucracy.
3. The team should not be an extension of any single agency.
4. Each person, agency, or program should be an equal member of the team.
5. There must be a chairman or liaison. If the initial request for the establishment of such a team came from a school district, it may be a better strategy to have a nonschool person be chairman. This reduces the possibilities of the team being associated as the school's rather than the community's.

6. Even in the smallest community, it should be assumed that agencies have never cooperated on anything before. Most agencies are not aware of all the services available for preschool handicapped children that could be put to coordinated use. For example, one community agency in Kansas screened about 300 children in one year, but none of these children were referred to any other program or agency!

7. Involve parents. They help keep the focus of the team's activities where it needs to be—*on the child.*

8. Minimize the professional jargon. If this is not done there is a possibility of losing the parents.

9. Initially, agencies, programs, or individuals may need to develop interpersonal communication skills in order to be encouraged to exchange ideas and to interact.

10. Do not use an agency's letterhead for team correspondence. This will minimize a team member viewing the team as belonging to a certain agency or program.

11. Establish goals and time lines. People will be asked to commit time to the planning sessions, and unless there are clear objectives and procedural steps outlined, the team will not survive.

12. Personal contacts are the key to active participation. Do not rely on the mail exclusively.

13. Choose a chairman who has excellent public relations abilities and is an assertive and energetic leader. There are instances when it is a good strategy to have a person from the school district appointed as chairman if the district is dragging its feet.

14. Request agencies and programs to appoint a representative to these planning sessions by official action. It establishes accountability. (See Appendix A.)

15. Give examples of how each program, agency, and individual can contribute to the preschool interagency team.

16. Seek out the decision makers in a community.

Financial Assistance

As a small "carrot" to encourage special education cooperatives and school districts to work together with other agencies, communities were offered financial assistance. First, Preschool Incentive Funds from Title VI-B of the Education of the Handicapped Act were made available on a grant basis. Second, the Kansas State Department of Education through Title VI-B Special Project Grants of the Education of the Handicapped Act made preschool handicapped children one of its priorities. In either case, the special education cooperative or school district was required to have an interagency team and demonstrate interagency planning to request such federal funding.

However, there are communities where preschool interagency teams developed without federal project money, either of their own choice or by the decision of school administrators and school boards. These communities were still eligible to receive technical assistance in the development and implementation of their community preschool plans from the Kansas State Implementation Grant for Early Childhood Education for the Handicapped. Technical assistance requests have ranged from identification of local needs, preparation of public awareness materials, and development of a local plan to staff training. Consultants were identified and utilized throughout the state to provide assistance to local interagency teams.

Problems Encountered

Many of the problems encountered in using an interagency approach can be defined as attitudinal or territorial. Such problems usually do not surface until 6 to 12 months after the team is formed. In the actual words of some team members, some of the examples of attitudinal barriers to cooperation are:

"Let the school do it all. They eventually will be mandated to do it anyway."
"School district, tell us the year you want to take full responsibilities for preschool services and we will organize our plans around you."
"The preschool coordinator hired by the special education cooperative can do all the work to coordinate services."
"Our funding resources are unstable." "Let the school replace those dollars."
"Our agency will only participate on the team if we receive more money."
"Our program can provide all the services that are needed."
"As a community-based agency, we are apt to lose our funding sources if the school begins preschool services."
"School programs are going to force the private preschool out of business."

Other misconceptions people have about interagency cooperation include the fear that an agency or program is going to benefit monetarily, or that other agencies and programs will get to know the actual state of affairs of their own program.

The struggles in initiating a preschool interagency team seem minimal when compared to the problems of maintaining the team. In almost all cases, communities realize that agencies need to cooperate and recognize each other's role. However, those teams without federal funding find implementing recommendations more challenging. Local constraints force them to become more innovative and aggressive. They also seek a greater commitment of time to achieve these goals.

Some people have commented that the first meetings were "blurred." Establishing goals should be the team's first charge. Defining a team's goals and purpose can be a difficult and trying process for some. The state liaison representatives provided a needs assessment to assist in the analysis of local services and the identification of children in need of or receiving services. There are team members who know exactly what the issues are; others know they need to spend a few hours establishing goals and priorities but do not have the procedural steps outlined. A workable solution for a local community, then, is to view a sample of another local community's goals and procedural steps that will facilitate the formulation of their own and to have other local team leaders assist them in this effort.

In implementing cooperative programs, the salaries of personnel may be secured from two or more agencies. Thus, the personnel often become confused as to which agency they are directly responsible to. Who will do the interviewing, evaluating, and terminating of employees, approve in-service days, approve materials and supply requests, and assign specific responsibilities? The solution is that the appropriate decision makers must maintain open communication. Responsibilities of each agency or program must be defined. The agency that will have the ultimate responsibility for services should also be specified. Subsequently, these responsibilities should be defined in an interagency agreement.

The level of trust that exists determines whether an agreement needs to be written before implementing a program. There are instances where people do not see a formal agreement as a priority. At the point they do, arrangements should be made to develop such an agreement. There is one advantage in writing an agreement after the program has begun. It allows the agencies and programs to field test a cooperative program and know the specific responsibilities that need to be included in the agreement.

In conducting many local meetings, the question *"How does my agency or program fit in?"* is invariably raised. Based on the Kansas experience, a portion of the meeting should be devoted to presentations on what and how each agency can contribute. Using various agency personnel from other existing teams is an excellent strategy to reduce the perception that this is entirely a school's team.

Another problem exists between the State Coordination Committee and local interagency teams. Very few State Coordination Committee members attend local level meetings; thus, it is difficult for them to identify with the process local teams use and the obstacles they encounter. This problem has a relatively simple solution. In the coming year, the state liaison representatives, in conjunction with the local teams, plan to personally invite State Coordination Committee members to attend these meetings.

With such attitudinal roadblocks in abundance, frequent attendance by the state liaison representative at local level meetings is mandatory. The representative's presence is felt to be stabilizing, neutral, and objective. In essence, the state liaison representative becomes a referee and a buffer. In almost all cases, the solutions to local problems are based around open communication, and the state liaison can facilitate such communication. To develop mutual awareness of each agency and its capabilities, this third party must be perceived as neutral.

Several of the interagency teams that were established were outgrowths of the regional meetings mentioned earlier. These first teams helped in the preparation for the more challenging and difficult development processes involved with some of the other teams. As stated earlier, not all teams were organized under the initiative of the special education cooperative. Some communities became interested in forming a preschool team only after they heard of the activities and results of another community's team. For example, in two particular communities, the teams became the instrumental agents in convincing their respective special education cooperatives to submit a proposal for a preschool incentive grant. Neither of these special education directors would have speculated a year ago that they would be planning and implementing preschool handicapped services.

In one community, a new special education director, who was overwhelmed with the school-age mandate problems, allowed the project staff to conduct a community preschool meeting, but promised nothing. The formulation of a preschool interagency team was the result of this initial meeting. In turn, this particular team collectively wrote the preschool incentive grant proposal. It was approved by the special education cooperative and was funded by the State Department of Education and has since become one of the strongest in Kansas.

In another community, various personnel were reluctant to come to a meeting. It became obvious that the head of agency A did not speak to the head of agency B. Certain people were opposed to attending these initial meetings if other agencies were to be invited. Nevertheless, representatives from all of the agencies were invited to the meetings. The strategy in this case was to invite middle level personnel plus individuals perceived by all agencies as neutral parties. To the community's amazement, the team was instrumental in having a preschool incentive grant proposal submitted and funded.

The preschool interagency team can be instrumental in convincing a school board and special education cooperative board to approve a preschool proposal. It is easy for a board to deny one or two agencies, but the presence of seven or eight agencies is an imposing front. The intent is not that the school or special education cooperative be pressured to do it all. Rather, the strength in developing a community plan is that the school and special education cooperative are not in such an endeavor alone. The community preschool plan shows the school administrators and board members that they contribute only part of the plan. While this approach is probably easier to achieve in a state that has a permissive preschool law, communities in states that mandate such services should not be discouraged from attempting to take this approach.

In summary, if a community anticipates developing an interagency team, the following points may prove helpful:

1. One agency or person must take the initiative to get things started.
2. All of the agencies, programs, and individuals involved must have a clear picture of the policies, constraints, and goals that cover each of the other agencies and programs.
3. As a group, the agencies should discuss their mutual goals and set objectives for their team effort. Will the team set up a cooperative preschool, make placement decisions, or simply share information and referrals?
4. Each agency is capable of providing certain services and performing certain tasks. Those tasks (roles) must be defined and clearly assigned. As a team, they may find they can "fill in the cracks" that are found when one agency tries to provide all of the services to a child and the family.
5. The team needs to give itself a generous amount of lead time to iron out difficulties. For example, weeks may be needed to reach an agreement on forms or procedures, or it may take a year to initiate a cooperative preschool. The pooling of resources and careful planning should make services less expensive, more comprehensive, and more appropriate to individual children's needs.

One of the keys, therefore, to successful preschool interagency teams is to demand local level planning power. Local leaders must be guaranteed local ownership and commitment. The strength of the Kansas program is in the local leaders.

EXAMPLES OF INTERAGENCY PLANNING EFFORTS

School Interaction

Special education directors, school boards, and administrators (especially in the areas where preschool interagency teams exist) are becoming aware that there indeed are handicapped preschool children and that early intervention is a pressing need. Prior to the State Implementation Grant, there were only four special education cooperatives in Kansas with Title VI-B Special Preschool Project Grants. There are now eight additional Title VI-B Preschool Incentive Grants and one new Title VI-B Preschool Special Project Grant. These nine additional projects have been required to establish preschool interagency teams as a condition of funding. All of these teams have encountered setbacks, obstacles, or prejudices. Most people, however, are accustomed to struggles, and if there is a commitment to the team's goals, the team will flourish.

With the advent of the State Implementation Grant and the component of interagency cooperation, direct services to preschool handicapped children have begun in some special education cooperatives. What is exciting is that the majority of special cooperatives are interacting with other community resources.

In one community a preschool interagency team addressed the criticism that preschool handicapped children were receiving services in a segregated setting. Clearly, one of the team's goals was to provide preschool services to young handicapped children in an integrated setting. During one of the interagency team meetings, the Head Start and the Developmental Disabilities Center directors suggested to each other that perhaps their two programs could work together. In subsequent meetings, it was the consensus that Head Start would be responsible for 3- and 4-year-olds and the Developmental Disabilities Center would focus on handicapped children from ages birth through 3 years. Since this Head Start program did not operate during the summer months, handicapped children needing services during that time would be continued through the Developmental Disabilities Center's home-based program. There was one major problem preventing the initiation of such a plan. More personnel were needed by the Head Start program for the additional handicapped children. At that point, the special education cooperative agreed to provide the needed staff. The Head Start program first served those preschool handicapped children mandated by its regulations, and the special education cooperative provided the required services for the additional preschool handicapped children. It was agreed by the special education cooperative, Developmental Disabilities Center, and the Head Start program that the total population of preschool handicapped children would not exceed 30% of the total Head Start enrollment. The 30% limit was agreed upon so as not to lose the goal of an integrated preschool. Once the program was at its capacity, referrals were made to the Developmental Disabilities Center.

In another community, a Developmental Disabilities Center had unstable funding. The special education director saw a quality program in severe constraints. When a preschool interagency team was formed, the members put their heads together to generate funds for improving preschool handicapped services. The special education cooperative agreed to provide the certified teachers, a speech-language therapist, the paraprofessionals, and certain support staff to this program. The facilities, materials, equipment, occupational therapist, physical therapist, preschool coordinator, and any excess education expenses became the responsibility of the Developmental Disabilities Center. The program doubled the number of children receiving services, and, for the first time, 40 handicapped children received free and appropriate educational services. The Developmental Disabilities Center continues to contribute one-third of the preschool program's funding with the county mill levy, United Way dollars, and donations. As a side note, the transition to this cooperative program was hardly noticeable since a good rapport already existed among these agencies.

Hays Interagency Planning Group

Some of the interagency teams have made strides without receiving grant funding. As an example, in Hays, Kansas, a public awareness meeting was held which focused on coordinating services for preschool handicapped children. At the conclusion of this meeting, a number of individuals agreed to develop an Interagency Planning Group for Preschool Children. Each agency committed 1 day a week for 4 months to develop this community preschool plan. As a procedural guide, the *Hays' Interagency Preschool Standards* was patterned after *A Plan for Coordinated Interagency Services for Children with Special Needs in Massachusetts* (1978). There was some criticism that this team simply adopted the Massachusetts plan without revisions. To the contrary, this team developed and adopted unique community preschool standards, identified its own service gaps, and formulated and initiated its own recommendations.

The first task of the Interagency Planning Group was to develop standards or ideal guidelines for providing services to preschool children. After writing the standards, the Interagency Planning Group compared each service delivery agency to the standards. (A recommended strategy is to have a third party perform the comparison in order to reduce paranoia.) After studying the services of each agency relative to the standards, the Interagency Planning Group conducted a needs assessment. Out of their assessments came recommendations in the form of procedural guidelines for providing interagency services. The following procedural guideline for the area of assessment is a sample of this planning group's standards and recommendations.

ASSESSMENT

A. Guidelines
Standard
All referred children should receive an assessment appropriate to the degree and type of suspected special need(s) as determined by the coordinating team. Appropriateness is defined as the selection and administration of instruments that determine the sequence and achievement of developmental levels and may include part or all of the following as determined by the referral data and the child's need(s):

General physical
Neurological
Ophthalmological
Audiological
Gross and fine motor development
Perceptual motor development
Receptive and expressive language
Cognitive development
Social and emotional growth
Formal and informal observations of the child including at least two visits to the home and any other settings where the child customarily spends waking hours
Complete social history including individual and family information

B. Timing
Standard
All referred children should have an initial assessment completed within 6 weeks of date of referral.
Needs
Make necessary arrangements so that all initial assessments will be completed in 6 weeks.
Avoid needless duplication—maximize the use of resources.
Coordination in case management/assessment.
Avoid needless duplication—share information.
Recommendations
A task force composed of volunteers from the Interagency Planning Group (IPG) should be in charge of developing materials that can be used across agencies. No financial reimbursement will be made to members of this task force for the time they donate to the IPG. Included in the materials to be developed are an interagency referral form, an interagency history form, and an interagency consent for release and exchange of information form. [See Appendices B, C, and D.]

The task force will be responsible for modifying or adding additional forms.

Each agency will ensure that assessments are completed within 6 weeks.

The agency that first sees the child will be responsible for coordinating the assessment of the child. Coordination will include the following:

1. Determine what additional evaluations are necessary.
2. Notify other agencies that the child is being referred.
3. Obtain proper release forms.
4. Follow up referrals when necessary.
5. Deliver the summary evaluation to the next referral agency.

(A complete list of the procedural guidelines developed by the Hays, Kansas, Interagency Planning Team is included in Chapter 9 as Appendix D.) A formal commitment to endorse and implement these standards and recommendations was sought. Fifteen out of the 18 various agencies and programs in Hays formally adopted the standards and recommendations. (See Appendix E.)

High Plains Special Education Cooperative

In a more rural area, another preschool interagency team has made tremendous gains in the first 12 months of existence. Having an area of 10,000 square miles to address in implementing services, the team members knew from experience that a carefully constructed plan was a necessity. They developed a 3-year planning outline to have, eventually, an impact on the entire 10,000 square miles, although the first year was limited to a single county. Ideally, it would be far better to look at a 5- or 10-year plan, but a 3-year plan was a major undertaking. A portion of the plan of the High Plains Special Education Cooperative, Garden City, Kansas includes:

Year One
*Develop and distribute <u>a resource guide for all appropriate agencies and parents containing information concerning services available to the handicapped child and his/her parents</u>

Provide awareness and education to the agencies in contact with preschoolers
and the public through the news media, posters, brochures, a resource
guide, and speakers

Organize a system of identification of preschool handicapped children
through local doctors, agencies serving preschool children, and screening clinics

Organize a system of referral to a central information center for services,
placement, and support of the child and his/her parents

Organize a system of follow-up and support to parents

Organize a system of providing necessary information, appropriate training,
and support to placement agencies

Organize a system of consistent testing and evaluation materials

Organize a system of appropriate assessments and individualized education
programs (IEPs) of each child identified

Organize a system of follow-up placement and services to the child recognizing specific needs of the child and his/her parents, such as transportation, speech-language therapy, and similar services

Organize a system of smooth transition into the public school system

Work with appropriate existing agencies for preschool program approval

Year Two and Year Three include the remaining counties of this special
education cooperative. It is exciting to realize this interagency team addressed
such a large list of objectives within the short time of 12 months.

The development and adoption of preschool standards and recommendations were added to the plan during the course of the first year. Rather
than attempting to develop their own preschool standards, the *Hays' Interagency Preschool Standards* guide, referred to earlier, was used as a
springboard. A section of the High Plains plan follows:

REFERRAL
Standard
A systematic process for referral should exist to ensure that children identified or suspected as high risk or special needs shall have screening or
further evaluation and appropriate services available.

Referral of children for screening shall be made to screening clinics or
agencies, as appropriate

Identification and referral of infants with special needs or high risk at birth to
appropriate agencies

Referral of children identified as high risk through the screening process for
further evaluation

Recommendations
A central referral number shall be maintained and publicized for information
to parents, agencies, and interested organizations

Recommendations and/or placement made through the central referral
number will be reviewed by a committee consisting of Task Force members.

In cases of direct approaches to an agency, that agency will consider the
child's total needs as to appropriate and comprehensive services and shall be
responsible for information to parents for other resources

This team was in dire need of such standards, but until they developed
and adopted them, they had no criteria or device to measure progress being

made. With the adoption of standards and recommendations, members of the team suddenly saw they had an active rather than a passive role.

All preschool interagency teams should develop and adopt such preschool standards and recommendations. As has been already shown by example, new teams can use existing standards as a reference point. Variations in the recommendations will be necessary in order to utilize varying local resources. For example, one special education cooperative is exploring the idea of using local preschool teachers as the local contact persons for preschool screening clinics while another special education cooperative uses public health nurses.

Northwest Kansas Education Service Center

Another example of a delivery model, the Northwest Kansas Educational Service Center, Colby, Kansas, is in a planning phase of organization. This preschool interagency task force is organizing a mutually agreeable and coordinated system of:

1. Seeking out preschool handicapped children
2. Providing comprehensive diagnostic services
3. Developing and implementing service delivery model alternatives
4. Conducting follow-up and support

In order to more fully understand the process involved, a sample description of the Colby project objectives, activities, and evaluation follows:

Objective 1:
Facilitation of the planning task force process.
Activities and Evaluation:

  1.10 Continue to facilitate the ongoing interagency task force process through: participation in the regularly scheduled planning meetings, resulting in preschool program standards and recommendations for improvement concerning 1) public awareness, 2) professional awareness, 3) screening, 4) assessment, 5) planning process, 6) service delivery, 7) technical assistance, and 8) program evaluation *as evidenced by documents on file.*

  1.11 Through personal visitation with member agencies, parent representatives, and unified school districts, involve them in the planning process *as evidenced by list of contacts made, the list of active team members, and the mailing list.*

  1.12 Coordinate the compilation and distribution of a monthly newsletter to all interested persons and agencies *as indicated by the file of newsletters.*

  1.13 Provide a data base for team decisions through an ongoing needs assessment and community research *as indicated by evidence on file.*

  1.14 Through ERIC searches and contact with NDN (National Diffusion Network) representatives, keep the team informed of innovative nationally validated preschool models *as evidenced by information on file.*

Objective 2:

Provide a clearinghouse service for information exchange and referral.

Activities and Evaluation:

2.10 Research, develop and disseminate a resource directory *as indicated by evidence on file.*

2.11 Assist the task force in developing a locally based Child Find network *as indicated by a list within the resource directory.*

2.12 Design and implement a follow-up or tracking system to follow the child once he/she has been referred *as indicated by evidence on file.*

2.13 Utilizing public media, develop an awareness of the referral and information service *as indicated by newspaper clippings and brochures on file.*

2.14 Establish and implement an incoming telephone monitoring service for referral and information exchange *as evidenced by the log of calls received and the action taken.*

Objective 3:

Coordinate and provide in-service and training to parents.

Activities and Evaluations:

3.10 Based on community research and needs assessment, develop a data-based plan for parent in-service and training *as evidenced by material on file.*

3.11 Implement this plan through workshops for parents *as indicated by log on file by January 1, 1980.*

Objective 4:

Assist agencies in meeting the state Department of Education's pre-school program standards for the area.

Activities and Evaluation:

4.10 Based on needs assessment, provide an ongoing in-service to participating agencies' personnel *as evidenced by having an in-service plan on file and a record of attendance.*

4.11 Coordinate an in-service plan for special education personnel that focuses on assessment and evaluation techniques and procedures for preschool handicapped children *as evidenced by having an in-service plan and record of attendance on file.*

4.12 Coordinate with colleges and universities for the provision of classwork toward certification in early childhood education for the handicapped in northwestern Kansas, *as evidenced by material on file.*

Objective 5:

Arrange, or provide for on an individual basis where existing services are inadequate, needed evaluations to preschool handicapped children with policies to be developed in conjunction with other agencies.

Activities and Evaluation:

5.10 Refer to appropriate agencies for evaluation services *as shown by referrals on file.*

5.11 Use and make available appropriate materials for evaluation and instruction *as shown by inventory of materials and their use.*

5.12 Provide evaluation services for preschool handicapped with the following criteria: 1) needs that other agencies are unable to meet with certified staff, 2) severity of the handicap, 3) type of handicap, 4) ineligibility for Title XX or other funding sources *as evidenced by information on file.*

Objective 6:
With the approval of the Unified School Districts and local Board of Directors, and in cooperation with local agencies, provide instructional services to preschoolers on an individual basis where no service now exists and when the age of the child and the type and severity of the handicap show the need for services.
Activities and Evaluation:

6.10 Screening and identification through a network set up in Objective 2, *as indicated by evidence on file by January 1, 1980.*

6.11 Diagnosis and comprehensive evaluation, utilizing certified and/or licensed personnel as assigned by the referral staffing *as indicated by an activities log on file.*

6.12 IEP staffings to determine the needs of the child *as indicated by IEPs on file.*

6.13 Meet identified needs of handicapped children upon local school board approval, utilizing support services (speech-language therapy, occupational therapist (OT), physical therapist (PT), psychological, personal social adjustment (PSA), vision impaired, hearing impaired, and audiologist) and self-contained classrooms for severely multiplied handicapped/trainable mentally retarded (SMH/TMR) students *as indicated by evidence on file.*

6.14 Coordinate direct instructional service with the interagency team, utilizing available certified resources *as indicated by IEPs on file.*

Comprehensive Evaluations

One of the primary difficulties in providing services is establishing a comprehensive evaluation after screening. In many screening clinics, recommendations are made for further evaluations. Unfortunately, many of those recommendations remain only on paper. A majority of the parents are unable to follow through because of cost, inability to contact professionals, unknown resources, and "mysterious" eligibility requirements for the various systems of funding. Some preschool interagency teams have proposed an evaluation team composed of preschool interagency members. The advantages of this approach are that it prevents parents from traveling to different locations over long distances to secure specific evaluations, it reduces the number of forms, and it hastens the entry process for a child into the appropriate program. It also allows for any participating agency to schedule a child for an assessment at no charge on a first-come, first-served basis. Referrals are made by the total team, thus increasing cooperation and communication by participating agencies/programs, and, most importantly, children receive a comprehensive evaluation from a multidisciplinary team. The evaluation may include the areas of psychological, medical, speech-language, motor, developmental, physical, vision, and audiological testing.

There have been problems in implementing this service. The first system proposed by the Preschool Interagency Task Force, Garden City, Kansas, was that each agency/program donate 100% of its time on specified days. Many agencies charge a fee for comprehensive evaluations or have only a specific number of community days. These community days are minimal in relation to the waiting list for the community assessment team. Private therapists must also charge a fee because there is no way to subsidize their salary. Hence, the consensus was the preschool interagency team could not donate 100% of its time on specified days to conduct assessments.

As an alternative, the High Plains Special Education Cooperative proposed to pay approximately 50% of the professionals' salaries to their agency through the preschool incentive grant. In turn, professionals would participate on the assessment team one day each week. Members of the team realize this funding arrangement is short term, but the outlined assessment procedures need to be field tested in order to demonstrate and establish a full commitment to a comprehensive interagency assessment team. This same team also serves as a program planning and referral committee.

Considerable time was spent in the preschool interagency meetings working on the details of implementing such a system, including who was responsible for contacting the assessment team members, confidentiality, wages per hour, and standardization of forms and procedures. Whether agencies and programs would commit their personnel to this assessment team, as well as whether staffing time was to be included as a part of the evaluation, became a concern. As a result, the assessment team procedures have been carefully outlined defining agency responsibilities. For example, the agency responsible for the referral is also responsible for sending the Preschool Program Coordinator social history and the medical information signed by a physician or health nurse. All members of the preschool task force have adopted standard forms for social history, request for comprehensive assessment, parent rights, individualized education programs, placement permission, and release of information.

Through the efforts of the Child Find project and various preschool interagency team members, five screening clinics were held in local counties during the first year. With the screening information, the screening coordinator and staff determine what areas need further evaluation. The preschool coordinator hired through the preschool incentive grant is responsible for scheduling and coordinating the assessment team. The flowchart in Figure 1 further describes the system used by this task force.

Cost Considerations

A great variety can be seen in the local level plans of the preschool interagency teams that are developing across Kansas. All of the communities are striving for similar outcomes, but the process varies in each community.

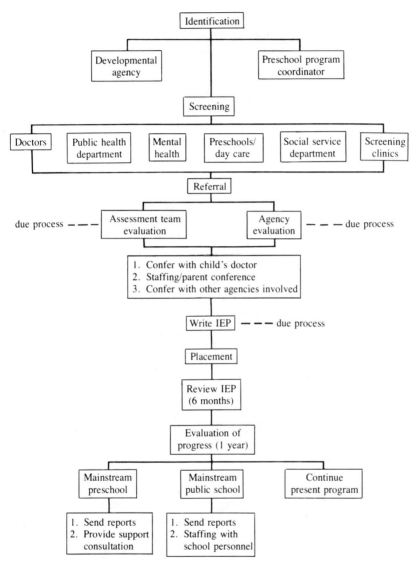

Figure 1. Flowchart of task force on preschool services to the handicapped. (Reprinted from: Punkin Patch Project, High Plains Special Education Cooperative, Garden City, Kansas, 1979.)

It is difficult to convince particular people, especially special education directors and school superintendents, to implement preschool services because of the costs. The answer to this objection is there are many agencies that can share expenses. Obviously, it is cheaper to do nothing. There are school districts and special education cooperatives that believe it is better to plan now in anticipation that a state mandate will be forthcoming. There is also a question of whether there would be any lead-in time if a mandate was passed since federal law already mandates preschool handicapped services.

In order for schools to meet the requirements set by federal and state laws, sharing expenses becomes a necessity. Equipment, materials, staff, transportation, facilities, and in-service training can all be shared.

All of the Preschool Incentive Grant projects have used interagency funding resources. One of the requirements in the grant application is to identify and utilize all of the community resources to strengthen an interagency approach to serve young handicapped children. A summary of one community's preschool agencies and their areas of fiscal responsibility includes:

Special Education Cooperative: through a written contract, provides psychological and speech consultants, audiological evaluations, vision- and hearing-impaired consultants, teachers, and paraprofessionals

Developmental Disabilities Center: provides transportation, staff development, equipment, materials, food services, operation and maintenance of plant, infant program, occupational and physical therapy

SRS: provides social services; funds purchase of service contracts

Mental Health: provides psychological evaluations paid by Medicaid or insurance, and offers family counseling

United Cerebral Palsy of Kansas: assists in the payment of adaptive equipment for children with cerebral palsy

Child Care Association: places children in day care on an individual basis if funding is available through SRS

County Health Department: offers immunizations; screens children who qualify through SRS or Title XIX; conducts child care classes

Recreation Commission: offers recreational activities for children with mild and moderate handicaps

City Commission: leases a building to the Developmental Disabilities Center for $1.00 a year

Head Start: conducts a summer program for children enrolled in the Developmental Disabilities Center during the school year

Hospital: provides a written contract for physical therapy consultation

Kansas Crippled Children's Program: offers medical services for eligible children based on a physician's referral

Home-Based Project: sponsored by the school district and working also with the Developmental Disabilities Center to provide assistance to children with special needs and their families when a strong supportive service is needed in the home

In addition, other direct funding sources in this community include United Way, the county mill levy, the Kansas Community Mental Health and/or Community Facility for Mentally Retarded Assistance Act, state categorical reimbursement funds, Title I–89-313 funds, and Title VI-B Preschool Incentive monies. Using all of the above funding sources except Title I–89-313 funds, the special education cooperative, in conjunction with the Developmental Disabilities Center, served 40 3- and 4-year-old children at a cost of $17.00 per day per child. At today's prices, that is a bargain. During the past year's operation, local, state, and federal agencies each contributed one-third to the total operating budget.

It is the intent of the special education cooperative that, at the end of the federal funding cycle, it will assume the amount that the federal government is currently paying. With or without a mandate, the special education cooperative plans to continue funding this portion of the total program. All signs indicate that this is the direction this special education cooperative will follow. For next year, the cooperative did not request an increase in federal funding. The increase will come from the local level. The advantage of this approach to schools is they do not have to fund this program alone, and may utilize the expertise in other community agencies and programs.

SUMMARY

In promoting preschool interagency teams, many communities have recognized the need to act and want to have input into new policies rather than having them dictated. These teams are breaking ground in a new frontier of education. This chapter has given an overview of how the program has evolved, problems encountered, the effectiveness of this program, and cost savings or avoidance for the school.

As stated earlier, the core of Kansas's efforts began at the "grass roots" level with the state level agencies and programs providing the technical assistance to accomplish the local objectives. It may appear that Kansas has local teams proceeding in any number of directions. Surprisingly, quite the contrary is true since local teams are ambassadors to other developing teams.

An interagency approach to serving preschool handicapped children can be achieved in a state with permissive legislation for services for preschool handicapped children. No single agency is ready to assume the comprehensive responsibility or cost of services to handicapped preschool children. After preschool services are mandated, achieving interagency cooperation will most certainly be more difficult.

REFERENCES

Early Childhood Interagency Planning Group. 1978 (January). *A Plan for Coordinated Interagency Services for Children with Special Needs in Massachusetts.* Special

Early Childhood Project sponsored by the Massachusetts Department of Education, Division of Special Education, and the Bureau of Education for the Handicapped. Boston, MA. (Available from the project, 31st James Avenue, Boston, Massachusetts 02116.)

APPENDIX A

Interagency Preschool Handicapped Task Force
Agreement

To join in a local coordinated effort to cooperatively develop services for preschool handicapped children, I, representing
_____, agree to: (circle any or all of the following)

1. Talk to others in my community about the August 9th meeting
2. Return with other appropriate people for the August 9th meeting
3. Help organize a local meeting concerning the need for preschool
   services for the handicapped
4. Participate in this Interagency Preschool Handicapped Task Force

Signed _____
Date _____
Agency/Program _____
Phone _____

Reprinted from: Interagency Preschool Handicapped Task Force, Salina, Kansas,
July, 1979.

APPENDIX B

Date _____

Interagency Planning Group
Referral Routing Form

Child _____ Birthdate _____

On the basis of _____

_____

the following recommendations are warranted:

1. _____
2. _____
3. _____
4. _____
5. _____

_____

Person making recommendations

_____

Agency

Reprinted from: Interagency Planning Group for Preschool Children, Hays, Kansas, 1978.

Consent for Release and/or Exchange of Information

Client's name _____ Birthdate _____

I hereby consent to the release and/or exchange of:

_____ Speech and language   _____ Family assessment
      information
_____ Audiological assessment   _____ School records/reports
_____ Medical information   _____ Social/psychological
                                 evaluation
_____ Discharge summary   _____ Individualized educa-
                                 tional program
_____ Intake/admission report   _____ Other (specify)

Among the following _____ (#) individuals or agencies:
(Parents should verify the agencies/programs named by initialing each agency listed)

(Name)	(Address)	(Phone)

for the above named client. The purpose of this request is: _____

I understand the information obtained will not be transmitted to another party without my specific written consent or as otherwise permitted by federal regulations.

_____   _____
                                                (Date)

_____   _____
(Signature of parent/legal guardian)   (Relationship of legal guardian)

_____   _____
(Address of parent/legal guardian)   (Phone)

This consent, unless expressly
revoked earlier, expires upon: _____

(specify date or condition)

Referral information provided by:

_____

(Name)   (Agency)   (Date)

———————
   Reprinted from: Interagency Planning Group for Preschool Children, Hays, Kansas,
1978.

APPENDIX D

Background Information

<u>General Information</u>   Date _____

Child's name _____ B/D _____
          (Last)   (First)   (Middle)

Address _____ Sex _____ Age _____
              (Street, P.O. box)

_____ Phone _____
      (City)   (State)   (Zip code)

Parent's or legal guardian's name _____
Relationship _____
Referral source _____
Area of major concern _____
When did you first become concerned? _____
_____

To be completed by clinic staff	Prenatal and Birth History
HR	1. Was your child born prematurely? Yes _____ No _____
Before 37 weeks	If *yes*, how many weeks early? _____
Less than 5 lbs.	2. Birthweight _____ lbs. oz.
	3. Did your child have any respiratory problems at birth? (problems breathing; incubator; etc.) Yes _____ No _____
Yes	4. Were there any complications with this pregnancy such as respiratory problems, incubator, etc.? Yes _____ No _____
	Comments:

Reprinted from: Interagency Planning Group for Preschool Children, Hays, Kansas, 1978.

Prenatal and Birth History *(continued)*

5. Did your baby have any birth defects? (examples: cleft palate; heart condition; etc.)

   Yes _____ No _____

   Explain _____

   _____

6. Did you have any illnesses or accidents (such as rubella) while you were pregnant with this child? Yes _____ No _____

   Explain _____

   _____

7. Were there any complications with the pregnancy? Such as rubella, blood type, premature, etc. Yes _____ No _____

   Explain _____

   _____

Medical History

List childhood diseases and serious infections, surgery, and indicate ages:

_____

_____

_____

_____

Has your child ever had a serious accident or injury? Yes _____ No _____

Describe _____

_____

_____

Has child had convulsions, "fits," or seizures? Yes _____ No _____

How frequent? _____

Is your child presently receiving medication or medical treatment?

Yes _____ No _____ What type? _____

Family physician _____

Address _____

Social History

Brothers and sisters	Age	Any problems? List
_____	_____	_____
_____	_____	_____
_____	_____	_____

Growth History (Indicate age accomplished) If available

Held head erect	_____	Fed self	_____
Sat unsupported	_____	Gave up bottle	_____
Crawled	_____	Cares for bathroom needs	_____
Walked alone	_____	Bladder control	_____
Ate baby food	_____	Bowel control	_____
Ate solids	_____	Dressed self	_____

Speech and Language

Did child babble or coo during first 6 months? _____
Does child respond to sound? _____
Does child respond to name consistently? _____
Does child speak in short sentences? _____
Does child speak in complete sentences? _____
Did child speak first words with meaning? _____
Does child use speech? _____
Frequently? _____ Occasionally? _____
Never? _____
Does child have any speech difficulties? _____
Please describe _____
Did anyone in the child's family lose his/her hearing before age 30? ___

Vision

Has child had a recent eye exam? Yes _____ No _____
When? _____ Where? _____

Hearing

Has your child had a recent hearing exam? Yes _____ No _____
When? _____ Where? _____
Results _____

Behavior

Do you feel that there is a problem with your child's behavior?
       Yes _____ No _____ If yes, explain _____

What types of services has your child received to this point? _____
_____

Is the child currently in a program? _____
Is there any further information you would like us to have? _____
_____
_____

School District # _____
Information provided by _____
_____
                    Signature

APPENDIX E

Agreement Between Participants in the
Interagency Planning Group for Preschool Children

It is recognized by the parties to this agreement that optimal delivery of comprehensive services to preschool children demands coordination, integration, and cooperation of service providers. It is the intent of this agreement to further such comprehensive service delivery.

For this purpose:

We, the undersigned, representing ourselves or our agencies, agree in good faith to follow to the best of our abilities the standards and recommendations set forth in the Interagency Approach to Comprehensive Services for Preschool Children submitted by the Interagency Planning Group for Preschool Children, Hays, Kansas, November 16, 1978.

This agreement shall become effective upon its total approval by the agencies/programs. This agreement may be terminated by written notification of all parties or any single agency/program may terminate its agreement by (60) days termination notice. Such notices shall be sent by certified mail to the governing board of the Interagency Planning Group for Preschool Children. The 60-day notice begins on the date of the postmark on the certified mail.

If one section of these standards is found inapplicable or amended, the entire standards will not be voided.

Each agency or program shall have (60) days to approve the standards and recommendations which are incorporated in the Interagency Approach to Comprehensive Services for Preschool Children effective,

_____.
(Date)

_____
(Name)   (Authority)   (Agency/Program represented)   (Date)

Reprinted from: Interagency Planning Group for Preschool Children, Hays, Kansas, 1978.

Chapter 7

Planning Issues in
Local Interagency Collaboration

Denise Humm-Delgado

When one enters into local interagency collaboration for the first time, issues arise that are slightly different from those prevailing in agency-specific planning. This chapter describes, from the perspective of one local interagency collaboration project in Massachusetts, some issues with which one may have to deal when undertaking interagency planning.

The areas covered include a review of some of the empirical and theoretical studies in the literature, selected to provide insight into what interagency planning is conceived to be by several authors; a description of one interagency planning setting; a delineation and discussion of interagency planning issues in that setting; and recommendations and conclusions relevant to planners involved in similar settings. The purpose of this description is to alert planners involved in similar situations to some of the issues that may confront them, and of which they should, therefore, be aware at the outset of their effort.

SELECTED LITERATURE REVIEW

In order to gain a broad perspective on interagency collaboration as concisely as possible, five key pieces of recent literature, each of which deals with interagency collaboration in more than one state, have been selected for review below. These articles highlight some of the conclusions concerning interagency collaboration that have been reached by several authors after consideration of data generated and analyzed within the past 6 years. Literature pieces related to just one state or locality, or interorganizational treatises, are not included here.

The author gratefully acknowledges the contributions of the present and past members of the Danvers-Salem Area Service Planning Team, on whose project this chapter is based.

The literature reviewed has a common historical thread in that it focuses at least in some way upon a federal thrust initiated through the U.S. Department of Health, Education, and Welfare (DHEW) to induce local interagency collaboration or integration in the form of so-called *services integration*. The first formal mention of this concept occurred in a 1971 policy memorandum by Eliott Richardson, then Secretary of DHEW. (Earlier, the concepts of interagency collaboration and service linkages had been encouraged in some federal legislation.) Principally during 1971–1974, DHEW funded 45 "Services Integration Targets of Opportunity" (SITO) grants to accomplish or to study state or local integration or coordination. This is the background from which the literature below has evolved.

Gans and Horton (1975) analyzed 30 case studies, done in 1972, of DHEW integration projects nationwide. The 1972 proposed federal Allied Services Act, aimed at integration and coordination, was also studied with regard to the application of its principles in six states, one of which was Massachusetts (Gans and Horton, 1975).

The case study findings revealed that services integration is not extensive, is a rather lengthy process, is not based on any one particular best model, and does have a positive effect on accessibility, continuity, and efficiency. Many variables influence the process, including the socio-political environment, the project director, the project staff, project objectives and priorities, service provider objectives and attitudes, mode of coordination, general purpose government and client input, and grant administration, policies, and procedures.

A taxonomy of possible services integration and coordination linkages includes the following categories (Gans and Horton, 1975):

1. Fiscal linkages (joint budgeting, joint funding, fund transfer, and purchase of service).
2. Personnel practices linkages (consolidated personnel administration, joint use of staff, staff transfers, staff outstationing, and co-location).
3. Planning and programming linkages (joint planning, joint development of operating policies, joint programming, information-sharing, and joint evaluation).
4. Administrative support services linkages (record-keeping, grants-management, and central support services).
5. Core services linkages (outreach, intake, diagnosis, referral, and follow-up).
6. Modes of case coordination linkages (case conference, case coordinator, and case team). (pp. xviii–xix)

These categories have become accepted terminology when discussing "services integration" and "interagency collaboration."

Mittenthal et al. (1974) conducted a descriptive research study of 22 of the SITO projects nationwide. Data were organized by the use of a system technology model, "the technology which deals with complex systems and which includes well-tested concepts, models, procedures, principles, and terms useful in the preparation of a meaningful description of any complex process'' (Mittenthal et al., 1974).

Examples of several, but not all, system variables described regarding the SITO projects included population served, governance, effect specification, management, client pathway and service delivery, funding mechanism, system initiation, detailed system design, and normal operations. Of services integration, Mittenthal et al. (1974) state: "Especially it is a goal-directed process whose objective is the establishment of an operating, integrated human service system that addresses a range of an individual's needs and contributes to his status of personal independence and economic self-sufficiency.''

Generally, they found that all of the projects studied lack some of the elements (variables) in the system technology model. With one exception, the "effect specification" element, that is, the identification of "those specific dimensions of human need community members want their system to address'' (Mittenthal et al., 1974), is lacking. The *desired* effects upon *individuals* therefore cannot be assessed, which the authors found to be a major drawback. Mittenthal et al. also found that most projects were part of a statewide reorganization, were organized at the substate level, involved elements of reorganization in public human service agencies, served only a particular clientele, and did not operate under legislation that supported integration, without its being directed at a particular agency.

Horton, Carr, and Corcoran (1976) analyzed four local case studies in four states, focusing on programs that attempt services integration by expansion of a one-category funded program to include other services, target groups, areas, and facilities. These findings were generalizable only to this particular type of services integration project, unlike other studies that deal with a variety of integrating or coordinating methods.

The factors that facilitate services integration in these four projects were identified as the following: stable, adequate funding; a strong project director; community receptivity; administrative structure; staff; and long term planning capability. Funding was cited as the single most important determinant, although other factors such as the project director and staff members can minimize funding problems (Horton, Carr, and Corcoran, 1976).

Morris and Lescohier (1978) reviewed the research and history concerning services coordination and integration efforts in order to develop a theoretical perspective on local planning efforts and to suggest alternatives. These authors distinguish between integration and coordination. *Integration* is "that action which brings previously separated and independent functions and organizations (or personnel, or resources, or clientele) into a new, unitary structure," while *coordination* is "various efforts to alter or smooth the relationships of continuing, independent elements such as organizations, staffs, and resources'' (Morris and Lescohier, 1978). They gave particular emphasis to local efforts (e.g., the DHEW-funded projects such as the SITO projects and the later "Partnership Grants"); however, they pointed out the lack of hard data about outcomes in local efforts.

The viability of services integration and coordination was analyzed in terms of the goals of accessibility, continuity, fragmentation, efficiency and cost, and better care with the same funds. In general, the authors believed that inducements for integration or coordination resulted from a failure to deal directly with problems of social organization or social distress.

Five major conclusions were reached by Morris and Lescohier (1978):

1. Coordination should be that of a "delimited coordination" model. It should contain these components: reinforcement of a loose network through better information and referral, limited external control over a marginal amount of funds, utilization of these funds to fill service gaps and induce agencies to reduce rates of client rejection, and central capacity to identify and monitor service gaps and client rejections.

2. A "limited integration" model could be used to bring together under one administrative structure a number of public social services currently scattered in several large bureaucracies.

3. Problems such as access, continuity, and cost control are not easily dealt with by integration. Rather, upper level changes, such as those in service categorizations, appropriations, and allocations, or in public policy, are proposed.

4. Coordination efforts such as case management, information and referral, or co-location may not be very useful in reducing service gaps and client rejections. Yet, they may help to increase exchange among complex but loose subsystems of providers, especially to orchestrate response to those clients who have multiple problems or are confused about the pluralistic service system.

5. Only the limited approaches appear feasible to the authors at this time at all government levels, because any coordination or integration is carried out in a situation in which service providers try to maintain their own interests and priorities. In order to carry out fuller integration and coordination, changes in service subsystems' relationships must receive attention from the level of DHEW; these changes would then provide impact for local service delivery.

John (1977) analyzed the findings from 20 of the SITO projects, as well as giving a historical perspective on services integration. The analysis utilized the categories of services integration linkages cited above (Gans and Horton, 1975) as descriptive categories. Goals of services integration projects were also analyzed: accessibility, availability, a holistic approach to clients, responsiveness to clients, impact on costs, and accountability (John, 1977).

Findings in terms of the categories of services integration linkages were as follows. Fiscal linkages, e.g., pooled funds, at the state or local level are tried or implemented successfully in relatively few cases. Constraints include federal regulations, state law, institutional barriers, and lack of funds.

Personnel linkages were tested by co-location projects in 12 cases, with mixed results. Accessibility to clients and staff communication are sometimes increased, but "turf" questions (regarding autonomy of programs, budgets, and identities), confusion, and conflict between agencies are also sometimes increased. The personnel linkage of joint use of staff was not tested extensively.

Planning or programming linkages were tested in most (18 of 20) projects. A fair degree of success was reported in five projects, ineffectiveness or counterproductiveness in eight. Joint planning and joint programming seemed viable if authority existed to enforce participation by members. However, voluntary planning could sometimes also work, especially if the work was focusing on developing *new* services.

Administrative linkages were tested by nine projects in the form of client information systems, i.e., the use of multi-agency eligibility and intake forms. Both quality and volume of referrals can be improved when the forms are regularly completed, and information can be gathered regarding referrals, dropout rates, and unmet needs among agencies. However, in many cases, direct services workers resist using the forms.

Core services linkages to clients of many agencies were conducted by 15 projects in terms of case managers, case teams, transportation, or other services. Accessibility, responsiveness to clients, and informal agency relationships increased. Yet these services did not replace agency-specific core services, partly because of federal regulations and reporting requirements.

Case coordination linkages, such as case conferencing, case teams, or case management, were tried in 12 projects. Case conferences did not seem to be effective. Case teams and case management did lead to better accessibility, comprehensiveness, and volume of services, especially when the teams could exercise some authority over the expenditure of resources, such as purchase of services, and did not duplicate other agency efforts.

The author cited three major lessons from the study (John, 1977). First, building interagency linkages is a difficult process that demands great political skill and can be approached best on an incremental basis. Second, interagency linkages can improve service delivery but are unlikely to cut costs. Third, future research and demonstration (R&D) efforts in interagency collaboration should be designed more carefully in order to generate useful research data.

DESCRIPTION OF THE SETTING

The interagency collaboration project described here was begun in the fall of 1977, and funded through the summer of 1980 by a federal 3-year demonstration project grant under PL 94–142 (Education for All Handicapped Children

Act of 1975). The Massachusetts Department of Education is the state agency that administers this and four other such local grants. The local agencies that received the grants are all educational "collaboratives,"[1] and their mandate under the grants is to coordinate services to children and youth with special needs who are served under the Massachusetts special education law, Chapter 766 of the Acts of 1972 of the Massachusetts General Laws (the state counterpart and predecessor to PL 94-142).

For this grant, the North Shore Special Education Consortium was the collaborative group funded to bring together six additional local public agencies with the seven agencies forming an "Area Service Planning Team" (ASPT) as an interagency board that would then hire a staff person, in this case, a Project Director/Interagency Coordinator. The interagency collaboration was to be done through planning, not a direct service method, within the five-community "Danvers-Salem Area" (Danvers, Marblehead, Middleton, Peabody, and Salem).

The agencies that had a representative on the ASPT were those designated by state level mandate: the Department of Mental Health (Danvers-Salem Area Office); the Department of Public Welfare (Peabody District Office); the Department of Youth Services (Region IV Office); the Massachusetts Commission for the Blind (Central Office's regional division); the Massachusetts Rehabilitation Commission (Lynn Area Office); the Office for Children (Heritage Area Office); and the Division of Special Education of the Department of Education (North Shore Special Education Consortium, the collaborative). In February, 1979, a municipal representative joined the ASPT (Danvers Human Services/Public Health) in anticipation of a planned state mandate to expand the ASPTs to include municipal government representation.

The demonstration project is part of a statewide interagency collaboration planning effort known as "Area Strategy," modeled after other efforts nationally known as "services integration" (Mittenthal et al., 1974; Gans and Horton, 1975; John, 1977). The state Department of Education agreed to fund the five Area Strategy demonstration sites as a cooperative planning effort with the Executive Office of Human Services (EOHS), the state secretariat which coordinates the human service departments represented on the ASPT. The EOHS has funded four other demonstration sites as well. This cooperation between education and human services departments is somewhat unique, in that services integration efforts have often been human services efforts alone.

Major goals of the Area Strategy process were to decentralize decision making to local areas; to identify, on an interagency basis, area service gaps, priorities, and resources; and to coordinate agencies' planning and budgets to

---

[1]Chapter 40 of the Massachusetts General Laws was amended in 1974 to allow for the formation of collaboratives, which are organizations formed by the agreement of more than one school committee to conduct educational programs and services jointly, e.g., special education collaboratives (see Chapter 40, 1974, and Education Collaborative for Greater Boston, 1975).

address the service gaps on an interagency basis, while avoiding duplication of services. The 40 ASPTs are the major statewide mechanism for Area Strategy activities; they are based in the 40 coterminus geographic areas used by the Department of Mental Health and the Office for Children. Support is given from seven regional teams, the state human services departments, the Executive Office of Human Services, and the state Special Projects Office of the Division of Special Education of the Department of Education.

Although the ASPT was mandated to meet the above goals of Area Strategy which relate to *all* clients, it also has had to work toward goals *specific to* children and youth with special needs under its federally funded demonstration grant. These latter goals were:

1. Increase area schools' referrals to, and the accessibility of, human services programs and services available for students and families, especially for those served under Chapter 766/PL 94-142.
2. Document area service gaps in human services agencies for children and youth, especially for those children and youth served under Chapter 766/PL 94-142.
3. Identify, document, and analyze interagency policy issues relevant to the implementation of Chapter 766, and make recommendations for remedying these.

These goals were arrived at after lengthy ASPT discussion, leading to group consensus as to the nature of interagency coordination the ASPT wished to pursue.

To integrate the Area Strategy goals and activities with those of the demonstration project, the former were conceptualized as separate from, but useful to, the latter. The Area Strategy state-mandated activities that the ASPT has found useful to the demonstration project are information sharing, interagency needs and service gap assessment, interagency needs prioritization, and the obtaining of citizen input through two public hearings on unmet area needs.

The major objectives accomplished or in process by the fall of 1979 regarding the demonstration project goals follow. The ASPT has participated in interagency planning and development of grant applications dealing with services and programs for children and youth with special needs. It has been involved with an interagency effort to identify, document, and disseminate information about successful methods of recruiting Portuguese and Spanish bilingual/bicultural staff to human services and educational agencies in the area. The ASPT has also compiled and disseminated a *Resource Directory* dealing with ASPT agencies and the Social Security Administration (Danvers-Salem Area Service Planning Team, 1978, 1979a). Finally, the ASPT had conducted in-service training workshops for special education and other staff regarding the use of the ASPT agencies and the Social Security Administration for assisting children and families.

Participation in interagency development of grant applications has been done with varying success and levels of involvement in the actual grant application and proposed services delivery. Factors that influenced this involvement included assessments of the needs of the target population, of the willingness or ability of local agencies to collaborate, and of the receptiveness of the potential funding agency or agencies. The levels, from least to most ASPT (interagency) involvement, were the following:

1. Provision of a letter of support to an individual ASPT agency applicant, if the grant related to ASPT interagency service priorities, based upon identified service gaps.
2. Active ASPT representation on an area-wide task force that was given the authority to determine at least a portion of the substance of the children's component of a grant application.
3. ASPT application for new-money funding of an interagency project, with the ASPT as the governing board and one ASPT agency as the single fiscal agent for the grant.
4. Provision of a forum for discussion, planning, and decision making about the exact components of a grant application that is to have an interagency focus, including ASPT agency cost-sharing via reallocation of area funds and "in-kind" services.

It was not generally feasible that cost sharing could occur. Yet, the other forms of interagency collaboration proved useful to area needs regarding services for children and youth.

The effort to identify methods of recruiting bilingual/bicultural staff was done by an ad hoc, local interagency "Multi-Cultural Services Committee," to which the ASPT had representation. The committee's effort took the form of fact finding regarding location of all bilingual/bicultural staff in the area and the successful method used for recruitment of these staff, for the purpose of educating other agencies about recruitment.

Agencies donated "in-kind" services to the effort, e.g., staff time, clerical support, mailings, and supplies. Since the ASPT had recognized bilingual/bicultural services as a pressing need of high priority within all child and youth agencies, it provided substantial support to this interagency effort from inception to completion.

The methodology used by the Multi-Cultural Services Committee was as follows. A research question was posed: "What are successful methods of recruiting bilingual/bicultural staff to area agencies?" Nineteen "successful" agencies were identified. Committee members then administered a structured questionnaire interview to representatives who knew about the recruitment procedures utilized. Data were analyzed, a report written, and a committee-sponsored interagency meeting was held to present, discuss, and disseminate the report. It was hoped that the report would serve as a building block for further interagency cooperation in meeting the needs of a multi-cultural community.

The compilation of the ASPT *Resource Directory* was a direct, interagency response to a stated need of the special education departments in the local schools to develop better access to human service agencies for students served by Chapter 766/PL 94–142. This project resulted in free distribution of hundreds of directories to schools, human services agencies, municipal agencies, and consumers; the first edition was updated after 8 months.

Both editions covered all ASPT agencies and the Social Security Administration, the latter to increase utilization of federal Supplemental Security Income (SSI) payments to children and youth with special needs. Topics covered for each agency were eligibility of Chapter 766 students for services, ages served, bilingual services available, programs and services available, basic referral procedure, and contact people.

Usefulness of the *Resource Directory* was evaluated by means of an anonymous questionnaire sent by the ASPT with the second edition of the directory. In general, it was learned that users considered it helpful for increasing knowledge of and access to agencies (Danvers-Salem Area Service Planning Team, 1979c). The evaluation did not touch upon cost savings for schools, since the goal of the directory was not to manipulate costs but rather to increase access to the most beneficial combination of interagency resources available for the student (or client).

After development of the *Resource Directory,* an in-service training workshop on utilization of human service and educational agencies was a natural next step to facilitate further access to agencies for students and families. Although the *Resource Directory* was useful in and of itself, it also served as a comprehensive hand-out material at workshops, for future reference about the resources described. Furthermore, the ASPT believed the directory would be better used if it was personally provided to potential users by representatives for the agencies covered in the directory, than if it was distributed through the mail.

Workshops were conducted for groups of school special education and guidance staff, special education collaborative staff, adult education staff, and municipal agency staff (e.g., librarians and visiting nurses). These persons attended the sessions by choice, after reviewing a written summary of the training content and goals, or meeting with ASPT staff.

The focus of the training was similar to that in the *Resource Directory,* but with additional detail, emphasis on agencies' overall philosophies and goals, and a question and answer session. The workshops were conducted by the ASPT's individual agency representatives, except for the section on the Social Security Administration, which was presented by the state Office for Children, the local Social Security Administration, and the state Department of Public Health. A local Elder Affairs agency representative also spoke at the workshop held for municipal agencies, since several staff members who were working with older adults attended that particular workshop.

Preliminary questionnaire evaluations filled out anonymously by participants at just two workshops indicated the training was considered very beneficial in gaining knowledge, personal contacts, and potential access to agencies (Danvers-Salem Area Service Planning Team, 1979b). Again, the cost-savings aspect was not researched, and could not even have been determined at the time of the workshops per se.

ISSUES IN THE PLANNING SETTING

Various issues have arisen in the Danvers-Salem Area Service Planning Team's experience that have influenced the attainment of interagency collaboration of services for children and youth with special needs, and coordination for other clientele. They arose from a variety of sources and, at the least, had to be recognized as constraints or catalysts to the ASPT's work, and thereby as components of the parameters of the planning process.

1. *The ASPT representatives have limited time in their already busy schedules, and the interagency collaboration mandate is superimposed on their schedules.* Although ASPT members are conscientious in their interagency work, time imposes a very real constraint on their participation. Agency-specific responsibilities may sometimes take precedence over interagency work, or state-mandated ASPT tasks may take precedence over tasks seen by the ASPT itself as more important.

These time constraints can assist the group to focus and work hard in a limited time period, but, to some extent, they also limit the *scope* of the *tasks* that can be accomplished. In addition, much time is taken up—appropriately and necessarily—in an interagency group with information sharing and group decision making about action to be taken, as well as by the more "concrete" tasks such as in-service training workshops or proposal development.

2. *The ASPT representatives perform different roles within their agencies.* They are directors of local agencies, regional clinical or administrative supervisors, and community organizers. Their outlooks on interagency collaboration differ not only as a result of their agency and client/student allegiances, but also because of their varied day-to-day insights, their diverse areas of expertise, and their separate vantage points regarding client/student needs.

This results in different interests and expectations about the value in working on specific issues. For example, a director of an agency may at times emphasize fiscal benefits, while a direct service worker may simultaneously focus upon individual student/client benefits. Sometimes the differing viewpoints result in irreconcilable differences. At other times, they provide a learning experience for all concerned, and represent two facets of a common concern.

(3) *Group membership changes.* Change in membership has occurred because of job mobility of members and, in one case, illness. This is conducive to upheaval within the group because the group loses a liked and respected member and also because there may be an interval during which an agency is unrepresented while the ASPT awaits the appointment of a new member. However, the process is virtually inevitable, and the new member can bring insights and skills to the group that may add a unique perspective to problem solving.

(4) *The interagency negotiating and planning process is a lengthy one, if the group wishes to operate upon a consensus, rather than an authoritarian, model at the local level.* At times, the reaching of consensus becomes tedious, and it seems as if objectives are taking second place to "working through" group procedural issues. Yet, the very process of agencies' representatives discussing issues can be a useful way of establishing better interagency working relationships and learning about other agencies.

Furthermore, if a consensus model is *not* used within a group that voluntarily chooses its objectives and tasks, coordinating efforts in which all or most agencies have an interest will not be accomplished. Only when consensus has been reached in the ASPT has work on a task moved forward, because work on a task without consensus would only result in the loss of participation of certain agencies.

(5) *The fiscal "clout" of the ASPT as a group lies in state level "respect" for its recommendations, not in full control over funds that can be earmarked for direct services to clients/students.* The federal demonstration project funding operates on a 3-year decreasing basis, with only two permanent staff positions (Project Director and Secretary), and funds are allocated for planning, not direct services. There is no flexible agency money that can be utilized for a pooling of funds, unless a request is granted through the regular agency budget procedures; there is no guarantee that this allocation will occur.

What *is* possible in terms of influencing funding is that the ASPT, as a regular, mandated, statewide planning group, is seen by state administrators as representative of the combined wisdom of more than one area administrator, with a broad knowledge of area needs. ASPT endorsement of a proposal then represents a marginal, although not necessarily strong, inducement to fund the plan through the regular agency budget procedure.

(6) *The ASPT agencies lack uniform philosophical, administrative, and fiscal structures, so planning within the agencies is done differently.* Budget cycles, services categories, amount of decentralization, geographic boundaries, client target groups, federal funding sources, and state and federal legislative mandates all vary. Therefore, the ASPT members attempt local collaboration under constraints upon collaboration that can only be remedied by state or federal authority. Generally, these have not been remedied.

From the outset, even in order to arrive at consensus on an issue, or to maintain group interest in it, the issue must survive the test of being pertinent to at least a majority of eight diverse agencies' representatives (and usually *all* representatives), and it must not infringe upon agencies' "turfs." It also must meet or not hinder the mandate of the federal demonstration grant, i.e., to target children and youth with special needs.

Issues being focused upon by the ASPT, such as in-service training, development of new funding sources, the documenting of service gaps, and information sharing, partially reflect the fact that the local area has too many constraints upon it to engage in activities such as extensive funds pooling, co-location, or an interagency case management system. Yet, keeping in mind the reality that the ASPT's work cannot go so far as to revamp local agencies' total budgets or structures, it can still coordinate certain more limited activities.

⑦ *The state level Area Strategy process, which has authority over some aspects of the ASPT process, is itself operating on an "experimental" level, like the ASPT.* As a result, the state mandates have changed, at times in response to area needs regarding the interagency collaboration process. This can be progressive and confusing at the same time, especially if directives, issued and defended in the face of ASPT opposition, are then later changed. Even if a change is useful, the earlier failure to admit the experimental nature of the previous directives is not conducive to ASPT seriousness about directives.

Interagency agreements at the state level that would allow for local cost sharing are not, with very few exceptions, in place. Feedback from the ASPTs has been encouraged as to interagency collaboration steps the state should take, and responded to by some state agencies, but the state's process of interagency collaboration is a slow one as well. (Undoubtedly, federal constraints on certain types of coordination hamper state level attempts at interagency collaboration.)

As an experimental process, changes in state administration can result in changes in the acceptance of the whole Area Strategy process, or its nature. The ASPTs at the time of this writing are awaiting directives as to their overall mandates from a new state administration, which results in leeway in the ASPTs' work due to a lack of state-mandated tasks, but also a confusion as to the philosophical and fiscal support from the state level for the continuation of the process.

RECOMMENDATIONS AND CONCLUSIONS

Recommendations and conclusions that may prove useful to planners in similar settings are presented below with respect to each of the seven above-described planning issues.

1. Regarding limited time in schedules, *when interagency collaboration*

is mandated or voluntarily entered into, it should be legitimized as a regular administrative function, and recognized as time consuming. The staff involved in the interagency collaboration should not be expected to carry out the project as a low priority "add on" to their schedules. If it is seriously assigned or entered into, then it should be conceptualized as part and parcel of the agency's administrative functions and costs, and as relevant to the agency's goals for its students/clients. Assigning it high priority on paper, yet making it a difficult activity on which to spend time, results in a constraint on the effort at its inception.

2. Regarding representatives' different agency roles, *the representatives on an interagency team, and their staff, should recognize and accept both the need for clarification of and openness to different viewpoints, and the possibility of irreconcilable differences between representatives.* Members will each be committed to their own specific clients/students, professional methods, and goals, and these should be respected and learned from by other members and staff. In fact, this understanding of other agencies is one of the desired outcomes of interagency collaboration.

In many instances, a common ground between agencies can be found by focusing on the students'/clients' benefit. However, it is also important to realize that there may be truly irreconcilable differences, and, when they occur, the process should eventually move on to a topic on which agreement about action can be reached. In that way, the points of agreement and group strength, rather than those of disagreement or weakness, can be utilized to build interagency linkages.

3. Regarding changes in group membership, *the interagency group must be accepted as a changing organization of people, just as a single agency has changes in personnel.* Although continuity of individuals does, no doubt, enhance the group's learning to work with each other, the interagency group must at some level be seen as consisting of representatives of agencies that remain involved even if individual members change.

Naturally, continuity and stability of membership should be stressed. However, certain procedures will help to minimize disruption of progress toward goals, regardless of the reason for the disruption. These include by-laws, regular meeting times, written agendas and minutes, and votes. New members should be briefed regarding the issues facing the group.

4. Regarding the choice of decision-making model, *the consensus model allows for respect for differing viewpoints and participation by all members.* It is acknowledged here that reaching a consensus may be time consuming, and still not result in each representative being pleased with the outcome or having had equal input into the decision. Yet, it does encourage a process of voluntary problem solving among agencies that are separate bureaucratic structures, with none having authority over the others.

In the Danvers-Salem ASPT, votes are taken that result in group accountability to uphold decisions, and closure on a topic. However, these are basically a formalization of a consensus already reached through discussion, and are not generally suggested until they will prove unanimous. The implicit understanding is that consensus, not conflict, is the operational mode of final decision making. This is not to say that disagreements do not occur, but rather that the group usually chooses to vote to work on those tasks on which there is consensus. Although controversial, and possibly innovative, actions are thereby avoided, certain actions mutually useful to the independent agencies involved are still accomplished.

5. Regarding a failure to have an ASPT control over funds, *it is extremely difficult or impossible to accomplish some types of interagency collaboration or linkages without the authority to affect funding on an interagency basis.* Unless some funds are mandated to be "pooled" with other agencies, or are flexible in their use, it will be a natural tendency with finite resources to fund agency-specific or continuation projects. The seriousness of the interagency collaboration mandate will be partially apparent in the commitment to interagency cost sharing, at the level of state government that makes funding decisions.

One feature of control over funds that can be of some limited use to an interagency effort is the provision of a staffing grant to an interagency group. This is an added expense to the collaboration effort, and as such may not be cost effective. However, it is a source of interagency planning funds and speaks to the problem of agency administrators' time constraints. It also represents a state level commitment to facilitation of collaboration.

6. Regarding differences in agencies' structures, *it is extremely difficult, if not impossible, to accomplish some types of interagency collaboration or linkages, because federal and state level structures and mandates put constraints on local planning.* The local interagency group must become knowledgeable about these constraints under which it attempts collaboration. Then the group can choose to work within them or try to have them changed. Change is more likely to occur if an aggregate of several areas and agencies reflects the same demands to the appropriate policy makers. Ideally, of course, the state or federal governments should seek out such feedback and respond to it.

In reality, many legislative mandates need to be coordinated at the state and federal levels in order to accomplish truly comprehensive interagency collaboration at the local level. For example, PL 94-142 and Chapter 766 make comparatively clear statements regarding the responsibilities of public schools toward students with special needs. Human services agencies' state and federal legislative and administrative mandates need to be coordinated with those of the schools. At this time, local administrators do not have clear guidelines to establish responsibility for "non-educational" services for students, for post-school-age services, or for cost sharing.

7. Regarding the experimental nature of the state level Area Strategy

process, *local interagency collaboration efforts often operate without specific state level expectations for them, and so are relatively free to try the coordinating method of their choice*. Despite any statement of goals or mandated tasks regarding interagency collaboration by the state level of government, the specific methods are generally left up to the local group. This happens by necessity, in that the "state of the art" of interagency collaboration or services integration is a relatively new one, with no best proven method to follow.

This does leave the local group in the position of having to react to changing mandates as the state experiment develops, as well as sometimes having little guidance at all. However, this also provides the local group with the opportunity for innovation and experimentation in planning or direct service delivery, as well as for research into the strengths and weaknesses of methods, or even the feasibility of the whole process.

SUMMARY

This chapter has used one local interagency planning effort under PL 94–142 to derive information that may be useful for planners in similar settings. A few selections from the literature on interagency collaboration or services integration were reviewed. The planning effort of the Danvers-Salem Area Service Planning Team, part of a statewide Massachusetts effort, was described. Issues were delineated from this setting regarding the local interagency group itself and the environment in which it functions. Recommendations and conclusions were presented which considered both constraining and facilitating factors in the local interagency collaboration process.

REFERENCES

Danvers-Salem Area Service Planning Team. 1978 (December) and 1979a (July). *Resource Directory*. Danvers-Salem Area Service Planning Team, Salem, MA.

Danvers-Salem Area Service Planning Team. 1979b (July). Evaluation of two in-service training workshops on utilization of human service and educational agencies. Danvers-Salem Area Service Planning Team, Salem, MA.

Danvers-Salem Area Service Planning Team. 1979c (August). Evaluation of the *Resource Directory*. Danvers-Salem Area Service Planning Team, Salem, MA.

Education Collaborative for Greater Boston. 1975 (April). *Approaches to Collaboration: A Handbook of Strategies for Serving Special Needs Children*. Education Collaborative for Greater Boston, Boston.

John, D. 1977. *Managing the Human Service "System": What Have We Learned from Services Integration?* Project Share Human Services Monograph Series, No. 4, Rockville, MD.

Gans, S. P., and Horton, G. T. 1975. *Integration of Human Services: The State and Municipal Levels*. Praeger Publishers, New York.

Horton, G. T., Carr, V. M. E., and Corcoran, G. J. 1976 (November). *Illustrating Services Integration from Categorical Bases,* Project Share Human Services Monograph Series, No. 3, Rockville, MD.

Mittenthal, S. D., Clippinger, J., Gotzman, H.-J., and Dixon, R. T. 1974 (April). *Twenty-Two Allied Services (SITO) Projects Described as Human Service Systems.* The Human Ecology Institute, Wellesley, MA. (Revised May, 1974).

Morris, R., and Lescohier, I. H. 1978. Service Integration: Real Versus Illusory Solutions to Welfare Dilemmas. In: R.C. Sarri and Y. Hasenfeld (eds.), *The Management of Human Services,* pp. 21–50. Columbia University Press, New York.

Section III
EFFECTING INTERAGENCY COLLABORATION

Chapter 8

Essential Components in Development of Interagency Collaboration

Jerry O. Elder

As illustrated by the examples delineated in Section II, there is no one best model for developing interagency collaboration in a community. Case study findings by Gans and Horton (1975) also reveal there is no one best model for services integration. The experience of Humm-Delgado (Chapter 7) leaves the specific methods of developing interagency collaboration up to a local group. Because the political, economic, and other environmental factors vary so much from community to community, there is no set road map for developing interagency collaboration. There are, however, essential components that need to be considered when a community is desirous of establishing an interagency collaborative effort to coordinate services for handicapped children. This chapter describes these components or factors that should be taken into consideration by agency personnel at both the state and local level when developing community interagency collaboration.

PROPERTIES OF INTERAGENCY BEHAVIOR

There are a number of critical and central properties that either directly characterize or may be inferred from interagency behavior. Steingraph (1977) lists these properties as: 1) power, 2) conflict, 3) cooperation, and 4) economic utility. Such properties should be viewed as complementary to other elements and are critical enough to describe separately.

Power

The essential perspectives on organizations as comprising systems of relationships is best described by Crozier (1964):

No system of organization can be constructed without power relationships, and all organizations are built around power relationships which afford the necessary link between the desired objectives and human means which are indispensable toward their realization.

The organization of power relationships, or the means of controlling human resources, condition the ability of the whole to cooperate and to develop. By studying it we can understand better the phenomenon of integration as an organizational entity.

Power relationships cannot easily be measured. To get an indirect, but fairly clear picture, we can analyze attitudes, feelings, and behavior of members of various groups comprising the organization. These attitudes and behavior reflect on the different roles that have developed within the organization considered as a social system. But behind these roles lie the components of power inherent in every organized relationship. The actors, therefore, cannot help expressing indirectly at least, their feelings about their position in this context, and one can use these expressions as indicators of the power setup. Their explanations and rationalizations are also signals pointing to the problems around which the power relationships crystallize (p. 87).

Steingraph (1977) views interorganizational power arrangements in two major ways: 1) as the in-fighting among actors from different organizations regarding such issues as status, prestige, and control of both resources and decision making, and 2) as the power that an interorganization might achieve through its collective influence relative to still other sets of organizational actors in the larger society.

Conflict

If power is considered a process of defining control and access to resources, then conflict inevitably emerges as a necessary dynamic property and corollary to power. Barth (1963) identified a set of conditions generating pressures toward interagency conflict in human services: 1) the existence of several relatively autonomous agencies working in the same general sphere, 2) the organization of the agencies on a bureaucratic basis, 3) the differentiation of such agencies on the basis of philosophy and goals as well as on the basis of the special skills of agency personnel, and 4) interagency competition for both financial and public support. It should be kept in mind that the presence of this set of conditions in negotiating interagency collaborative arrangements for handicapped children would be more prevalent in a large urban setting than in small rural communities. Therefore, the presence of conflict should be less of a factor in negotiating interagency working relationships at the local community level.

Cooperation

This property means that actors in interagency collaboration are willing to work together for mutual benefit of the handicapped child. Since all agencies involved should have a common goal toward this end, the level of cooperation in developing interagency working relationships would be quite high.

Economic Utility

This final property refers to the calculation of costs and benefits by individuals and organizations relative to interagency working relationships. Cost-benefit analysis in the area of interagency collaboration is difficult to determine because the immediate results are not readily evident. The initial costs of establishing interagency working relationships are high both in time consumed by staff from various agencies and in the turmoil created within agencies by the factor of change in the way services are provided in a different manner.

In order to overcome the initial resistance to the cost of establishing interagency efforts, Kazuk (Chapter 5) used a matrix of community resources and services to show where duplications and gaps in services existed prior to collaboration. The expense of funding a facilitator or staff in the initial stages of establishing an interagency effort, as mentioned by Humm-Delgado (Chapter 7), may not be cost effective. However, in the long run, the creation of the interagency efforts should prove to be cost effective because of the cost avoidance that will be enjoyed in future years as duplicative services are eliminated and coordination efforts are facilitated by staff through interagency negotiations. A more thorough discussion of cost-benefit analysis is considered later in this chapter.

COMMUNITY CRITERIA

The experience of the Canadian government in developing their COMSERV Projects for the mentally retarded population indicates there are 12 criteria that are essential in any community in order to generate a successful interagency effort (Neufeldt, 1979). The 12 criteria used for the selection of COMSERV Project sites are:

1. Suitable service region (within 1 hour's driving distance to service)
2. Establishment of a plan for a wide range of services
3. Community receptivity
4. Strong consumer organization
5. Presence of activists and change agents
6. Strong collective leadership
7. Strong project direction
8. Provincial (state) government support and good prospects for local fund matching and continuance
9. Commitment to demonstration role
10. Willingness to accept consultation

11. Wide applicability of the demonstration
12. Specific applied research mission

The presence of these 12 criteria does not guarantee a successful interagency effort in any community. However, if a majority of these criteria are present in a community, the chances of an interagency effort succeeding are increased dramatically.

ELEMENTS REQUIRING COORDINATION

Basic Elements

The two basic elements requiring coordination in human resource service delivery systems are *clients* and *resources*. The concept of how these elements are coordinated among agencies has been termed *organizational exchange* by Levine and White (1961). They use the concept of exchange as a basis for understanding the impetus for the movement of resources among health agencies. It was also used to explain relationships among community health and welfare agencies by viewing them as being involved in an exchange system. Organizational exchange is defined as any voluntary activity between two organizations that has consequences, actual or anticipated, for the realization of their respective goals or objectives. These same authors further break down the element of resources into labor services and resources other than labor services. Theoretically, if these two elements along with clients were all of the essential elements required and were in infinite supply, there would be little need for organizational interaction or subscription to interagency collaboration. Under the conditions of scarcity, however, interagency collaboration or interorganizational exchanges are essential to goal attainment.

Aiken et al. (1975) contend that, in addition to clients and resources, there are two other elements that require coordination in human resource service delivery systems: *information* and *programs*. They point out that information about clients and the programs of the various agencies, along with clients and resources, needs to be coordinated in a different way. They propose a structure based upon their examination of five research and demonstration projects, whose purpose was to bring about coordination of services for the mentally retarded in five different metropolitan areas. This structure, which they caution will only work in an urban setting, contains three key elements: 1) a unit to do case coordination, 2) a coalition of organizations, and 3) a community board. With the exception of Direction Service described by Zeller (Chapter 4), which is a unit of case coordination itself, none of the examples of local interagency collaboration described in Section II utilizes a separate case coordination unit. This function is one that seems to be shared among the various agency staff members involved in the interagency collaboration network in each of the three other examples. The second element, coalition of organizations is definitely present in all of the interagency collaboration networks described in this book. Although the last element of a community board is not always present in a formalized fashion, the functions performed by this element are present in each of the examples. In the Colorado model, a formalized community council serves as a decision-making body which acts as a steering committee for the project. The Kansas experience utilizes preschool interagency teams to fulfill this function. In Massachusetts, the Area Service Planning Team (ASPT) serves as an interagency board to approve policies for coordination of services for handicapped children.

Coordination of Individualized Education Programs

The one single element that is key to providing coordinated services for school-aged handicapped children is the individualized education program (IEP) process. The experience of Direction Service (Zeller, Chapter 4) shows that the IEP process in schools cannot be treated separately. Since the IEP is a critical piece of client information, this is one of the elements that needs to be coordinated. At the same time, the process of developing and following an IEP is an important coordination element in and of itself. It is crucial that agencies' staffs work together both to plan for the IEP and to ensure that the provisions in it are carried out in a coordinated fashion.

Confidentiality

An aspect that needs to be wrestled with in establishing working relationships among agencies is the handling of confidentiality of client information. As Kazuk (Chapter 5) points out, agencies in the Colorado experience were reluctant to provide information to other agencies even with a release form signed by the parents. An element of trust and respect, described by Hall (Chapter 3), for each other's work needs to be developed to facilitate exchange of client data. If agency staffs can get together to increase their awareness level about each other and work out a joint release form, many of these problems can be overcome. If a community is organized under one unified voice as it speaks to release of information, the question of confidentiality and release of such data will not be such a concern.

Needs

As Mulvenon (Chapter 6) notes, the process of establishing a community interagency effort accelerated when there were recognized needs or problems within that community. If agencies within the community do not recognize these needs, then it may be necessary to increase the public's awareness of such problems through community meetings or special interest groups. The use of a "workbook" as described by Kazuk, Greene, and Magrab (1979) in *Planning for Services to Handicapped Persons* is one method that can be used to determine community needs.

Duplication

Zeller (Chapter 4) points out that many service agencies duplicate efforts in the areas of intake, assessing needs, determining eligibility, finding clients, and so on. The existence of interagency collaborative efforts can eliminte much of this duplication of effort and make the administration of these functions more efficient.

LEVELS OF COORDINATION

It is important to recognize the existence of different levels of coordination. Baumheimer (1979) describes three types of interagency linkage mechanisms.

> *Policy management* linkages are those goal-oriented interactions between two or more agencies or units that support identification of needs, selection of options in selecting a particular course of action, and making allocative choices on a jurisdication-wide or cross-agency level. As such these linkages are those designed to help general purpose government develop more coherent policies that look at broader concerns than those of individual agencies.
> *Administrative* linkages are those goal-oriented interactions between two or more agencies that are designed to facilitate the organizational, administrative, or management dimensions of agency relationships. These linkages are designed to facilitate goals of policy management by providing facilitative administrative arrangements that can support such policy aims.
> *Service delivery or case management* linkages are those interactions between agencies that serve better individual client case coordination, such as case conferences, case teams, case management, and case consultation.

Most of the interagency linkages that are established at the community level will be of the administrative or case management types. Policy management linkages are most likely to be decided at the state level, although there may be some policy management linkages at the community level if agreements are entered into between two locally controlled autonomous agencies.

Of the three levels of coordination described above, the most attractive and easiest to implement is the services delivery or case management mechanism. Individual case management, however, is misleading in nature because agency staff can be lured into a false sense that once they are able to establish this level of coordination, that is all they really have to do. Nothing could be further from the truth. Unless individual case management is also coordinated across agency boundaries through interagency collaboration, there is bound to be duplicative effort and a resulting waste in human resources. There is need for further research and study to improve the technology needed in case management. A thorough discussion of this approach is found in Zeller's chapter on Direction Service (Chapter 4).

QUALITY OF WORK COORDINATION

Another approach to looking at different levels or types of coordination is one developed by Benson et al. (1973). They developed three elements that are used to define the quality of work coordination among agencies.

Agency Interaction

The first of these elements is the extent of agency interaction that can be assessed by using a variety of indicators such as referrals, providing information about services, sharing clients' files, collaborating in the formulation of programs, and joint planning of services to specific clients. The adequacy of these services to clients should in general relate positively to the frequency and breadth of such interactions. There could possibly be some outer limit beyond which interactions become so extensive that they inhibit the delivery of services. However, it is seldom that such a limit would be approached.

Program Articulation

The second element is program articulation, which relates to the extent agencies coordinate programs with each other. It can be measured by: 1) analyzing the effective division of labor between agencies, 2) the way in which several programs are interconnected, and, 3) the way in which competitive features between programs are minimized. Program articulation would be important in reducing the number of problems destructive to a client's interest. Examples of poor articulation include poorly conceived referrals based on inaccurate understanding of programs in other agencies; the provision by two or more agencies of contradictory, incompatible services to the same client; the provision of services as discrete items unrelated to services provided by other agencies; and the overtaxing of the client's time and determination by making him/her the principal link between agencies, that is, by placing the burden of coordination upon the client or the family.

Flexibility Relationships

The final element used by Benson to describe the quality of work coordination among agencies is flexibility relationships. This refers to the extent to which agencies are free from formal rules or guidelines that inhibit the services to eligible clients. Interaction among the agencies is more adaptable and flexible when it is dependent on the judgment of personnel rather than dictated by complex sets of rules. Flexibility can be lost by extensive formalization of agency relationships. Some agreements developed by agencies to facilitate their relationships may become unworkable from a client's standpoint because of their rigidity. This is particularly true when interactions between agencies are narrowly prescribed in a written format that is elaborately spelled out to the minute detail. This brings about relationships that may be carried out mechanically with little opportunity for the exercise of rational judgment by the agency staff worker. Personnel may end up going through the motions of collaboration and of fulfilling the rules and lose sight of the client and his/her unique problems in this process. Such an approach should be guarded against in all interagency dealings.

ESSENTIAL CHARACTERISTICS

Target Population

The chances of succeeding in interagency collaboration are improved greatly if the effort can be focused on a small age group such as the early childhood population in the Colorado and Kansas experiences (Chapters 5 and 6), and if it can be limited to a specific community or small geographic area. Obviously, the fewer the number of agencies involved in an interagency collaborative effort and the fewer the number of clients to be served, the more likely effective lines of communication and working relationships can be established that will lead to effective interagency linkages. Gilbert and Specht (1977) conducted a study which showed that interagency coordination projects in which less than a dozen agencies were involved are more likely to achieve positive results than those in which a larger number of agencies take part. They found the number of agencies participating in the program is related negatively to the success of coordination. One can imply from this that unless collaboration attempts in large urban areas are broken down into efforts by smaller subgroups, the initiators' chances for success are severely jeopardized.

Client characteristics can play an extremely important role in the organization of any interagency collaboration effort. For example, the lines of communication in agencies that need to be involved for services to preschool handicapped children would be entirely different from those that are needed to assist adolescent, disruptive, or emotionally disturbed populations.

Family

Another key element that needs to be considered in interagency collaboration is the cultural, social, and educational differences of families. The cultural and social environment of a community plays a central role in how problems of the handicapped child are handled. The differences between rural and urban areas in the way families are organized as a unit are great enough to make a program that works well in a rural setting impracticable in an urban setting and vice versa. Rural residents do not have the advantage of anonymity that urban residents do, and, therefore, pride often prevents them from seeking the services they need. Fear and social pressure will often inhibit families from seeking assistance for their handicapped child because they may be ashamed to have friends and neighbors recognize the existence of a "cripple" as a member of their family.

Urban and Rural Characteristics

There are obvious problems of communication and transportation in the rural areas that are rarely encountered in urban areas. Telephone service is sometimes a luxury for a remote rural area, and public transportation is usually lacking. The distances are great and the availability of a car is often unpredictable. Professionals who operate at the tertiary level need to recognize these differences and be made aware of them so that when they prescribe treatment or services they are not inappropriate with respect to the location of the child's residence. Resources in rural areas to meet the needs of handicapped individuals are sparse. Traditionally, human services in rural areas have been delivered by friends or neighbors. There is, moreover, a large concentration of elderly people in more distant places. As a consequence of these factors, frustration is often experienced when human services personnel receive requests for assistance that they cannot provide, either because of the lack of training or because of the lack of facilities in rural communities.

Characteristics of Delivery System

The characteristics of the delivery system and the professionals who work in it also play an important role in the organization of interagency collaboration. Each of the major service delivery systems has its own model of service delivery, and years of tradition and experience, based upon this model, have to be dealt with when crossing over into other service delivery models.

The relationship between the educational and medical models in providing services to handicapped children is one example of this potential for differences in approaches and opinions when interagency collaboration is undertaken. Each of the service delivery systems was developed independently in response to needs within its areas of specialty over the past decades. Professionals in the education field consider their education model, which concentrates on the educational and behavioral aspects of the handicapped individual, the most appropriate mechanism for providing services to the handicapped. At the same time, those in the health field argue that their medical model, which concentrates on the health problems of the handicapped individual and the physician's role in meeting those needs, is the most appropriate service delivery model. It must be recognized that each of these service delivery systems has a place and role in providing services to the handicapped child and that the models can work together harmoniously. For example, in the early childhood years of a physically handicapped individual, the medical model of service delivery might be the most appropriate service delivery mechanism since the child is not normally in contact with the schools. Once the child reaches school age, the educational model may well be more appropriate.

The key factor is to allow the professionals and administrators who are involved in delivering services to children in their community to decide which approach is more appropriate for service delivery in that particular community. What is decided in one community may be entirely different from that decided and acceptable in another, and these differences should not be discouraged. As Hage (1975) states, a joint program, as a definition for interdependence, makes an implicit technological assumption—that the production process requires joint efforts or teams that transcend organizational boundaries. This seems plausible whenever a client, such as the handicapped child, has a multitude of problems. Crossing over and combining service delivery models should be encouraged in developing interagency collaborative arrangements.

Uninformed or misinformed professionals in a local community, especially professionals in private practice, are often roadblocks to effective interagency collaboration. The physician in private practice who is not aware of the latest treatment programs available for various types of handicapping conditions may misinform the parents of their child's potential for habilitation. Physicians in private practice are also less willing to accept the input of other professionals in the areas of special education, social work, psychology, and so on. This is not so much the case for physicians who have recently completed their medical school training program, especially those who have gone through interdisciplinary training as part of a University Affiliated Facility (UAF) training program for the developmentally disabled. Most professionals in private practice in smaller communities have neither the time nor the interest to stay informed of the latest advances in caring for handicapped children. Many are also uninformed of the complexities of the delivery system required to provide services for these children. The primary care physician, such as the pediatrician or general practitioner, and other private practicing professionals in a community who provide services to handicapped children need to be involved as an integral part of the interagency collaborative network if it is to be a successful system.

COALITION OF ORGANIZATIONS

In developing interagency collaboration, there arises a need for a group of organizations to work together toward the common benefit of the client, in this case, the handicapped child. The organizations involved in such a coalition must give up some of their autonomy in order for this to be accomplished. Hage (1975) concludes that when one strikes a balance between organizational needs for autonomy and coordination needs for the solution of complex problems, then the proposal that a coalition of organizations arranged in some service delivery system tends to make sense. Organizations lose some autonomy but greatly enhance their power to obtain resources from their environment.

Based upon the experience of five urban network strategies, Hage (1975) recommends an optimal strategy for a coalition of organizations with joint programs and central record-keeping for the delivery of services to clients who have multiple problems and must receive services across discipline lines within an organization as opposed to the awarding of funds to a single organization to meet these needs. As long as the funds go to more than one organization, agency fear of losing autonomy, a strong potential inhibitor of collaborative efforts, can be reduced. He also points out that a single organization, whether old or new, does not have a big enough power base to gain sufficient resources from the community. Organizations for specific clients have never done well because they cannot mobilize enough power to overcome the elite segment of the community and their arguments for efficiency. Therefore, specialized organizations tend to become dominated by elite values and invariably move toward rigid, bureaucratic control in a concern for efficiency. Any single organization cannot be very successful in a fight for scarce resources. These arguments all support the position of developing a coalition of organizations in a local community.

Hage (1975) also points out the following inducements for organizations to participate in a coalition. Obviously, better funding is a key benefit and inducement for participating. The multiply handicapped child provides a technological basis or rationale, and it is important to recognize that a delivery system proposal by any one agency to provide comprehensive care for these children would not get very far. The client problems of both a longitudinal and lateral nature would be beyond the scope of any one agency to handle. It is assumed that the client's needs would be best served if handled simultaneously in joint programs, rather than piecemeal in some sequential or chainlike fashion. There is also a desire created to cooperate whenever there is a clear technological imperative or functional necessity such as the coordinating responsibility for schools under PL 94–142 and other recent federal legislation mandating interagency collaboration. This force, however, is not strong enough to overcome the inherent strain toward autonomy, especially given the conflict between competitors. Therefore, Hage contends one needs to provide a sustained basis for entering into an exchange, one that recognizes the autonomy needs of agencies. By suggesting the creation of stable and relatively permanent coalitions to meet new and complex problems of handicapped children, and the delivery systems' need to handle their needs, one creates new channels of funding that leave undisturbed agency identities and traditional funding avenues. Something is added, rather than subtracted or rearranged. Therefore, a proposal to create a coalition of agencies maximizes organizational benefits and minimizes organizational costs. However, it is a proposal that has meaning only when there is relatively clear functional necessity, such as the need to create a delivery system of agencies in a technological imperative like the need to work concurrently in providing services for the client. The client in this case would be a handicapped child; the need to create a delivery system of organizations would be the need to work in a cooperative manner because of the requirement to provide coordinated services under PL 94-142.

Guidelines

Mulvenon (Chapter 6) offers a comprehensive list of guidelines that need to be considered when undertaking the development of a coalition of organizations. Such a list is long and many factors need to be considered. This is just another indication of the complexity of establishing interagency collaborative arrangements.

Initial Concerns

Also in the early stages of interagency collaboration, a coalition of organizations needs to consider a number of questions about client population, geography, eligibility, services, and other related factors. These initial concerns are addressed in more detail by Kazuk (Chapter 5) and Mulvenon (Chapter 6).

Role of Schools

Since this volume is concerned with coordination of services for handicapped children, the role of the schools in establishing or maintaining such a coalition of organizations needs to be considered. As Zeller points out in his chapter on Direction Service, the schools have a legal responsibility under PL 94-142 for becoming the community's responsible agent for facilitating child development. It seems to be very appropriate for the school to assume a leadership role in forming the coalitions of organizations to develop interagency collaborative efforts that center on the care of the handicapped child.

Separate Authority

Deinstitutionalization programs centered around the deveopmentally disabled population in Michigan and Massachusetts, along with Canada's COMSERV Program, utilize a separate authority to operationalize interagency collaboration. However, there are a number of unanswered critical issues that need to be addressed before this becomes a viable alternative for interagency collaboration. Among these questions are:

Who should have authority at the regional level?
Should the regional authority provide hard services or just offer case management?

How long should such an authority be established?

What reinforcers can be exercised to encourage continued development of a coordination system under such an authority?

All of these issues need to be addressed. In the meantime, the voluntary unstructured coalition of organizations approach seems to be the most appropriate and most expeditions. Generally, local communities are not able to exert sustained efforts toward more effective coordination through the creation of a new authority because not enough is known about how to do it. John (1977) concludes that joint planning works better when planning is to fill a gap in services, but not very well when the issue is the restructuring of the delivery system, such as the case would be in establishing a separate authority.

Coalitions of organizations, however, should be cautioned to guard against becoming just another level of bureaucracy between the client and the services he/she needs. The term *interorganization* infers that a group of autonomous organizations or parts thereof are interacting for a purpose, in this case to coordinate services for handicapped children over a period of time and space. However, when the coalition of organizations or network coheres sufficiently to look and behave like a single organizational system, the question arises as to whether the agencies are fulfilling the original purposes of their interorganizational relationship.

ESTABLISHING INTERAGENCY COLLABORATION

Creating a Base of Knowledge

One of the most essential elements in establishing interagency collaborative arrangements is the education of agency staffs to the scope and types of services provided by participating agencies. The degree that an organization's members are aware of the existence and functions of other agencies in a community will determine, to a large extent, the success of establishing an appropriate referral mechanism and other interagency functions. Greenley and Kirk (1976) report that a number of researchers have described agencies that failed to refer to each other because they lacked an understanding of, or agreement on, the other agency's jobs. Knowledge of the existence of other agencies in the service delivery systems that provide services to the handicapped child was found to be surprisingly limited. Levine and White (1961) reported that leaders of agencies in one community knew of the existence of only 40%-50% of other organizations. Such a percentage would be higher in a rural community, but in urban communities similar results could probably be found. Initially, representatives of all the agencies involved in the interagency collaborative network need to meet on several occasions to define the scope, functions, and specific services of their agencies in relative detail. Through the process of asking questions for purposes of clarification, previous misunderstandings of agencies' functions can be clarified. As Hall (Chapter 3) concludes, it is through such understanding and mutual appreciation that the defensive tone within a coalition of organizations will be rapidly diminished.

Client Coordination

Experience in numerous integration projects nationwide has shown there is no one best model for developing services integration (Gans and Horton, 1975). The models delineated in this book in Chapters 3, 5, 6, and 7, along with the experience of Direction Service (Chapter 4), all provide helpful hints for developing this capability in a local community. The existence of Direction Service or some similar entity or function is needed by the handicapped child and his/her family to help them identify needs and access to services in the various service delivery systems. A small proportion of clients, particularly those with relatively few problems, may be able to gain access to the necessary services individually and obtain sufficient support to meet their needs. However, others who need more resources, due to the multitude of their problems, require the assistance of an agent, such as Direction Service, a case manager, or a service coordinator (Kahn, 1978). Virtually all attempts at developing client-based mechanisms of service coordination and interagency linkages have been dependent on voluntary concurrence of service providers. There is evidence, however, that such client level service coordination will deteriorate to being simply one of information exchange, rather than a realistic and reliable coordination of resources on behalf of the client, unless it takes place within the context of an umbrella or coalition of organizations at the system level to provide coordination of services among agencies (John, 1977; Baumheier, 1979). As Zeller points out (Chapter 4), some entity or function must be established within the service delivery system that works with families and handicapped children to help them identify their needs and gain access to a full range of appropriate services regardless of who provides those services.

Effective Communication

> Communication is the cement that makes organizations. Communication alone enables a group to think together, to see together and to act together. Also sociology requires the understanding of communication (Wiener, 1963, p. 77).

The importance of good communication in establishing and maintaining effective interagency collaboration cannot be overly stressed. In a study on interorganizational relationships of agencies that deal with problem youth, Hall and Clark (1975) found that conflict between organizations is positively related to good communication as is frequency of interaction. It appears that communication patterns can be of good quality, be used frequently, and be based around conflict situations. Coordination is also positively associated with good communication, which suggests that communication can perhaps play a dual role, leading to coordination and also serving in the resolution of conflict situations.

Hage (1975), in response to a question about an appropriate coordination mechanism, indicates that a communication perspective is by far the better coordination mechansim. The idea of communication as a coordination mechanism seems logical based on the implicit assumption that the major problem involved in coordination is that the situations are always changing too fast. This means an almost continuous flow of information is required from a coordinating point of view. To a large extent, society is moving away from punishments and rewards as coordinating mechanisms. The trend is away from using sanctions to control student behavior in universities. Instead of saying there is another system whereby we can provide control and coordination simultaneously, the trend seems to be toward coordination through communication. The use of open, direct communication by agency staff leads to trust and mutual support (Hall, Chapter 3).

Community Boards

Membership on boards or councils that are created as a result of a coalition of organizations to establish interagency arrangements needs to be determined in the beginning stages. Mulvenon (Chapter 6) provides a practical list of participants who should be involved in local interagency councils or teams. Hage (1975) proposes that such councils' members should be comprised of one-third elite, one-third professionals relevant to the handicapping conditions, and one-third individuals representing the needs of the client/consumer. This membership distribution recognizes various power groups in larger communities and also avoids focusing on one or the other interest group. If one-half or more of the council members represent the clients, then professional-client conflict will become too great. If there are only one or two representatives of clients, they will not talk and represent the interests of their group. There is a certain reluctance on the part of everyone to admit that elites exist and especially to state that their interests should be represented. Each of the interest groups represent values that should be represented on any interagency council or board. Elites, as suggested, emphasize efficiency and a concern about a reduction of costs. Professionals, on the other hand, are more concerned about quality care, while the representatives of the consumers are more concerned about the social/emotional needs of the client/consumer.

Hage points out that a dialectic can be created if there are about five to ten members representing each of these interests. Each interest group needs to check on its own power, but it also needs a forum to present its viewpoint.

Denying the existence of the power structure is no more credible than denying the lack of expertise on the part of most people, be they elites or representatives of consumers.

The purpose of an interagency council or board should be exactly those of any corporate board: to make policies about interorganizational relationships, transfers and exchanges, joint programming, and the like, and to protect the interest of the larger community regarding the allocation of funds. As Hage points out, however, the above-stated purpose of function is theoretical; boards may aspire to this ideal, but in actual practice they are seldom able to operate this way. Their purpose, instead, is to provide a way for agencies at the local level to fight the larger environment and gain resources from it. They are the basis on which the agencies build political support. Thus, the interagency board or council will primarily spend its time trying to get more money, staff, and prestige for the delivery system. The essential point is that there should be local control of interagency collaboration at the community level.

Role of Facilitator-Coordinator

A case could be made for the delineation of separate functions for a facilitator versus a coordinator. A facilitator could be viewed as an independent third party who assists the community in establishing interagency collaborative arrangements. Once an interagency communication network is established, the role of the facilitator might be ended. A coordinator, however, is someone who would have to carry on from where the facilitator left off and ensure that interagency collaborative arrangements continued to exist and operate to the benefit of the handicapped child. However, for the purpose of discussion in this chapter, a distinction will not be made between these roles, and the person filling the role will be referred to as a facilitator.

A facilitator is a key element to establishing and maintaining interagency collaborative arrangements. This person should be an independent contractor so that he/she is not unduly influenced by any particular agency or program. If such a person were employed by one of the agencies involved in a community, there would always be a tendency to yield to pressures that might be placed upon such a person by the agency director. By having a facilitator employed by and responsible to an interagency council and not responsible to any particular agency, relationships to agencies are clearer and remain equal.

Such a person has to be knowledgeable about the total service delivery system. Although he/she would probably come from one of the major service delivery systems and be well versed in that system, it is essential that one of the first tasks of the facilitator be to become familiar with the other major service delivery systems to the extent that the facilitator can be conversant in the types of services provided, how they are provided, the makeup of the professional staff, and how they relate to other service delivery systems.

A facilitator should work from a client-centered base rather than from any specific agency or program base. In a sense it can be said that the facilitator is an advocate for the client rather than the agencies. At the same time, the work of the facilitator cannot be to the detriment of the agencies in order to benefit the client.

The facilitator should be conversant in and able to deal effectively with the human factors as described by Hall (Chapter 3). Skills in interpersonal relationships, effective communication, group dynamics, and change agents are some of the prerequisites for this person. The facilitator would work with both state agency heads and local community agency heads and service providers, but his/her primary interest should be in obtaining services for the handicapped child through community agencies.

There are numerous roles that a facilitator should fill in establishing interagency collaborative arrangements. Kazuk (Chapter 5) provides a list of some of these functions.

EVALUATION

Basic Considerations

A key element in interagency collaboration is an independent evaluation of how well such efforts are succeeding. Because interagency efforts in the area of coordinating services for handicapped children are relatively new, there has been little effort at providing third party evaluation for these systems. The Colorado model as described by Kazuk (Chapter 5) does have an evaluation component provided by the John F. Kennedy University Affiliated Facility in Denver. The criteria used for evaluating success were 1) the satisfaction of the participating agencies, and 2) an increase in children and families served.

A number of the University Affiliated Programs for the Developmentally Disabled have the capability of providing technical assistance and evaluation components to interagency efforts in communities. It is an appropriate role for the UAFs to pursue. The Nisonger Center at Ohio State University has done considerable work in developing an evaluation scheme for interagency collaborative arrangements in the area of developmental disabilities. The correct evaluation format for this area is still evolving, and further research and evaluation design are required.

Cost-Benefit Analysis

One of the areas in need of evaluation that is often mentioned as a criticism of interagency efforts is the cost-benefit of establishing interagency collaborative arrangements. The initial cost in establishing an interagency collaborative effort in a community is quite high. Depending on the size of a community, the cost of services of a full- or part-time facilitator with secretarial and other related support services needs to be established. These are only the direct costs, however. An even greater cost is the indirect cost in the amount of time devoted by various agency representatives to numerous meetings and the commitment of their time and agency resources to the interagency effort. Because these initial start-up costs are high, there needs to be a careful needs assessment in a community to show where duplication and gaps in service exist. Such a procedure was used in the Colorado model (Chapter 5) where a matrix of services and handicapping conditions was developed to show the community there was a need for an interagency effort. Ideally, these start-up costs, at least in the initial stages of establishing models of interagency collaboration, will be picked up through grants from various federal agencies that see the need to avoid duplication in the services they provide. A number of such efforts have been funded by the Bureau of Community Health Services to coordinate health and education services in six states. The author directs one of these model projects in the state of Oregon.

The biggest problem in conducting a cost-benefit analysis of interagency collaborative efforts is the assignment of cost avoidance factors because the potential benefits derived from interagency collaboration are long term and not immediately evident. As Zeller (Chapter 4) points out, it is very difficult to assign costs that are saved through avoiding expensive hearings under PL 94-142, or the costs that were saved by keeping a handicapped child out of an institution and in the community. The number of dollars saved by agencies working together to develop early assessment programs for handicapped children that might prevent problems that would be very costly to overcome later in life is difficult to determine. It is safe to say that through interagency efforts future costs are avoided. The question remains, however, as to whether or not they are sufficient to match the cost of developing and maintaining interagency collaborative efforts. Considerable study and research must be done in the area of cost-benefit analysis to answer these questions.

CONCLUSION

Interagency collaborative efforts can be of benefit to the community, to the parents and children, and to agencies involved in the delivery of services. The community can benefit from a coordinated needs assessment that has been formed by all the agencies involved, from the establishment of a resource directory, and from the maximization of resources through the sharing and elimination of duplicative services. Parents and children benefit because they have better access to services and their point of view can be represented on an interagency council that provides direction to interagency efforts in a community. The agencies themselves, of course, benefit because their awareness of services in each of the agencies is increased; the level of communication among agencies and the efficiency of each agency also increase since they are now working primarily in their own area of expertise in a coordinated fashion.

A couple of cautionary notes should be sounded, however, for those whose primary concern is the application of the knowledge and techniques described in this book. As described by Benson et al. (1973), it first should not be assumed that the system of interagency relationships is subject, to any large degree, to rational manipulation and control. Clearly, some of the variables that have been identified are susceptible to some rational manipulation. Because of this, modest improvements in interagency collaboration can be achieved by careful attention to them. However, it seems likely that the limits of such rational manipulation and control are quite restricted. Some of the tensions and changes that are encountered in developing interagency efforts are probably related to transformations of the entire social order of American society. Changes, for example, in the valuation of work and leisure, in the basic trust in public officials, in the concepts of social responsibility, and in the ideas about equal rights for all handicapped citizens are all involved in this process. The question needs to be asked: to what extent are we, author and readers alike, caught up by social forces that we cannot control and perhaps can only dimly perceive?

Second, it should be recognized that interagency collaboration and coordination are not necessarily good under all circumstances. The major focus of this book has been the establishment of interagency efforts around the needs of the handicapped child who requires services from various agencies and service delivery systems. Agencies, however, must remain accountable and responsible to all their target populations that may only require programs and services provided by a single agency. The main focus of the education system has and always will be education of today's children and youth. Public health departments will continue to place their primary focus on preventive health care, and social service agencies must continue to remain accountable and responsible to each other and be responsive to the needs of the public. Interagency collaboration and coordination are designed to handle the problems of a relatively small segment of our population and should be viewed as such in the total light or services to the total population of this country.

What has been described in this chapter is based upon empirical approaches to establishing model interagency efforts. At the same time, much work remains to be done in order to develop a better theory of interorganizational relationships that will take full account of the integral place they have in the community as well as in societal structure. Adamek (1975) indicates over 150 articles and books have appeared over the past 18 years and at least 130 variables thought to be relevant to interorganizational analysis have been identified along with some seven major paradigms. It is no surprise then that, while existing maps have given us a better idea of the lay of the land, none of them has given us a comprehensive, unified picture or generated agreement about the best way to "get from here to there." While interorganizational scholars and researchers have sketched parts of the interorganizational landscape in broad outline, there remains much detailed exploring yet to be done in this area and much uncharted territory to cover. Researchers in interorganizational theory seem to have raised as many questions that require further study as they have answered.

The same can be said of the empirical approaches to developing interagency collaborative arrangements that have been explored in this book. There is a wealth of practical information available in this book, and it is up to you, the reader, to combine these practices with the theoretical concepts in this chapter to create a workable solution that will promote comprehensive, coordinated services for handicapped children in your community.

In summary, it can be said that establishing interagency collaborative arrangements is, first of all, a difficult process that demands great political skill. Second, it should be approached in incremental steps and not hurried. Next, there needs to be further research and demonstration in interagency collaboration and coordination of services with carefully designed objectives that can provide a better measurement of the success and cost-benefit of these efforts. Finally, it must be recognized that the human element needs to be recognized as clearly the major variable in determining the success or failure of any interagency collaborative effort.

REFERENCES

Adamek, R. 1975. Mapping the interorganizational landscape: A critical appraisal. In: A. Negandhi (ed.), *Interorganization Theory,* pp. 71–76. Kent State University Press, Kent, OH.

Aiken, M., Dewar, R., DiTomaso, N., Hage, J., and Zeitz, G. 1975. *Coordinating Human Services.* Jossey-Bass, San Francisco.

Barth, E. 1963. The cause and consequences of interagency conflict. *Soc. Inquiry* 33:31–33.

Baumheier, E. 1979. Interagency linkages in the field of developmental disabilities. Unpublished paper presented at the Interagency Evaluation Conference, May, Miami Beach.

Bensen, J. K., Kunce, J., Thompson, C., and Allen, D. 1973. *Coordinating Human Services.* The Curators of the University of Missouri, Columbia.

Crozier, M. 1964. *The Bureaucratic Phenomenon.* The University of Chicago Press, Chicago.

Gans, S., and Horton, G. 1975. *Integration of Human Services: The State and Municipal Levels.* Praeger Publishers, New York.

Gilbert, N., and Specht, H. 1977. Quantitative aspects of social service coordination efforts: Is more better? *Admin. Soc. Work* 1:53–61.

Greenley, J., and Kirk, S. 1976. Organizational influence on access to health care. *Soc. Sci. Med.* 10(6):317–322.

Hage, J. 1975. A Strategy for creating interdependent delivery systems to meet complex needs. In: A. Negandhi (ed.), *Interorganization Theory,* pp. 210–234. Kent State University Press, Kent, OH.

Hall, R., and Clark, J. 1975. Problems in the study of interorganizational relationships. In: A. Negandhi (ed.), *Interorganization Theory,* pp. 111–127. Kent State University Press, Kent, OH.

John, D. 1977 (August). Managing the human service "system": What have we learned from services integration? Project Share Human Services Monograph Series, No. 4, Rockville, MD.

Kahn, L. 1978 (October). A case management system for the mentally retarded citizens of Rhode Island: A model, a needs assessment and recommendations. Unpublished report, Prepared by Social Planning Services, Inc., under contract to the Rhode Island Department of Mental Health, Providence.

Kazuk, E., Greene, L., and Magrab, P. 1979. Case study for planning coordinated services. In: Magrab, P., and Elder, J. (eds.), *Planning for Services to Handicapped Persons*, pp. 211–245. Paul H. Brookes Publishers, Baltimore.

Levine, S., and White, P. 1961. Exchange as a conceptual framework for the study of interorganizational relationships. *Admin. Sci. Q.* 5: 583–601.

Neufeldt, A. 1979. Evaluating interagency linkages: Some experiences from the Canadian COMSERV experiments. Unpublished paper presented at the Interagency Evaluation Conference, May, Miami Beach.

Steingraph, H. 1977. *Interorganizational Theory and Practice: Interpretation and Annotation.* The University of Texas, Austin.

Wiener, N. 1963. Communication. As quoted in: K. Duetsch, *The Nerves of Government.* The Free Press, New York. p. 77.

Coordinating Services to Handicapped Children:
A Handbook for Interagency Collaboration
Edited by Jerry O. Elder and Phyllis R. Magrab
Copyright © 1980   Paul H. Brookes Publishers   Baltimore • London

Chapter 9
Writing Interagency Agreements

Jerry O. Elder

The principal purpose of this chapter is to provide examples of the various types of interagency agreements that have been written throughout the country. Although it is not expected or even advised, that the reader will adopt word-for-word the examples provided here, they are designed to present ideas that can be modified and adapted for use in other states. Some states may be restricted in the design of interagency agreements by requirements of contract offices at various levels of government. The design of an agreement, however, is not as important as the contents of the agreement itself.

The primary purpose of an interagency agreement is to put in writing the collaborative elements that have been developed in the form of policy and procedures and working relationships among agencies. The agreement itself is the final step in establishing interagency working arrangements. It is wise to develop and then test interagency procedures so that they can be refined and codified before putting them down in writing in the form of an interagency agreement.

LEVELS OF AGREEMENTS

There are basically two levels of interagency agreement that can be developed. The first of these, which is more or less a philosophical statement of the major purpose of each agency, but which also spells out areas of responsibility and financial arrangements, is developed by agency heads at the state level. The establishment of this type of interagency agreement is essential both to give those involved in constructing interagency collaborative arrangements at the local level something on which to base their deliberations and to establish boundaries as to which agency will provide services for which type of handicapping conditions, i.e., when, where, and how these services will be provided. Such agreements provide the overall structure for determining the basis for interagency relationships at the community level. These agreements also serve to exemplify the commitment of the state level agency heads who are a party to such agreements to the concept of interagency collaboration.

Two examples of this type of interagency agreement are provided in this chapter. Appendix A is an agreement that was developed by the author between the Oregon State Department of Education and the Crippled Children's Services Program which, in Oregon, is administered through the Oregon State System of Higher Education through the University of Oregon Health Sciences Center, Crippled Children's Division. The second state level agreement, Appendix B, is one developed under the supervision of Judy Schrag, Supervisor of Special Education for the Idaho State Department of Education. This is an agreement between the State Department of Education and the State Division of Vocational Rehabilitation and the State Division of Vocational Education.

The second level of agreement includes those agreements usually developed between specific agencies at the local community level. These agreements spell out specific working relationships in such areas as referral, exchange of information, service provision, evaluation, and financial arrangements, among others. Since these types of agreements vary widely, depending on specific purpose, only one example is given in this chapter. Appendix C illustrates a working agreement for physical therapy services provided to a local school district by the Crippled Children's Program in the state of Oregon.

CLASSES OF AGREEMENTS

Another way of looking at different types of interagency agreements was described by Audette in Chapter 2. He indicates there are three significant classes of interagency agreements. The first and most important, he feels, are those agreements centered on common or baseline standards for the conduct of different agencies' programs that are similar in their purpose and scope, but are conducted separately. Such agreements represent promises by different agencies to adopt defined, common criteria in the provision of services to handicapped children and their families. Essentially, these standards constitute "multiple-agency adoption of explicit program understandings regarding who does what to whom, when, where, how often, under whose supervision, and to whose advantage" (p. 30). Audette feels that agreements to establish such standards are prerequisite to all other agreements concerning the provision of services to handicapped children and their families. An example of this type of agreement is found in Appendix D. This is a list of standards developed by the Interagency Planning Group for Preschool Children in Hays, Kansas. These standards were patterned after *A Plan for Coordinated Interagency Services for Children with Special Needs in Massachusetts* (Early Childhood

Interagency Planning Group, 1978). The development of this type of a list of standards is very time consuming. Almost a year of semimonthly meetings of the Hays Interagency Planning Team were needed to develop and agree upon the standards listed in Appendix D.

The second class of agreements defined by Audette consists of promises regarding the allocation of various agency resources in the accomplishment of mutually agreed upon objectives. He describes at least six methods of cooperatively allocating resources. Please refer to Chapter 2 (p. 31) for a list and description of these methods.

Audette's third class of agreements includes promises of uniform processes, forms, and activities by multiple agencies offering comparable services. He feels that agreements regarding standards (class 1) and allocation (class 2) are absolute prerequisites to process and activity (class 3) agreements. Promises can be made concerning some 12 or more areas of activities that might be managed cooperatively. Each of these areas directly links the needs of individual children and families to the capacity of the cooperating agencies to respond. Child and family service agreements can be addressed in a systematic manner if the promises clearly articulate how each participating agency administers client entitlements. Examples of this third type of agreement are also listed in Chapter 2 (pp. 32–33).

ELEMENTS OF AGREEMENTS

There are any number of elements than can be included in an interagency agreement. The eight elements listed below are considered important components of interagency collaborative agreements. Not all agreements, however, will require all eight elements, and some agreements may require elements that are not mentioned here. Nonetheless, it is the author's experience that these are the major elements that should be considered as part of any interagency agreement. Most of these elements are based on an unpublished study by Smith (1978) conducted at the Nisonger Center at Ohio State University.

Statement of Purpose

A statement of clear purpose for agreement between the parties should be one of the first items listed. It should include a delineation of goals and measurable objectives for the term of the agreement. The writing of objectives in measurable units will greatly facilitate the later evaluation of the success of an agreement.

Definition of Terms

Many times the terminology used by one agency is familiar to that agency alone. The word *evaluation* may mean one thing to a health agency, but have a different meaning for educators. Therefore, it is essential to define any ambiguous or unfamiliar terms as part of the document.

(3) Program Delineation

In order to facilitate a clear communication of the need for and the intent of an agreement, there should be a clear delineation of the specific program, service, or focus for which the document in being written. Such statements do not need to be long, drawn-out descriptions written in minute detail, but enough information should be included to describe sufficiently the program or service to enable a first time reader to grasp its meaning.

(4) First Dollar Responsibility

Much confusion exists among various federal and state programs providing services to handicapped children as to which program or agency is responsible for paying the first dollar for a service and which agency only pays when no other program is responsible. The determination of which agency has the first dollar responsibility for the payment of services needs to be spelled out in an agreement. The specification of other financial or funding arrangements for payment of services also should be addressed.

(5) Roles and Responsibilities

The specific actions, roles, and responsibilities of each party to an agreement should be written clearly so there is no confusion as to who does what, when, and where. At the same time, mutual responsibilites to be shared by all parties need to be set forth.

(6) Designation of Responsible Positions

The major fault of many past agreements between agencies can be traced to the failure to assign to a designated staff person the responsibility of ensuring that the provisions of the agreement were carried out. Too many times an agreement will be written, filed away, and forgotten until a major crisis or problem comes along. To prevent this from occurring, a staff member from each agency who is party to the agreement should be designated in the terms of the agreement. This person would be responsible for:

1. Implementing the agreement as specified
2. Monitoring the implementation to ensure its success
3. Negotiating change in the agreement when it becomes necessary to update it

(7) Administrative Procedure

There are numerous general administrative procedures that need to be a part of every agreement. These items include a specified starting and ending date for the agreement, a mechanism for updating/revising it, confidentiality safe-guards, referral mechanisms, information sharing, nondiscrimination clauses, and other ensurances.

Evaluation Design

In order to determine the success or failure of an interagency agreement, it is extremely helpful to build into the agreement itself an evaluation mechanism. The design of this mechanism should be specified and agreed upon by all parties. The person(s) responsible for the evaluation should be identified in the agreement, and sanctions need to be agreed upon to ensure its implementation.

SUMMARY

Interagency agreements may be designed and written in almost any format that will fit the purposes of the parties involved. This chapter has suggested different levels or classes of agreements that can be developed and has pro-vided a review of various elements that can be included in such agreements. Since situations differ so much from community to community, there is no recommended format or content design that will work for every interagency agreement. In developing interagency agreements, the reader is encouraged to relate his/her own situational requirements to the elements and examples provided in this chapter in order to arrive at the level or class of agreement most appropriate to the specific needs of the community and collaborative effort under consideration.

REFERENCES

Early Childhood Interagency Planning Group. 1978 (January). *A Plan for Coordinated Interagency Services for Children with Special Needs in Massachusetts.* Boston.

Smith, C. B. 1978. Interagency agreements as a mechanism for coordination. Unpublished manuscript. Ohio State University, Columbus.

Interagency Agreement Between the Oregon State Department of Education and the Crippled Children's Division, University of Oregon Health Sciences Center, Oregon State System of Higher Education

I. STATEMENT OF PHILOSOPHY AND PURPOSE
   A. All handicapped children must be provided appropriate services for their habilitation, including, especially, health and educational services so they can develop to their maximum potential as productive and contributing members of society. The Oregon State Department of Education (SDE) and the Crippled Children's Division (CCD), University of Oregon Health Sciences Center are strongly committed to cooperate to achieve this goal.

   A continuum of appropriate programs and services must be available for each handicapped child from birth to adulthood. Major areas of services include prevention, early identification, screening, diagnosis, information and referral services, medical treatment, developmental programs, recreational and leisure time activities, special education, transportation, vocational training, and income maintenance. No single agency or organization has the capability of providing all necessary programs and services for handicapped children.

   B. It is the purpose of this agreement to clarify the responsibilities of the SDE and the CCD in the provision of appropriate education, health, and related services for handicapped children throughout Oregon which are required by federal and state law and regulations. This process will lead to the coordination of health and education resources for handicapped children.

      1. The first objective of this agreement will be to instruct special education administrative and professional staff in local school and education service districts and staff of the State Department of Education about the services available through CCD. This will be carried out by CCD through informational brochures and in-service training programs that will be developed through the Interagency Collaboration and Rural Outreach projects.

      2. The second objective of this agreement will be to instruct administrative, professional, and support staff of CCD and consultant professionals to CCD about the role and responsibilities of the SDE under PL 94-142 and ORS Chapter 528 as they relate to CCD services. This will be

carried out by the SDE through informational brochures and in-service training programs.

II. DEFINITION OF TERMS
A. In order to avoid any misunderstandings arising from this agreement, the following terms which may be ambiguous are defined:
1. *Handicapped children* under PL 94-142 means those children evaluated in accordance with the provisions of PL 94-142 as being mentally retarded, hard of hearing, deaf, speech impaired, visually handicapped, seriously emotionally disturbed, orthopedically impaired, other health impaired, deaf-blind, multi-handicapped, or as having specific learning disabilities, who because of these impairments need special education and related services. The terms used in this definition are further defined in Section 121a.5 of the rules and regulations for PL 94-142 and are found in Appendix A of this agreement.
2. *Related services* under PL 94-142 means transportation and such developmental, corrective, and other supportive services as are required to assist a handicapped child to benefit from special education, and includes speech pathology and audiology, psychological services, physical and occupational therapy, recreation, early identification and assessment of disabilities in children, counseling services, and medical services for diagnostic or evaluation purposes. The term also includes school health services, social work services in schools, and parent counseling and training. The terms used in this definition are further defined in Section 121a.13 of the rules and regulations for PL 94-142 and are found in Appendix B of this agreement. Under Oregon law, related services are part of the definition of "Special Education."
3. *Crippled children* under Oregon Crippled Children's Services means children ages birth to 21 who require medical and rehabilitative care for the following chronic classifications: chronic orthopedic problems, cleft lip and palate and other craniofacial disorders, burns and their resultant scars, congenital heart disease and operable rheumatic heart disease, cerebral palsy and other neurologic disorders, organic communication disorders, certain metabolic disorders.
4. *Management* under the Crippled Children's program is the responsibility of long term coordination and/or provision of health care. It implies: a) periodic evaluation to

determine patient's needs, b) professional intervention to facilitate meeting identified needs, c) medical eligibility for possible financial assistance.

5. *Consultation* under the Crippled Children's program is the responsibility for rendering an opinion and suggesting a course of management regarding a problem or problems presented. The definition implies that intervention or initiation of treatment should be done only with the agreement of the referral source and patient.

6. *Diagnosis* under the Crippled Children's program requires an evaluation adequate to indicate appropriateness for a child to be served in an established CCD program. Diagnosis under the State Department of Education is covered under the Minimum Eligibility Criteria (Oregon Administrative Rules 581-15-051) which are found in Appendix C of this agreement.

7. *IEP*—Individualized Education Program—is an individual plan of education that is written annually for each child requiring special education services. Such plans must be developed and implemented in accordance with paragraphs 121a.341–121c.349 of the Federal Register implementing PL 94-142.

8. *ISP*—Individualized Service Plan—is an annual written plan of service or treatment that is required for each child followed in the SSI Disabled Children's Program. Such plans include specific education, social and medical service needs to each child.

9. *IMP*—Individualized Management Plan—is a written plan of treatment that is required for each child followed in one of CCD's Management Programs. Such plans include specific medical and psychosocial needs of each child.

III. STATEMENTS OF GENERAL RESPONSIBILITY
A. Oregon State Department of Education
1. The SDE under PL 94-142 has overall responsibility for all educational programs for handicapped children and ensures compliance with regulations relating to this law.
2. The SDE under Chapter 343 of the Oregon Revised Statutes is responsible for general supervision of all educational programs for handicapped children and ensures compliance with state administrative rules relating to special education within limits set by the Legislative Assembly of Oregon.

B. Crippled Children's Division, University of Oregon Health Sciences Center
   1. The CCD under Sections 504–507 of Title V of the Social Security Act is responsible for providing a system within the State which ensures the accessibility of diagnosis and treatment needed to correct or ameliorate defects of chronic conditions of children.
   2. The CCD under Chapter 444.010–444.050 of the Oregon Revised Statutes is responsible for the administration of a program "to extend and improve services for locating crippled children and for providing medical, surgical, corrective and other services and care, and facilities for diagnosis, hospitalization, and aftercare for children who are suffering from conditions which lead to crippling."

IV. STATEMENTS OF SPECIFIC PROGRAM ROLES AND RESPONSIBILITIES
   A. The Oregon State Department of Education will be the lead agency in the planning and implementation of educational programs for school-age handicapped children. Through Oregon Administrative Rules for Special Education 581-15-005 through 581-15-840, it will encourage local school districts, who have the ultimate responsibility for carrying out special education programs for handicapped children residing in their districts, to carry out their legal mandate. Oregon Administrative Rules of the SDE which relate to services provided by CCD include:
      1. Definitions of terms used in these rules (581-15-005)
      2. Criteria for approving school district special education programs (581-15-035)
      3. Identification, location, evaluation, and census of handicapped children (581-15-037)
      4. Parental consent (581-15-039)
      5. Equipment and supplies (581-15-043)
      6. State reimbursable costs (581-15-046)
      7. Minimum eligibility criteria (581-15-051)
      8. Confidentiality of handicapped children's records (581-15-055)
      9. Alternative placements and supplementary services (581-15-060)
      10. Placement of the child (581-15-061)
      11. Individualized education program (581-15-064 through 581-15-069)
      12. Evaluations (581-15-071 through 581-15-074)

13. Prior notice for change in status (581-15-076 through 581-15-078)
14. Hearings (581-15-081 through 581-15-092)
15. Independent educational evaluation (581-15-094)
16. Selecting persons as surrogate parents for handicapped children (581-15-098)

B. The Crippled Children's Division is a specialized health program whose services are limited to the diagnosis and treatment of certain crippling conditions. General medical care is not provided. Children with crippling conditions are diagnosed and managed under one of nine CCD clinical programs. These programs are Cerebral Palsy, Child Development, Orthopedic, Paralytic (including myelomeningocele), Neurology, Congenital Heart and Respiratory, Genetics (including Hemophilia), Communication and Craniofacial Disorders, and Primary Evaluation. Diagnostic and treatment services are offered through clinics held in various parts of Oregon or by CCD consultants in their private offices. These consultants are certified specialists. Ancillary services for patients include medical social casework, occupational therapy, physical therapy, speech pathology and audiology, clinical psychology, community health nursing, pedodontics and nutrition.

Eligibility requirements for diagnostic services are that the patient is:
1. Under 21 years of age
2. A resident of the United States
3. Suspected of having one of the crippling conditions covered by the program

Eligibility requirements for treatment services are that the patient is:
1. Under 21 years of age
2. A resident of Oregon
3. Determined medically eligible
4. Financially evaluated

C. The Supplemental Security Income Disabled Children's Program is administered by CCD. It provides to low-income blind and severely disabled children, eligible for Social Security and referred by the State Disability Determinations Unit, services at two levels by age group. Children under seven (7) years of age are provided direct, comprehensive, individual services and treatment not available elsewhere. The development of an Individualized Service Plan (ISP) is mandated for all SSI eligible children ages birth through 15. (Currently, the

212

expenditure of funds for this purpose on those children ages 7–15 is severely limited.)

V. STATEMENTS OF COMMON ROLES, RESPONSIBILITIES, AND FINANCING MECHANISMS

    A. Evaluations of children are mandated under laws and regulations of both SDE and CCD. Evaluations carried out by schools are for the primary purpose of determining the educational capabilities of a child. Evaluations carried out under the auspices of CCD are for the primary purpose of determining the child's medical diagnosis and plan for management. Handicapped children, however, require assessments by both educational and health related disciplines. A medical examination is required by the SDE under ORS 343.227 and may be waived only for children with speech defects, learning problems or mild behavioral problems. The coordination of such evaluations is ideally carried out by personnel in the community or county where the child resides. When these evaluations are necessary for the development of a child's educational program, the financial responsibility for payment rests with the local school district.

    B. Federal and state laws require schools to provide related services if such services are designated in an IEP. Many of these same services are provided by CCD staff or paid for when authorized by CCD. Regardless of which agency provides these services, the financial responsibility for payment of such services should be the local school district's when they are a necessary part of a child's educational program as specified in the IEP. If such services are deemed necessary by CCD staff and relate to the child's medical needs, the financial responsibility for payment should be with CCD. The coordination of these services should be carried out in the community or county where the child resides.

    C. The writing of annual Individualized Education Programs (IEP) is required by the State Department of Education for students receiving special education services. The writing of annual Individualized Service Plans (ISP) is required for clients receiving benefits under the SSI Disabled Children's Program. In addition, the Crippled Children's Division requires that Individualized Management Plans (IMP) be developed for each patient it follows in one of its management programs. The SDE and CCD wish to avoid duplication in the preparation and content of IEPs, ISPs, and IMPs. To guard against duplication, it is assumed that the IEP, representing the educational programming for the child, and being the responsibility of education, should be incorporated in the ISP and made a part thereof when appropriate. It is also assumed that the IMP, representing the medical treatment and rehabilitation program for a child and being a responsibility of CCD should be incorporated in the ISP and made a part thereof for SSI eligible clients. For CCD clients who are not SSI eligible, the program outlined in the IMP should be made available to the child's school district for possible inclusion in the IEP, when appropriate. The coordination of these functions should be carried out by school personnel in the child's home school district and in communication with CCD personnel. It is further assumed that close working relationships between medical and ancillary personnel performing direct services in the child's community on behalf of CCD and SSI Disabled Children's Program clients, and local school district personnel will be the best means of achieving continuity of planning efforts. CCD as part of the Interagency Collaboration Project will take a leadership role in working with local school district, ESD, and other community agency staff to encourage such relationships.

D. It is recognized that when the SDE through local school districts, CCD and its SSI Disabled Children's Program all order similar or identical services for mutually eligible clients, the clients may be enrolled in or be eligible to receive payments for such services from a third party payor program or plan. In such cases, the third party payor should be looked to first for payment of services provided. Third party payors may consist of private health insurance plans or federal and state financial assistance programs that are not party to this agreement.

VI. PROCEDURAL AND CONFIDENTIALITY SAFEGUARDS

Policy and procedure for identification, screening, evaluation/assessment, prescription, placement, and program change of each handicapped child and confidentiality of client records are spelled out in Oregon Administrative Rules for Special Education 581-15-005 through 581-15-840 and in the Oregon State Plan for Crippled Children's Services. The implementation of SDE Administrative Rules and coordination of these provisions with those of CCD will be the responsibility of the local school district. If there is conflict between existing policy of the SDE and CCD, such matters will be referred to the Director of Special Education for the SDE and the Director of CCD for joint resolution.

VII. ADMINISTRATIVE CONSIDERATIONS
   A. This agreement will take effect as of September 15, 1979, and will continue in effect until September 15, 1980.
   B. Individuals occupying the following positions in each agency are hereby designated and given responsibility for
      1. Implementing the provisions of this agreement
      2. Monitoring the implementation of this agreement
      3. Negotiating any change when necessary to renew or update this agreement:
         a. Representing CCD—Director, Interagency Collaboration Study Project
         b. Representing SDE—Director, Special Education
   C. The evaluation of this agreement will be mutually carried out under the direction of the above named agency representatives and will be based on the completion of the objectives listed under Section I-B of this agreement.
   D. Planning for the needs of handicapped children requires that accurate data be maintained by both agencies. Management information will be shared by the SDE and CCD in order to evaluate the impact of services and for the purpose of ongoing program planning and development. Client information will be shared as long as it does not conflict with policies pertaining to confidentiality and informed consent of either agency.
   E. Additions, deletions, and other amendments to the provisions of this agreement may be made during the effective dates specified above upon signature of the undersigned parties.

OREGON STATE BOARD OF
HIGHER EDUCATION
on behalf of the UNIVERSITY OF
OREGON HEALTH SCIENCES CENTER
CRIPPLED CHILDREN'S DIVISION

by _____(Signed)_____
    Director, CCD
Date ___12/10/79___

by _____(Signed)_____
    President, UOHSC
Date ___12/11/79___

OREGON STATE DEPARTMENT OF
EDUCATION

by _____(Signed)_____
    Deputy Superintendent
Date ___12/5/79___

APPENDIX B

Interagency Agreement Between the State Department of Education,
the State Division of Vocational Rehabilitation,
and the State Division of Vocational Education

Statement of Philosophy and Purpose

It is the philosophy of the Idaho State Department of Education, Special Education Section; Idaho State Division of Vocational Rehabilitation; and the Idaho State Division of Vocational Education that all handicapped/exceptional students be provided an appropriate education and other necessary related services so that they can develop to their maximum potential as productive and contributing members of society. PL 94-142 mandates that the state and local education agencies "provide a free, appropriate public education and related services to all handicapped children." Public Law 94-482, Title II of the 1975 Education Amendments, makes specific provision for the vocational education of handicapped persons in occupational areas which require less than a baccalaureate degree. The Rehabilitation Act of 1973 (PL 93-112) requires that the State Division of Vocational Rehabilitation provide, or otherwise arrange for, services necessary to render eligible persons employable.

It is the purpose of this interagency agreement to clarify the areas of responsibilities, as well as areas of coordination and collaboration between the three agencies.

Statement of Responsibility

As required by PL 94-142, the State Department of Education will be the lead agency in the planning and implementation of educational programs for school-age handicapped/exceptional children. Educational and vocational training may take place in regular vocational education programs, special needs classrooms, and/or within special education programs. Through *Administrative Rules and Regulations for Special Education* and through other state policies and guidelines, the State Department of Education will support and assist local school districts to carry out their legal mandate to provide for the education and training of school-age, resident handicapped/exceptional students. The State Department of Education, Special Education Section; and the State Division of Vocational Education recognize the need for medical, social, rehabilitative and other related services for secondary handicapped/exceptional students to ensure an appropriate educational opportunity. The State Division of Vocational Rehabilitation may provide such support services as needed to ensure that eligible handicapped students approaching an employable age are adequately prepared to bridge the gap between the public schools and employment.

Target Population

Within this agreement the target population for cooperative services is defined as those students who qualify for special education and vocational education and who are eligible to receive vocational rehabilitation services. Eligibility for vocational rehabilitation and special education is defined within *Administrative Rules and Regulations for Special Education* and by local board policy. Eligibility for vocational rehabilitation is determined by:

a. The presence of a physical or mental disability which is a substantial handicap to employment;
b. The provision that Vocational Rehabilitation services will aid towards employment; and
c. The person must be of employable age.

Individualized Education Plans/Programs

Federal legislation (PL 94-142, PL 94-482, and PL 93-112) requires that individualized plans or programs be developed for handicapped persons served by the respective agencies included within this agreement. State policies issued by the State Department of Education, Special Education Section; the State Division of Vocational Education and the State Division of Vocational Rehabilitation will encourage coordination of individualized plans at the local program level.

A representative of Vocational Rehabilitation and Vocational Education should be involved as a member of the local district Child Study Team when individualized education plans/programs are written for handicapped/exceptional students at the secondary level. It is especially important that Vocational Rehabilitation personnel be involved in the last year of program planning conducted by the public school Child Study Team prior to leaving the school system. If the individual education plan/program for a handicapped/exceptional student specifies services from a regular vocational program and/or from Vocational Rehabilitation, specific written individualized plans required by those agencies will coordinate and be compatible with the student's individualized education plan/program.

Related Services/Vocational Education Support

In the development of individual education plans/programs for target population students within this agreement, related services may be provided by Vocational Rehabilitation. These services are available under the Vocational Rehabilitation program to those individuals who meet the eligibility criteria of Vocational Rehabilitation and are in need of such services as determined by the Vocational Rehabilitation specialist. The Division of Vocational Rehabilitation is required to explore all other resources that exist applicable to each case from private companies or federal legislation.

Support services may be provided by the Division of Vocational Education to those students enrolled in a state reimbursable vocational education program.

Following is a list of possible services and the agency under which the services may be provided:

Service	Agency		
	DVR	DVE	SP. ED.
Information, consultation	X	X	X
Evaluation of potential, when critical to development of individual plan	X		X
Counseling client/student	X		X
Medical restoration	X		
Vocational training	X	X	X
Maintenance of client	X		
Placement of client/student	X	X	X
Transportation of client/student	X		X
Telecommunications	X		
Salaries of selected personnel involved in delivering special program		X	X
Supplies and instructional materials over and above standard school resources		X	X
Instructional staff travel needed for workshops, pre-vocational meetings, or work placement coordination		X	
Staff development	X	X	X
Specialized support services contingent on student/client condition, program circumstances and problem	X	X	X

Procedural Safeguards

The State Department of Education agrees to continue to encourage, assist, and require through policy as given in appropriate federal regulations and the *Administrative Rules and Regulations for Special Education* that local school districts use procedural safeguards in the identification, placement, and programming of handicapped/exceptional students.

The State Division of Vocational Education agrees to support compliance with the standards and safeguards provided in the *Administrative Rules and Regulations for Special Education.*

The State Division of Vocational Rehabilitation agrees to comply with procedural safeguards given in appropriate federal and state regulations. All client records are completely confidential and are released only through strictly enforced guidelines.

In-Service Training

In order to provide quality programs and services for handicapped/ exceptional students, service providers and appropriate administrators must receive continual and ongoing opportunities for staff development and professional growth.

The Department of Education, Special Education Section, the Division of Vocational Education and the Division of Vocational Rehabilitation will plan cooperative in-service training activities at the state and local levels so that appropriate administrative and service providers can benefit from existing staff expertise, share additional in-and out-of-state resources and provide for ongoing opportunities for communication and professional interaction.

Management Information

Planning for the educational, vocational, and rehabilitation needs of handicapped/exceptional individuals will require that accurate data be maintained by the respective agencies. Management information will be shared by the Department of Education, Special Education Section, Vocational Education, and the Division of Vocational Rehabilitation in order for federal reporting purposes to evaluate the impact of services and for the purpose of ongoing planning and program development. Information will be shared within departmental policies pertaining to confidentiality and informed consent.

Additions, deletions, and other amendments to the provisions of this Agreement may be made upon signature of the undersigned parties.

(Signed)	(Signed)
State Superintendent of Public Instruction	Administrator, Division of Vocational Rehabilitation

January 27, 1978	January 25, 1978
Date of Signature	Date of Signature

(Signed)

Administrator,
Division of Vocational Education

January 25, 1978

Date of Signature

DIVISION OF VOCATIONAL REHABILITATION

Description of Services

Eligibility: Clients must demonstrate the following: 1) a physical or mental disability that is a substantial handicap to employment, 2) that it is reasonable to expect that Vocational Rehabilitation Services will lead to employment, and 3) that they are of an employable age, i.e., 16 and above.

Contact Person: There are managers and Vocational Rehabilitation Specialist Counselors in each of the seven regions of the State.

Priorities: The severely handicapped individual receives first priority.

Description of Services: The services to be provided by the Division of Vocational Rehabilitation include:

1. Information/Consultation: The Vocational Rehabilitation Specialist will provide information/ consultation to the public and potential clients/ families regarding eligibility requirements for receiving services from the Division of Vocational Rehabilitation.

2. Evaluation of Rehabilitation Potential: When critical to the development of the Individualized Rehabilitation Plan (IRP), the VR Specialist will identify and recommend the most appropriate method of evaluating the rehabilitation potential of each client.

3. Counseling Clients: The VR Specialist is available to provide the client guidance in such areas of need as identifying career goals, assistance with family concerns, use of recreational time, etc.

4. Medical Restoration: Based on the judgment of the VR staff, the law does allow the Division of Vocational Rehabilitation to be involved in the reducing of a handicap. That is, the Division of Vocational Rehabilitation may provide financial assistance to purchase those medical services necessary in order for clients to qualify for job placement. Examples of such assistance

include physical therapy, the purchase of a wheelchair, the purchase of prosthetic devices, etc.

5. Vocational Training: The training provided by the Division of Vocational Rehabilitation might include:

   a. Academic training (academic training outside the public school setting, e.g., education in a community setting for graduation in a GED)

   b. Post-secondary training

   c. Vocational technical schools

   d. Apprenticeship training programs

   e. On-the-job training

   f. Rehabilitation facilities (sheltered workshops)

   g. Correspondence schools (subject to approval by the SDE)

6. Maintenance of Client: A client may be provided food, clothing, transportation, and other subsistence through VR financial assistance if this need occurs based on an increased cost to the client due to his/her being involved in the VR process. This need must be demonstrated by VR staff through a state agency developed process.

7. Telecommunications: A client may qualify for VR assistance in purchasing communicative devices (such as a teletypewriter) if it is needed by the client to communicate with other individuals in the job placement setting.

8. Placement of Clients: The VR Specialist will provide clients with assistance in job analysis, job development, and job placement if a client is unable to locate his/her own job.

9. Occupational Services and Special Program Support: Those services which are provided by the Division of Vocational Rehabilitation in support of a client's progress on a job, i.e., tools, supplies, uniforms, etc.

The agency cannot and is unable to provide any type of services to an individual who would be able

Interface: to secure and be provided those same services in a secondary educational setting.

The Division of Vocational Rehabilitation suggests that for those individuals that school district person-nel realize will be in need of further assistance be-yond the secondary educational program, that a VR Specialist be invited to participate as a member of the Child Study Team—particularly during the last year that the student will spend in the school dis-trict's program.

Additional Information: See a copy of the form used to document an individ-ualized written rehabilitation program and the due process safeguards for each client.

The following are Managers of District Offices serving the seven major areas of the state:

I. Coeur d'Alene: _____, 667-7666

II. Lewiston: _____, 746-2326

III. Caldwell: _____, 459-6343

IV. Boise: _____, 384-2310

V. Twin Falls: _____, 733-0865

VI. Pocatello: _____, 233-0626

VII. Idaho Falls: _____, 523-9220

DIVISION OF VOCATIONAL EDUCATION

Description of Services

Eligibility: To qualify for support services from the Division of Vocational Education, a school district must have handicapped students enrolled in a state reimbursable vocational education program. These programs include:

1. Vocational agriculture
2. Office occupations
3. Distributive education/multi-occupations
4. Trade and industrial
5. Home economics
6. Industrial arts (only those approved by the Division of Vocational Education)

The Division of Vocational Education defines a handicapped individual as:

> ... persons who are mentally retarded, hard of hearing, deaf, speech impaired, visually handicapped, seriously emotionally disturbed, crippled, or other health impaired persons who, by reason thereof, require special education and related services, and who, because of their handicapping condition, cannot succeed in the regular vocational education program without special educational assistance or who require a modified vocational education program.

The handicapped student must be 14 years of age or older.

Contact Person: To determine eligibility, contact the school district superintendent/business manager, or the Division of Vocational Education, Len B. Jordan Office Building, Boise, Idaho 83720, 384-3876.

Priorities: School districts must apply for funds on an annual basis. Those applications which identify content/strategies and on-the-job placement activities which will lead directly to job placement will receive the highest priority.

Description of Services: This program functions primarily to assist Idaho school districts with needed support services to maintain vocational education programs for those handicapped students who cannot succeed in the regular vocational program but will be able to succeed in a special vocational education program. These support services include:

1. Curriculum development
2. Materials development
3. In-service training of program staff
4. Specialized program support like rental of facilities
5. Staff travel needed for work placement coordination, workshops, and pre-approved meetings
6. Salaries of selected personnel
7. Vocational training of students
8. Information to the public
9. Placement of students
10. Equipment needed for program/student success
11. Supplies and instructional materials over and above standard school supplies

A school district must make application for the above support services by March 1, for the following school year beginning in September. Applications are reviewed and approved on an individual basis. It is suggested that as school district personnel prepare applications for this program, they become familiar with Curriculum Guide #142 from the Division of Vocational Education. The guide will be of assistance in determining course content that has been approved by the Division of Vocational Education.

When appropriate, the Division of Vocational Education will conduct summer workshops for district personnel who are implementing a secondary vocational special education program model.

The Department of Education and the Division of Vocational Education will plan cooperative in-service training activities to provide ongoing opportunities for communication, professional interaction, and growth in skills.

It is suggested that districts refer to pages 56–57 in the 1977 Certification Standards Handbook for vocational education certification requirements.

Interface: For those students enrolled in both a special education program as well as a vocational education program, it is suggested that the development of the student's IEP be coordinated between the two programs.

It is the recommendation of the Division of Vocational Education that district special education programs be responsible for prevocational skills training to include exposure to a wide variety of vocational skills, settings, and prerequisites, and that the district vocational education program be responsible for the direct vocational training in preparation for job placement.

Additional Information: It is very important that handicapped students at the secondary level be provided prerequisite, prevocational, and vocational training toward that time when, as adults, independence is achieved by joining the labor force. Data for FY 1975 suggests that less than 2 percent of those enrolled in vocational education programs are reported as handicapped. The concentration of enrollment in education programs shows a sharp decline from ages 17 through 20. The existing need is represented by that deficit for appropriately designed vocational programs and related services. There are substantial numbers of handicapped students leaving the education system without occupational skills or prerequisites to satisfactorily take advantage of other services.

The Education for All Handicapped Children Act (PL 94-142) mandates a free and appropriate education. The Education Amendments of PL 94-482 require that a percentage of vocational education monies be granted to provide programs and services in vocational education that are consistent with state plans for special education. To this end, coordination and planning must support the handicapped student. Vocational and interdisciplinary efforts must be expanded which are also supported by PL 93-112, Section 504.

The Federal Bureaus of Education for the Handicapped and Occupational and Adult Education have notified the U.S. Commissioner of Education that such coordination will occur. The Idaho Department of Education and the Division of Vocational Educa-

225

tion have committed by agreement that coordination will take place. It is most important the coordination and support of prevocational and vocational education for the handicapped be in place at the local level for Individualized Education Plans to be effective.

Agreement Between the Crippled Children's Division, University of Oregon Health Sciences Center, Oregon State System of Higher Education and the Creswell School District #40

I. STATEMENTS OF GENERAL RESPONSIBILITY
    A. The Crippled Children's Division (CCD) is responsible for the administration of a program to extend and improve services for locating crippled children and for providing medical, surgical, corrective, and other services and care facilities for diagnosis, hospitalization, and aftercare for children who are crippled or who are suffering from conditions which lead to crippling.
    B. The Creswell School District #40 (CSD) is responsible for providing services and facilities, including but not limited to, curriculum material, special teachers, and special programs for handicapped children who reside in the CSD.

II. STATEMENT OF PURPOSE
    It is the purpose of this agreement to provide arrangements for physical therapy services to physically handicapped students who reside in the CSD.

III. STATEMENTS OF SPECIFIC ROLES AND RESPONSIBILITIES
    A. The CCD will provide a part-time registered physical therapist ten hours a week (.25 FTE) who will be a salaried employee of CCD. This person will provide physical therapy evaluations, consultation, and treatment to physically handicapped students in the CSD.
    B. The staff of the CCD regional office in Eugene will provide medical direction and therapy supervision and coordination to the physical therapist hired under this agreement in the performance of the service function. Medical direction will consist of an annual chart review of all physically handicapped students residing in the CSD and provision for prescription of physical therapy services by a licensed physician. Physical therapy supervision and coordination will consist of an annual chart review of all physically handicapped students residing in the CSD and consultation as needed by a supervising physical therapist.
    C. The CCD will provide equipment and supplies for students that may be required by the physical therapist in performance of the service function.

D. The CCD will provide in-service training opportunities for the physical therapist through attendance at regional physical therapy/occupational therapy meetings.
E. The CCD will provide suitable office space and office supplies for the physical therapist in the Clinical Services Building on the University of Oregon campus.
F. The CSD will provide:
    1. Program supervision to include, but not limited to, management of time, communication with staff and parents, and
    2. Job related travel reimbursement for the physical therapist.

IV. FINANCIAL CONSIDERATIONS

The CSD will pay to CCD upon billings from CCD the basic salary and fringe benefits of the physical therapist in the amount of $2,522 for salary and $681 for fringe benefits. This payment will be made no later than December 31, 1979. The CSD will pay to CCD upon billings from CCD for the cost of providing medical and physical therapy supervision in the amount of $25 per hour for medical supervision and $12.50 per hour for physical therapy supervision. The maximum amount CSD will pay for this supervision will not exceed $375. The CSD will also pay to CCD upon billings from CCD for the cost of student equipment and supplies. The maximum amount CSD will pay for such equipment and supplies will not exceed $88. The final billing from CCD to CSD for supervision, equipment, and supplies will be submitted no later than 15 days after the ending date of this agreement.

V. ADMINISTRATIVE CONSIDERATIONS

A. This agreement will take effect as of October 1, 1979, and will continue in effect until June 30, 1980.
B. The terms of this agreement may be modified during the time period mentioned above if both parties mutually agree to suggested changes.
C. Both parties to this agreement will comply with confidentiality requirements of state and federal law to ensure the confidentiality of individual client data.
D. The individuals occupying the following positions in each agency will be responsible for 1) implementing this agreement as specified, 2) monitoring the implementation, and 3) negotiating change when necessary to update agreement
    1. CCD—Director, Regional Services Center, Eugene
    2. CSD—Director of Special Education

OREGON STATE BOARD OF HIGHER
EDUCATION
on behalf of the
UNIVERSITY OF OREGON HEALTH
SCIENCES CENTER,
Crippled Children's Division

CRESWELL SCHOOL DISTRICT #40

by _____(Signed)_____
Director, CCD
Date _____11/5/79_____

by _____(Signed)_____
Superintendent
Date _____10/25/79_____

by _____(Signed)_____
Business Manager, UOHSC
Date _____11/29/79_____

APPENDIX D

Program Standards
Interagency Planning Group for Preschool Children,
Hays, Kansas

PUBLIC AWARENESS

Standard

There should be a comprehensive *ongoing* public awareness program which should include:

Parent and child legal rights
Knowledge of normal growth and development
Nature of handicapping conditions and their causes
Advantages of early diagnosis and intervention
Services available and the appropriate contacts

This program should communicate effectively with all segments of the population. In order to ensure this total communication, the program should utilize a variety of materials, media, methodologies, and all languages necessary to reach the total population.

Need

To disseminate preschool information to parents and to the general public especially in regard to knowledge of normal growth and development and services available.

Recommendations

A task force composed of volunteers from the IPG should be in charge of developing public awareness programs. No financial reimbursement will be made to members of this task force for the time they donate to the IPG. The task force should develop a brochure as a first step in meeting the needs for public awareness. Payment for the first printing of the brochure shall be borne by funds of the State Department of Education, Early Childhood Education. Sources of funds for subsequent printings will be determined as the need arises. The task force should consider sources of public service communication, including, but not limited to, school newsletters, unit newsletter, Hays Daily News, KAYS, KJLS, Plains Talk (High Plains Comprehensive Community Mental Health Center), hospital newsletters, Answering Service, etc.

The task force will be responsible for distributing the public awareness material.

PROFESSIONAL AWARENESS

Standard

There should be a comprehensive professional awareness program designed to increase skills and awareness for the purpose of preventing and identifying handicapping conditions through:

Impact on preservice curricula of professional schools in education, physical and mental health, dentistry, optometry, social work, and religion

Development of multidisciplinary in-service programs for all persons involved in the provision of care of young children and their families

Need

To increase and coordinate multidisciplinary in-service programs for persons involved in the provision of care to young children and their families.

Recommendations

A task force composed of volunteers from the IPG shall be in charge of developing professional awareness programs. No financial reimbursement will be made to members of this task force for the time they donate to the IPG. Interagency newsletters, notification of interagency meetings, and organizing professional in-services will be included in the responsibilities of the professional awareness task force. The cost of interagency mailings will be borne by the agencies comprising the task force.

SCREENING

Standard

A systematic process for screening should exist to ensure that all children from birth to age 6 receive periodic, comprehensive, health, and developmental screening in order to identify possible special needs. This system should include:

Identification of special needs at birth

Mass screening programs for the total population and referral system for further assessment

Individual screening of children suspected of having special needs and referral for further assessment

Need

To organize and increase the identification of high risk infants and to implement procedures for mass screening programs for all children from birth to age 6.

Recommendations

(A task force is being selected to examine recommendations to meet the needs for screening.)

ASSESSMENT

A. *Guidelines*

Standard

All referred children should receive an assessment appropriate to the degree and type of suspected special need(s) as determined by the coordinating team. Appropriateness is defined as the selection and administration of instruments that determine the sequence and achievement of developmental levels and may include part or all of the following as determined by the referral data and the child's need(s):

General physical
Neurological
Ophthalmological
Audiological
Gross and fine motor development
Perceptual motor development
Receptive and expressive language
Cognitive development
Social and emotional growth
Formal and informal observations of the child including at least two visits
    to the home and any other settings where the child customarily
    spends waking hours
Complete social history including individual and family information

B. *Timing*

Standard

All referred children should have an initial assessment completed within 6 weeks from date of referral.

Needs

Make necessary arrangements so that all initial assessments will be completed in 6 weeks.

Avoid needless duplication—maximize the use of resources.
Coordination in case management/assessment.
Avoid needless duplication—sharing information.

Recommendations

A task force composed of volunteers from the Interagency Planning Group (IPG) should be in charge of developing materials that can be used across agencies. No financial reimbursement will be made to members of this task force for the time they donate to the IPG. Included in the materials to be developed are an interagency referral form, an interagency history form, and an interagency consent for release and exchange of information form.

The task force will be responsible for modifying or adding additional forms.

Each agency will ensure that assessments are completed within 6 weeks.

The agency that first sees the child will be responsible for coordinating the assessment of the child. Coordination will include the following:

1. Determine what additional evaluations are necessary.
2. Notify other agencies that the child is being referred.
3. Obtain proper release forms.
4. Follow up referrals when necessary.
5. Deliver the summary evaluation to the next referral agency.

C. *Conditions*

Standard

The assessment process should be conducted under conditions which foster optimum performance (as distinguished from typical performance) by the child. Such conditions include:

The avoidance of unnecessary duplication or irrelevant testing
Flexibility regarding the environment in which the individual measures are administered
Comfort and convenience for the child and the family including the order in which the measures are administered and the selection of the individuals who administer them
Consideration for the child's age and attention span

Needs

To avoid duplication of assessment across agencies.
To coordinate the order in which measures are administered across agencies.

Recommendation

The agency that first sees the child is responsible for coordinating the assessment of the child and, when necessary, for determining the order in which measures are administered across agencies.

D. *Due Process*

Standard

The assessment program should ensure that all due process procedures, specified by state and federal law, are fully met. These procedures protect the rights of parents or surrogate parents.

Need

To ensure that due process procedures are fully met during assessment.

Recommendation

The agency that first sees the child will be responsible for seeing that due process procedures are met.

E. *Personnel*

Standard

Persons who conduct formal assessments of children will meet certification and licensing standards of the state or operate under the supervision of a certified or licensed agency or person.

Need

To ensure that persons who conduct formal assessments meet the criteria set forth in the standard.

Recommendation

Each agency will ensure that those staff who conduct formal assessments meet the criteria set forth in the standard.

F. *Nondiscriminatory Instruments*

Standard

All instruments administered will be as free of discrimination as possible considering the population upon which they are standardized and the population to which they are administered.

Need

To ensure that assessments are as free of discrimination as possible.

Recommendation

Each agency which conducts assessments will be responsible for using nondiscriminatory instruments.

G. *Confidentiality*

Standard

To ensure compliance with confidentiality requirements and to ensure the confidentiality of individually identifiable data, all treatment of assessment data should be consistent with federal and state law.

Need

To allow interagency communication that complies with confidentiality requirements.

Recommendation

Develop an interagency release of information form.

H. *Feedback to Parents*

Standard

A post-assessment conference should be held including parents, the assessment team, program planners, and the implementor to discuss the results of the assessment. The post-assessment conference should:

Provide parents with the opportunity to discuss the assessment with individual team members.

Provide participants, including the parents, with an explanation of all testing.

Allow participants to discuss possible interpretations with regard to both age level norms and the child's own pattern of development.

Need

To coordinate interagency feedback to parents and other members of the assessment team.

Recommendation

An interagency staffing involving all members of the assessment teams will precede a full staffing with the parents. The staffing schedule will be coordinated by the agency which first sees the child.

I. *Reporting Results*

Standard

All assessment data should be integrated into a single file reflecting the child's strengths and weaknesses and recommended intervention strategies to respond to those strengths and weaknesses. This file should meet the following guidelines:

Be completed within 2 weeks after the final assessment is completed
Be available to the parent, written in the native language
Be submitted to those individuals responsible for program planning for the individual child

Needs

To integrate the assessment data into a single file.
To have someone or some agency serve as custodian of the file, whereby the responsibilities of the custodian will include dissemination of information in the file to parents with translation into the parents' native language when necessary and to those responsible for program planning.

Recommendations

An assessment file will be initiated by the agency that first sees the child. When each agency completes its evaluation of the child, the agency will summarize its findings and include the summary in the file. The file will then be delivered to the next referral agency. More comprehensive reports will later be delivered to the custodian of the file.

The agency with the primary treatment responsibility will be designated as custodian of the file.

PLANNING PROCESS

A. *Team Membership*

Standard

The planning team membership should be determined by the needs of the child and family and should include:

Parent(s) or surrogate parent
Appropriate assessment team members
Possible implementors
Appropriate others upon request

Need

Coordination of interagency team.

Recommendation

The agency that first contacts the child will coordinate the team except in those instances when assessment staffing and planning staffing are separate. In those cases, the agency designated as having primary treatment responsibility for the child will coordinate the planning staffing.

B. *Parental Involvement*

Standard

There should be active parental involvement throughout the planning process. Administration of the planning process should provide for:

Full advance information to the parent(s) regarding mutually agreed upon times and places, purpose of meetings, process of meetings, and the parental role in the meeting

Interpreter to provide information in the native language or model of communication when necessary

Active parent involvement in the determination of all program decisions

Need

Someone/agency to communicate with parent, in sufficient time, to fulfill requirements set forth in standard.

Recommendation

The agency that first contacts the child will coordinate the team except in those instances when assessment staffing and planning staffing are separate. In those cases, the agency designated as having primary responsibility for the child will coordinate the planning staffing.

C. *Access to Services*

Standard

Planners should have complete knowledge of and access to a full range of services (e.g., a current directory of "approved" local and statewide services available).

Needs

Planners need current directories of services.
Planners need knowledge of local services.

Recommendations

The Kansas Department of Health and Environment will compile and distribute to agencies the sources of various directories. Each agency is responsible for obtaining copies of the directories.

A task force composed of volunteers from the IPG will outline the services available at the local level. No financial reimbursement will be made to members of this task force for the time they donate to the IPG.

D. *Statement of Goals*

Standard

The written program plan should include a statement of measurable goals and objectives. The plan should specifically:

Be based on strengths and weaknesses of the child
Include sequential objectives necessary to reach each stated goal
Designate any direct and related services to be provided to reach the
    goals and objectives, and the extent and duration of those services
Designate service providers
Include a program review and re-evaluation schedule:
—Quarterly review and revision based on on-site evaluation and periodic
    recording of the child's achievement and specifically stated ob-
    jectives and goals
—Formal re-evaluation of the program plan at least annually

Need

Agency to ensure that standard is met.

Recommendation

The primary treatment agency as designated at assessment staffing or planning staffing is responsible for ensuring that standard is met.

E. *Coordination and Accountability*

Standard

There should be a clear assignment of responsibility for coordination and accountability of program planning. Such responsibility includes:

Collecting of assessment data
Scheduling the planning team meetings
Chairing the meetings
Contacting the parents
Ensuring implementation of the plan
Ensuring the development of an appropriate program
Monitoring service delivery
Coordinating review and re-evaluation

Need

Standard is met.

F. *Timing*

Standard

Development of the written program should take place within 4 weeks of the completion of the written assessment report.

Need

Agency to ensure that standard is met.

Recommendation

The primary treatment agency ensures that the written program takes effect within 4 weeks.

SERVICE DELIVERY

A. *Integrated Delivery Model*

Standard

Service delivery should be designed on a noncategorical, integrated model and should reflect the child's total environment. To ensure this, the service delivery should include:

A continuum of services ranging from individual planned environment to an integrated environment
Opportunities for the child to experience situations most closely approximating "normal" life settings
Services to ensure provisions for basic needs to the child and family
Support services to the family
Services to primary care providers
Services to other significant people in the child's life

Need

To ensure that standard is met.

Recommendation

The planning team will use the standard as a planning guide.

B. *Implementation*

Standard

The total program implementors should have a clear understanding of all elements of the child's program plan and of their responsibility as stated in the plan. In addition, services should be provided in the least disruptive manner. To facilitate these goals:

Services should be located as near as possible to the child's residence
Service delivery should respect the child's daily routine
Service delivery should be designed to facilitate the family's dignity and respect

Need

To ensure that standard is met.

Recommendation

Planning team will use the standard as a planning guide.

C. *Relationship of Plan to Service*

Standard

The service should be a direct result of the written program plan and should begin within 4 weeks of completion of the plan.

During the assessment period, interim services shall be provided based upon the most apparent needs of the child.

Needs

To designate interim needs.
To ensure that standard is met.

Recommendations

Each agency conducting an assessment will provide its own interim services if such needs are apparent.

The primary treatment agency is responsible for implementation of the written program plan according to standard.

TECHNICAL ASSISTANCE

Standard

Local, state, and federal resources for technical assistance in serving preschool handicapped children with special needs should be sought for such areas as in-service training, program organization, finances, facility planning, and development of case management.

Need

A system to recognize weaknesses in interagency plan and to solicit assistance to eliminate those weaknesses.

Recommendation

A representative body will be elected from the participating agencies. The responsibility of this body will include those mentioned in the above-stated need.

PROGRAM EVALUATION

A. *Consumer Input*

Standard

There should be consumer input into the planning, implementation, and evaluation of all program components and of the total program.

Need

To develop a method obtaining consumer input.

Recommendations

A questionnaire covering the program components will be developed by the representative body and distributed to various consumers. The representative body will consider the information obtained from the questionnaire in their program planning.

B. *Independent Review*

Standard

Independent review should be made of the area services for preschool children with special needs, and of each agency's individual service for that child.

Need

To develop an objective review of program development for preschool children with special needs.

Recommendation

The elected representative body will solicit technical assistance for objective review.

C. *Internal Evaluation System*

Standard

Each individual service delivery should use its own internal evaluation system built within its structure.

Need

Standard is met.

INTERAGENCY AGREEMENTS

Standard

There should be a clear designation of roles, including fiscal responsibilities among all service providers.

Need

To develop a formal interagency agreement that designates each agency's role and fiscal responsibility.

Recommendation

The interagency plan will state each agency's role and fiscal responsibilities. Each agency participating in the plan will sign a formal agreement to abide by the plan.

Index